KNOWING VICTI

Knowing Victims explores the theme of victimhood in contemporary feminism and politics. It focuses on popular and scholarly constructions of feminism as 'victim feminism' – an ideology of passive victimhood that denies women's agency – and provides the first comprehensive analysis of the debate about this ideology which has unfolded among feminists since the 1980s.

The book critically examines a concerted movement away from the language of victimhood across a wide array of discourses, and the neoliberal replacement of the concept of structural oppression with the concept of personal responsibility. In derogating the notion of 'victim', neoliberalism promotes a conception of victimization as subjective rather than social, a state of mind rather than a worldly situation. As a result, victims of poverty, inequality, discrimination and violence are discursively constructed as the authors of their own suffering, or as genuine victims of incomprehensible crime.

Drawing upon Nietzsche, Lyotard, rape crisis feminism and feminist philosophy, Rebecca Stringer situates feminist politicizations of rape, interpersonal violence, economic inequality and welfare reform as key sites of resistance to the victim-blaming logic of neoliberalism. She suggests that although recent feminist critiques of 'victim feminism' have critically diagnosed the anti-victim movement, they have not positively defended victim politics. Stringer argues that a conception of the victim as an agentic bearer of knowledge, and an understanding of resentment as a generative force for social change, provides a potent counter to the negative construction of victimhood characteristic of the neoliberal era.

This accessible and insightful analysis of feminism, neoliberalism and the social construction of victimhood will be of great interest to researchers and students in the disciplines of gender and women's studies, psychology, sociology, politics and philosophy.

Rebecca Stringer is Senior Lecturer in Gender Studies at the University of Otago in Dunedin, New Zealand, and is co-editor, with Hilary Radner, of *Feminism at the Movies: Understanding Gender in Contemporary Popular Cinema* (Routledge, 2011).

WOMEN AND PSYCHOLOGY
Series Editor: Jane Ussher
School of Psychology, University of Western Sydney

This series brings together current theory and research on women and psychology. Drawing on scholarship from a number of different areas of psychology, it bridges the gap between abstract research and the reality of women's lives by integrating theory and practice, research and policy.

Each book addresses a 'cutting edge' issue of research, covering topics such as postnatal depression and eating disorders, and addressing a wide range of theories and methodologies.

The series provides accessible and concise accounts of key issues in the study of women and psychology, and clearly demonstrates the centrality of psychology debates within women's studies or feminism.

FEMININITY AND THE PHYSICALLY ACTIVE WOMAN
Precilla Y. L. Choi

GENDER, LANGUAGE AND DISCOURSE
Anne Weatherall

THE SCIENCE/FICTION OF SEX
Annie Potts

THE PSYCHOLOGICAL DEVELOPMENT OF GIRLS AND WOMEN
Sheila Greene

JUST SEX?
Nicola Gavey

WOMAN'S RELATIONSHIP WITH HERSELF
Helen O'Grady

GENDER TALK
Susan A. Speer

BEAUTY AND MISOGYNY
Sheila Jeffreys

BODY WORK
Sylvia K. Blood

MANAGING THE MONSTROUS FEMININE
Jane M. Ussher

THE CAPACITY TO CARE
Wendy Hollway

SANCTIONING PREGNANCY
Harriet Gross and Helen Pattison

ACCOUNTING FOR RAPE
Irina Anderson and Kathy Doherty

THE SINGLE WOMAN
Jill Reynolds

MATERNAL ENCOUNTERS
Lisa Baraitser

KNOWING VICTIMS

Feminism, agency and victim politics
in neoliberal times

Rebecca Stringer

Routledge
Taylor & Francis Group

LONDON AND NEW YORK

First published 2014
by Routledge
27 Church Road, Hove, East Sussex BN3 2FA

and by Routledge
711 Third Avenue, New York, NY 10017

Routledge is an imprint of the Taylor & Francis Group, an informa business

© 2014 Routledge

The right of Rebecca Stringer to be identified as author of this work has been asserted by her in accordance with sections 77 and 78 of the Copyright, Designs and Patents Act 1988.

British Library Cataloguing in Publication Data
A catalogue record for this book is available from the British Library

Library of Congress Cataloging in Publication Data
Stringer, Rebecca.
   Knowing victims : feminism, agency and victim politics in neoliberal times / Rebecca Stringer.
      pages cm
   Includes bibliographical references and index.
   1. Women–Crimes against. 2. Women–Violence against. 3. Victims–Political aspects. 4. Feminism. I. Title.
   HV6250.4.W65S79253 2014
   362.88082–dc23   2014002346

ISBN: 978-0-415-63492-2 (hbk)
ISBN: 978-0-415-64333-7 (pbk)
ISBN: 978-1-315-88012-9 (ebk)

Typeset in Times
by Keystroke, Station Road, Codsall, Wolverhampton

For Dylan

CONTENTS

ACKNOWLEDGEMENTS

I am extremely grateful to Jane Ussher for her support of this project, and I would like to thank Michael Strang and Michael Fenton at Routledge for their astute guidance and advice, and Ken McLaughlin and Nicola Gavey for their constructive feedback at the proposal stage. I am grateful to Lisa Marr for her terrific work on the index, Susan Dunsmore for her thorough copy-editing, and Valonia Dsouza for kindly granting permission to use her photograph for the cover. I would also like to thank the many people who have provided inspiration and support over the years as I worked on this research, helping me to bring this project to fruition.

As an undergraduate at the University of Western Sydney I benefited enormously from the knowledge and wisdom of Sue Best, who first uttered the word 'victimology' to me and sparked my interest in contemporary understandings of the victim. This book began life as graduate research at the Australian National University and it was a privilege to be supervised in that research by Barry Hindess and Barbara Sullivan, whose rigour, dedication and humour are ongoing sources of inspiration. I am grateful to Penny Deutscher, Rosalyn Diprose, Vikki Bell, Dougal McNeill and David Owen for engaging with my graduate work and providing useful feedback, and Alan D. Schrift and Chilla Bulbeck for encouraging me in my early publications. Anna Yeatman's mentorship and acuminous engagement with my work down the years have been indispensable and are lovingly appreciated, and I thank her and Linda Trimble for enabling me to undertake a visiting fellowship at the University of Alberta in 2008, where I worked on the book amidst the stimulating intellectual life of the Department of Political Science and the Interdisciplinary Political Theory Group, and was able to connect as well with the Department of Women's Studies, finding in Lise Gotell a true companion in the debates of feminism today. I thank her for her encouragement and useful feedback on the parts of this book she read in draft.

I feel very fortunate to have forged nourishing friendships and spaces of intellectual exchange with a number of colleagues, each of whom has contributed invaluably to this project. Simone Drichel provided a very welcome invitation to present some of this work at her 'Vulnerability: A Symposium' in 2010, and I have since benefited enormously from her support and insightful discussion of the themes in which we share a common fascination. I am also grateful for her skilful editorial advice on the version of Chapter 2 that appeared in the publication arising from the symposium. Working with Hilary Radner on our co-edited book, *Feminism at the Movies*, was for me a delightful apprenticeship, and I am very grateful to her and all our contributors for making that project such a positive and intellectually rich experience. In the years since we found we would be embarking on the academia/early motherhood combo at around the same time, Catherine Smith has been a mensch, her wisdom and wit often providing welcome inspiration and reprieve. Over many years Heather Brook's uplifting friendship and cerebral might have helped to light the way. On both sides of the Tasman and elsewhere I have benefited enormously from sharing interdisciplinary spaces of debate and exchange with David McInerney, Tony Burke, Nelly Lahoud, Jo Faulkner, Barbara Baird, Damien Riggs, Alissa Macoun, Elizabeth Strakosch, Cameron Duder, Barbara Brookes, Shayne Grice, Anita Brady, Bronwyn Boon, Catherine Dale, Louise Pearman, Vicki Spencer, Brett Nichols, Vijay Devedas, Brendan Hokowhitu, Nalani Wilson-Hokowhitu, Kevin Fisher, Paul Raemaker, Chris Prentice, Di Smith, Rachel Spronken-Smith and Cheryl Wilson. I am also grateful to Keridiana Chez, Randy Cota and Kelley C. Kawano, then graduate students at the City University of New York, for inviting me to present some of this work at their conference 'Resentment In/Of Women's Studies' in 2007.

My colleagues in the Gender Studies Programme at the University of Otago, Chris Brickell and Annabel Cooper, have been encouraging and accommodating as I completed the book – I thank them for this, and for the great pleasure of creating with them a thriving place for interdisciplinary gender studies teaching and research. I also want to acknowledge our colleagues in the Department of Sociology, Gender and Social Work more broadly, and all those who assist us in our work, and thank in particular Hugh Campbell, Martin Tolich, Anita Gibbs, Melanie Beres and Amanda Barusch for their encouragement along the way. Over the years it has been my privilege to encounter many outstanding undergraduate and postgraduate students, and among these I want to thank in particular Gabby Hine, Georgia Knowles, Marita Leask, Nell O'Dwyer-Strang, Anna McMartin and Fiona Douglas, for sharing their research journeys with me.

Words are less easy when it comes to my debts to those closest to me, my partner, son, family and dear friends not already mentioned. Suffice it to say that for me, nothing in life would be either possible or pleasurable without my partner, Brian Roper, and our darling son, Dylan Stringer. Brian has provided every kind of assistance, reading drafts and providing the characteristically direct and acuminous feedback every writer needs, inspiring me with his own intellectual work, and sharing the care of our son to provide space for me to progress and complete the book. He and Dylan have supported me consistently and with patience, and for this I am truly grateful. Life would be impoverished indeed without my friends, Peta Morris, Julie MacLeod, Donna Royden and Juanita Kenny – I am immensely grateful to them for being constant sources of wisdom, support and humour. My mother, Judy Stringer, and my late father, Ken Stringer, filled my youth with learning and laughs and have always been terrifically supportive, and I am grateful to them and to my sister, Sheridan Wakeman, my nieces, Isabella and Scarlett, and my nephew, Angus, my uncle, Robert Field, and my grandmother, Violet Field, for their love and encouragement over many years.

An earlier version of Chapter 2 was originally published as: Stringer, R. (2013). Vulnerability After Wounding: Feminism, Rape Law and the Differend. *SubStance* *132*, 42.3: 148–168. © 2013 by the Board of Regents of the University of Wisconsin System. Reproduced courtesy of University of Wisconsin Press.

INTRODUCTION
Feminism and victim politics in neoliberal times

'WE ARE NOT VICTIMS! STOP TRYING TO RESCUE US!' So read the first slide in a conference presentation I attended recently, given by a sex worker activist. The slide announced a blistering critique of the way efforts to rescue sex workers trade on a representation of sex workers as 'helpless victims'. This representation, the speaker explained, elides the personal and political agency of sex workers and feeds the demonization and criminalization of sex work, promoting prohibition. This representation should be replaced, the speaker argued, with a more accurate and respectful understanding of sex workers as active agents engaged in erotic labour, deserving of the labour rights enjoyed by other workers. While I concurred with this political argument for decriminalization and labour rights, I became increasingly intrigued by the stories of victimization the speaker told as their talk continued. The speaker began by denouncing victim identity and establishing that sex workers are not victims; yet his argument for decriminalization was nourished by vivid stories of intense victimization. In support of decriminalizing sex work, he described the multiple victimizing effects of prohibition in the everyday lives of sex workers, surveying a spectrum of forms of diminished citizenship, stigmatization and dramatic loss of legal protection. He stressed, for example, the inability of sex workers to complain of rape without facing charges of soliciting; and he described a condition of acute vulnerability to phobic violence and police violence, telling a particularly poignant story of the violent arrest of a sex worker who was targeted by police on account of her ethnicity. His compelling presentation closed with him describing this woman fallen on the side of the road, injured and traumatized, before being taken away by police. He reminded us that the racist violence this woman suffered was conducted with impunity.

In this talk, what began as a defiant rejection of victim identity soon developed into a far more ambiguous position within the language of victimhood, as the speaker rightly unveiled sufferings that are not duly recognized, implicitly framing sex workers as victims of criminal prohibition. This ambiguity, however, was not avowed, and when in question time I queried his rejection of the victim label, he held firm to it, repeating the message: 'Sex workers are not victims.' What actually took place in this talk is a critical rejection of the framing of sex workers as victims of sex work, and the replacement of this with a different and indeed persuasive

1

framing of sex workers as presently victimized in conditions of criminal prohibition. Why could this not be avowed? Why in this particular discursive situation did it seem more politically exigent, and certainly more resonant, to hold firm to the denunciation of 'victim' as a viable identity and category of analysis, than to explore the different framing and usage of this category that took place, implicitly but noticeably, in the speaker's political argument for decriminalization and labour rights? If sex workers clearly suffer an array of forms of victimization, why does it still make sense to reject the idea that they can be regarded, in any way, as 'victims'?

The ambiguity at play in how this speaker deals with the category 'victim' – the telling of politically significant stories of victimization, amidst strident denouncement of 'victim' as a worthy descriptor – is indicative of a much wider predicament. As Fatima Naqvi (2007) observes, a 'persistent anxiety about victims and victimhood has been present in a variety of cultural manifestations over the past thirty years' (p. 1). Since the 1980s, across a wide array of discourses in media, academia, official politics and movement politics, there has been a concerted movement away from the language of victimhood, prompted by the emergence of a surprisingly widely shared critique of the very notion of 'victim'. This movement away from the language of victimhood has not meant talk of victimhood has ceased. Rather it has meant that talk of victimhood primarily assumes the form of negative critique of the notion of 'victim': the proliferation of discourses in which the notion of victim arises in order to be critiqued, and is generally unseated by 'agency' as the trope of legitimacy and preferred analytical choice. Our ways of thinking and talking about victims, victimization and victimhood have been reorganized around the dominance of anti-victim talk.[1]

This rather profound shift has never gone unnoticed. There have always been those who have questioned the contemporary proliferation of discourses in which victim identity, victim politics and the language of victimhood are described in predominantly negative terms, imposing new limits on the way victimization can be signified and discussed. But the work of providing sustained critical analysis of contemporary anti-victim talk – the work of tracking its transformations in the meaning of victimhood and of weighing its political, ethical and social sensibilities and implications – has only recently begun.[2] As the scholarship emerging in this area suggests, the dominance of anti-victim talk is not exactly a progressive development, instead marking a largely conservative intervention upon the language of suffering and social being. Coinciding historically with the rise and consolidation of neoliberal hegemony, much anti-victim talk powerfully reflects the values of neoliberal thought, in particular the concept of 'personal responsibility'. The ideal neoliberal citizen is often explicitly figured as one who avoids 'victim mentality': one who assumes personal responsibility for guarding against the risk of victimization, instead of focusing on their right not to be victimized. Complementing this conception of the ideal citizen, much anti-victim talk discursively constitutes victimization as a matter of individual responsibility, psychology and will, endorsing a fundamentally conservative conception of victimhood as a state of mind rather than a worldly situation – an unhealthy attitude of resentment brought on by an individual's lack of personal responsibility, rather than a circumstance occasioned by wider social forces and the workings of power. This redefinition of victimhood is noticeably victim-blaming and, as such, profoundly depoliticizing. It drains all legitimacy from the idea that suffering can be social, political and collective, rather than merely subjective, psychological and individual. Thus, as critics of this trend warn, the neoliberal turn in victim talk carries serious political consequences, serving no less to 'suppress, negate, and erase most victim claims' (Cole, 2007, p. 6), especially those arising from radical and progressive political projects – even as these projects themselves participate in anti-victim talk. Foregrounding the dominant influence of neoliberal values in contemporary anxieties about the victim, this book undertakes sustained critical analysis of the presence of anti-victim talk in feminism.

Anti-victim talk

With the rise of what Alyson M. Cole (2007) has called 'anti-victimism', the notion that one should 'choose to refuse to be a victim' (Talbot, 2005, p. 167), and choose to refrain from identifying others as victims, has attained deep cultural, political and intellectual resonance, such that it has become unremarkable that individuals and groups who have endured all manner of violence, injustice and misfortune routinely publicly refuse to be perceived as 'victims', or find themselves hailed by others as agents, survivors or resilient, resistive subjects, rather than as 'victims' (Van Dijk, 2009; Rock, 2004).[3] Such acts of fleeing public identification as a 'victim' are visible alongside strikingly derisive efforts to psychologize 'victim identity' as a form of mental frailty. The virtues of renouncing 'victimhood' are perhaps most visibly extolled in the discursive output of the professional positive thinkers, life coaches and celebrity judges populating fit-for-export American TV, such as Tony Robbins, Oprah, Dr Phil and Judge Mary Ann Gunn, for whom the effort to dissuade others from succumbing to 'victim mentality' presents a rich vein of core business.[4] The virtues of renouncing victimhood are also very visibly extolled in the 'victim-panic tracts' (Davis, 1997, p. 225) produced by right-wing think-tanks such as London's Civitas, which dedicates itself to combating the ever-looming threat that political correctness may yet transform civil society into a 'victocracy' (Pizzey, Shackleton and Urwin, 2000, p. ix), where citizens take up victim identity instead of taking personal responsibility, seeking 'special treatment' through false claims that they are systemically disadvantaged, in this way obstructing the proper workings of market freedom and meritocracy.[5]

Rather than being confined to venues of conservative political expression, the virtues of renouncing victimhood and 'société victimale' (Baudrillard, 1997, p. 30) are also strongly extolled in venues of progressive political engagement, among radical thinkers and public intellectuals in the adjacent spheres of academia and social justice movement politics. What Gudrun Dahl calls the 'Agents Not Victims trope' is strongly evident in the academic humanities, particularly sociology and anthropology, where the gesture of framing the subjects of research as 'agents' is posited as the successor to an 'earlier' and 'ethically inferior' practice of repre-senting the subjects of research as stereotypically 'passive victims' (Dahl, 2009, p. 391). Shifts away from the language of victimhood and towards the language of agency are visible within human rights advocacy (Wilson, 2011), development politics (Dahl, 2009) and in the venues of Indigenous politics and policy (Coulthard, 2012), where particular populations – such as victims of human rights abuses, the labouring subjects of globalized neoliberal capitalism and Indigenous political actors – are exhorted to identify with positive, forward-looking 'agency' instead of negative, backward-looking 'victimhood'.

That anti-victimism is prominent not only in the venues of conservative populism, but also among academic scholars and progressives, raises the question of whether the latter draw 'the victim problem' in a more progressive and compelling way, in comparison with the contentious construction of this problem as one of 'victim mentality' and 'victocracy' in conservative anti-victimism. While it seems reasonable to expect that progressives will problematize the notion of 'victim' progressively, as Jan Van Dijk's (1999, 2009) analyses warn, this expectation is unrealistic. Unless they also engage in explicit and thoroughgoing examination and critique of bias within established constructions of the victim – that is, unless they recognize the problem of secondary victimization, or the way negative constructions of the victim set the scene for harmful and unjust social responses to victimization – scholarly and progressive accounts of 'the victim problem' are likely to traffic uncritically in these biased constructions, enjoining instead of interrogating the operations of secondary victimization. In short, we cannot expect that anti-victimism among scholars and progressives will be less problematic than anti-victimism among conservatives. Those who address the question of 'victim-hood' need to scrutinize the already powerful meanings the word 'victim' is carrying into their analysis when they use it. But they often do not.

Feminism and anti-victim talk

Feminism features prominently right across the field of textual hostilities against the notion of 'victim' outlined above, occupying an ambiguous position as target, critic and proponent of anti-victim discourse. Feminism is a principal target of conservative anti-victimism, routinely held up as the prime exemplar of the ills of 'victimism'. According to our friends at Civitas, for example, civil society and its free market have been brought to the brink by victocracy's 'ultra feminists' and their tenacious but entirely fictional claim that gendered inequality and systems of masculine dominance actually exist in liberal-capitalist societies. Such extreme depictions of feminist politics – as steeped in fictions of gendered victimhood, as institutionally dominant and pervasive – have never gone uncontested by feminists. Accordingly, feminism is also prominent as a site for critiquing conservative anti-victimism. Such critiques have focused on the way these kinds of extreme depictions of feminism promote an anti-feminist 'backlash': a revenge of 'mainstream' values against the gains made by women's movements across the West. Surprisingly, however, this line of critique tends to enjoin textual hostilities against the notion of 'victim'. Against the backlash depiction of feminism as 'victimism', feminists have declared, 'we are not victim-feminists' (Lamb, 1999, p. 1). This response challenges the idea that all feminists are 'victimists', but leaves the kernel of anti-victimism – the idea that the notion of 'victim' is harmful and gives rise to problematic identifications, attachments and practices – undisturbed.

This reflects the third aspect of feminism's ambiguous position in relation to anti-victimism. As well as being a target and critic of conservative anti-victimism, feminism has also been a key venue for articulating anti-victim discourse. In contemporary feminism, rejecting the notion of 'victim' as giving rise to reductive feminist identifications of women with woundedness, passivity, oppression and innocence, has become commonplace. Even among feminists who in other moments are interested in polysemy and resignification there is consensus that the words 'victim', 'victimhood' and 'victimization' are incurably connotative of passivity, helplessness, dependence and innocence. The language of victimhood appears to call forth a reviled subject: woman as powerless victim of domination. Such a subject is equally unacceptable from the perspective of popular postfeminism, which emphasizes contemporary Western women's apparent graduation to self-determining agency, and from the perspective of scholarly postmodern feminisms, which reject the notion that 'women are powerless as such' (Allen, 1998, p. 23) and analyse the way gendered subjects are governed through agency rather than its lack. Discussing the way neoliberalism and postfeminism jointly emphasize agency and individual choice, Rosalind Gill and Christina Scharff (2011) observe that:

> Even in feminist scholarship, an older vocabulary that spoke of structures, domination, inequality and oppression sometimes seems to be giving way to something more celebratory, as though the feminist theorizing were itself inflected by a postfeminist sensibility and had come to believe the hype.
>
> (p. 9; see also Gill, 2007a, 2008)

The dynamic these authors identify of an existing feminist scholarly vocabulary 'giving way' to an implicitly neoliberal language that champions agency is, I suggest, older and more firmly established than they imply.

In his anti-victimist classic, *The Culture of Complaint* (1993), the American-based Australian cultural critic Robert Hughes accused his feminist contemporaries of 'abandoning the image of the independent, existentially responsible woman in favour of woman as helpless victim of male oppression' (p. 12). In an interview that same year, when asked about the future of feminism, leading American feminist theorist Judith Butler similarly envisaged contemporary feminism as mired in a woman-as-victim theme, advising that feminists move beyond 'the paradigm of victimization' (Osborne and Segal, 1996, p. 125). Before Hughes and Butler uttered these words, the notion that some or all feminists are improperly invested in a paradigm of victimization had already begun to resound strongly within feminism, not only among feminist writers like Naomi Wolf and Katie Roiphe whose critiques of 'victim feminism' also appeared in 1993, but among feminist scholars and theorists in debates concerning postmodernism and power, the politics of identity and difference and the politics of pleasure. The idea that feminists should choose to refuse the 'paradigm of victimization' has continued to resound in feminist theory in the decades since, in ongoing critique of feminism as characterized by 'myopic focus on women as victims' (Gruber, 2009, p. 607), arguments for 'letting go of the abstract figure of woman as victim' (Hall, 2004, p. 15) and in critiques of the notion of victim itself as 'disempowering' (Ronai, 1999, p. 142) and unable to 'accommodate multi-layered experience' (Kapur, 2002, p. 10). There is now a large and diverse body of feminist work that critiques the theme of victimhood in feminist theory and politics, seeking to move feminism 'beyond victimhood'. This work primarily assumes the form of intra-feminist critique – launched from a position that is critical of feminism, but that, as Butler describes, is 'still "in" and "of" feminism' (Osborne and Segal, 1996, p. 125). This body of work forms my focus in this book.

The notion of victim, in particular the notion of 'woman-as-victim', has been the subject of multiple and sustained critique among feminists since the 1980s, coinciding historically with the rise and consolidation of neoliberalism as a hegemonic political form. What is the relationship between this body of feminist work critiquing the notion of victim, and the concurrent neoliberal turn in victim talk? Given that the most visible forms of anti-victimism reorganize victim talk in ways that legitimate and normalize the values of neoliberalism, have feminists shown the way to a progressive anti-victim stance? Or is it, rather, that the border between feminism and neoliberalism has proved permeable in the matter of the victim, with feminist objections to the notion of victim – and the near absence of feminist defence of the language of victimhood – serving to support neoliberal values, unwittingly or otherwise? Prior to the appearance of a wealth of popular and scholarly feminist texts critiquing 'victim feminism', did a paradigm of victim-ization prevail in the heterogeneous domain of feminism? Is it true that the language of victimhood stands immune to polysemy and resignification, and can only hold a single set of meanings – passivity, powerlessness, dependence and innocence? Has the language of victimhood held only these meanings in the context of feminism? Is it possible or desirable, amidst the dominance of anti-victim discourse, for feminists to develop a counter-hegemonic 'pro-victim' stance?

To address these questions in this book, I analyse a wide selection of feminist texts that critique the notion of victim, probing their conceptions of and objections to 'victim identity' and 'victim politics' and analysing these in relation to the rhetoric and motifs of conservative anti-victimism, which I term *neoliberal victim theory*, foregrounding the role of neoliberal values in contemporary anti-victim discourse. Rather than aiming at a global analysis, I focus closely on venues of feminist writing where the most prominent and influential critiques of the notion of 'victim' have been voiced. I analyse feminist texts in which neoliberal victim theory is very strongly and obviously present, namely the critiques of 'victim feminism' that were produced as media-courted blockbusters on international release in the 1990s, which promote a neoliberal version of feminism that is problematically focused on personal responsibility and individual transformation rather than collective politics and structural change. I make new observations about these texts and their ongoing legacy in conservative feminism, while acknowledging that many feminists before me have also critically analysed them. My analysis moves on, however, to also examine influential critiques of 'victim feminism' that have not been accorded the same critical scrutiny as those of the popular press, namely, postmodernist and poststructuralist feminist critiques of victimhood produced in feminist theory – texts in which we expect to find a progressive anti-victim stance that will critique rather than embrace the values of neoliberalism.

Rather than assume that scholarly feminist critiques of the theme of victimhood in feminism are necessarily more progressive than those of conservative populism, my analysis critically examines the claims about victimhood that appear within postmodern feminist critiques of anti-rape feminism, Nietzschean accounts of feminism as a 'politics of *ressentiment*' in feminist political theory, and anti-racist and postcolonial feminist versions of the anti-victim critique. I find that all but the last venue of feminist writing host complaints about victimhood that bear the hallmarks of neoliberal victim theory. The only genuinely progressive engagement with the theme of victimhood in feminism has come from anti-racist and postcolonial feminist critiques, which do not so much espouse a movement 'beyond victimhood' as advance a critique of the way themes of victimhood and agency are racialized at the junctures of feminism and imperialism, with 'agency' problematically marking empowered feminine whiteness. Though originally prompted by anti-racist and postcolonial challenges to Western feminist universalism – the notion of a universal 'sisterhood' with shared vulnerabilities, sufferings and political interests – scholarly Western feminist critiques of the notion of 'victim' are characterized more strongly by the agency-affirming rhetoric and anti-victim motifs of neoliberal victim theory than by the task of interrogating the racialization (and other intersecting forms of identificatory particularization) of victimhood and agency within and beyond feminist discourse.

While popular press critiques of victim feminism are very deliberately wedded to neoliberal conceptions of the ideal citizen, scholarly feminist critiques of victim feminism instead demonstrate the circumstance David Harvey (2005) describes as 'vulnerability to incorporation into the neoliberal fold' (p. 42), or the making of analyses and interventions that unwittingly echo and support the values and cultural syntax of neoliberalism. Neoliberal values now significantly shape the language of social suffering and social being, necessitating careful handling of the themes of autonomy, freedom, liberation, agency, privacy, choice, responsibility, victimhood and oppression. Postmodernist and poststructuralist feminists are among the most subtle, cautious and illuminating theorists of subjectivity and the theme of autonomy, actively critiquing strong individualism and developing a 'thick view of female autonomy' (Gruber, 2009, p. 607) that moves beyond the binaries of

7

agent/victim, and free will/determinism. But in the body of work I examine we see a lapse in theoretical caution around the cognate themes of victimhood, agency and responsibility – the same kind of lapse Van Dijk (2009) discerns in the field of victimology, which has since its inception trafficked uncritically in established and rather problematic ways of depicting victims, becoming 'trapped into repeating prevailing misconceptions about victims' (p. 20) instead of acting as a venue for critically interrogating those depictions.[6]

My analysis in this book demonstrates that there is considerable overlap between feminist and neoliberal depictions of 'the victim problem'. I argue that feminism needs to act more strongly as a site of counter-hegemonic victim talk, instead of ceding ground to neoliberal values in the contemporary meaning of victimhood. Reflecting this argument, I also marshal an archive of progressive conceptions of the victim that help make the case for rethinking feminist abandonment of 'victim' as a worthy category of feminist theory and politics. Carine Mardorossian (2002) has argued that, instead of enjoining textual hostilities against the notion of 'victim', feminists need to 'reconceptualise and reappropriate the word victimi-sation and its meaning' (p. 771). Agreeing with this, I argue that feminists need to examine, hone and defend the language of victimhood, not just in order to avoid following suit with the wider conservative trend of derogating the notion of victim, but in order to provide a potent counter to this trend. In the following section I describe the hallmarks of neoliberal victim theory and indicate how they are present within feminist anti-victim discourse, before finally describing the overall structure of the book.

Feminism/neoliberalism and the victim subject

Writing in the context of neoliberal educational reform, Michael W. Apple (2001) underlines the discursive impact of neoliberal philosophy – the way in which it remakes 'our common sense, altering the meaning of the categories, the key words, we employ to understand the social and educational world and our place in it' (p. 9). Similarly, David Harvey (2005) observes that neoliberalism has 'become hegemonic as a mode of discourse. It has pervasive effects on ways of thought to the point where it has become incorporated into the common-sense way many of us interpret, live in, and understand the world' (p. 3). The category 'victim' is a significant example of the discursive impact of neoliberalism described by Apple and Harvey. Rosemary Hennessey (2000) has argued that while analysing the economic impact of neoliberal programmes of structural adjustment – gaping inequality and the upward distribution of wealth – is important work, just as important is work that analyses the 'ways of knowing that accompany neo-liberalism's advance' (p. 78). In the matter of the victim, these tasks are related: neoliberalism's intensification of economic inequality is accompanied by discourses that derogate and pathologize complaints against inequality. Rejection of 'victimhood' as a worthy place from which to forge personal identity and wage political struggle has been essential to this process.

8

The neoliberal remaking of the category 'victim' is profoundly capricious and paradoxical, but its signature features are sufficiently predictable to be discerned and analysed. In this book I develop an analysis of the main features of neoliberal victim theory, outlined below, as they take shape in feminist critiques of the notion of victim: the victim-bad/agent-good formulation, the pattern of reverse victimology, and the motif of resentment. All of these features are strongly present in popular press critiques of 'victim feminism', which use the notion of victim as a venue for introducing neoliberal values into feminist discourse, making 'feminism' available as a political sign on the right as well as the left of politics. In scholarly feminist critiques of the notion of victim, on the other hand, the features of neoliberal victim theory outlined below are present but are so ambiguously, as a result of a lapse in theoretical caution in the handling of the theme of victimhood – a problematic but largely unwitting trafficking in the anti-victim discourses established in neoliberal victim theory.

Neoliberal victim theory is characterized first and foremost by a victim-blaming conception of victimization as subjective and psychological rather than social and political. According to this conception, victimization does not so much happen 'to' someone as arise from the self – through the having of a 'victim personality', through the making of bad choices, through inadequate practice of personal vigilance and risk management, through the failure to practise the rigorous discipline of positive thinking (see Ehrenreich, 2009). This way of knowing victimization transforms social vulnerability into personal responsibility, erasing the social foundations of suffering in order to mask rising inequality, and making it seem logical to regard victims of poverty, inequality, discrimination and violence as the authors of their own suffering. The concept of social suffering as arising from individual fault (and as ameliorable through individual self-improvement) is most clearly active in the context of neoliberal welfare reform, where the requirement of public assistance is thoroughly discursively constituted as a personal failing rather than as an effect of embedded socio-economic inequality exacerbated by fiscal austerity. But the idea that social suffering indicates inner 'victim mentality' and failed risk management on the sufferer's part is active wherever the rubric of personal responsibility prevails, and my analysis attends to the way feminist issues, especially gendered violence and economic inequality, have been reconceptualized around the anti-victim rubric of personal choice and responsibility. In this book I refer to the values expressed in the neoliberal redefinition of victimhood broadly as the *victim-bad/agent-good formulation*. It is remarkably easy to participate in this formulation without explicitly ascribing to a conception of victimhood as self-made, namely, by situating 'agency' (including the notion of 'constrained agency') over 'victimhood' as the seat of personal or analytical promise and possibility. Pairing derogation of victimhood with celebration of agency as the category of personal or analytical virtue affirms what is essential to neoliberal victim theory: the victim/agent dichotomy, or the understanding of 'victimhood' as agency's opposite and demise.

In neoliberal victim theory, the rather uncompassionate conception of victimization as self-made – the idea that winners win and losers lose because they have simply chosen to do so – fairly obviously evacuates sociological explanation of social suffering, directly subverting progressive political efforts to make victimization through poverty, inequality, discrimination and violence visible as collective and socio-economically embedded in an array of intersecting engines of social hierarchy and difference: class stratification, gender segregation, ethnic hierarchy, ableism, homophobia. But the concept of victimization as self-made is made more palatable by being couched within an appealing narrative of liberation borrowed from the very forms of progressive politics that neoliberal victim theory notionally subverts. The second primary feature of neoliberal victim theory is that it coopts and reverses, in order to rival and replace, progressive narratives of liberation from established orthodoxy and structural oppression. Neoliberal victim theory depicts society as awash with fraudulent claims to victim status and paints the state as held to ransom by victim politics promulgated by progressives, even as it is these depictions themselves, in their 'putative self-evidence and sheer pervasiveness' (Dean, 2010, p. 7) – and not prolific victim claims – that actually dominate. Neoliberal victim theory always assumes the form of an anti-establishment liberation narrative in which we free ourselves from the yoke of oppression brought on by Leftist political correctness and its 'power victims'.

In this book I develop a reading of this aspect of neoliberal victim theory as marking a form of *reverse victimology* – a reverse discourse that serves to reorganize the way suffering and the sufferer are perceived, in which those claiming victim status for themselves or for others are recast as non-credible victimizers. Reverse victimology is akin to the form of scapegoating Van Dijk (2009) describes as 'reactive victim scapegoating', or the performance of a dramatic withdrawal of compassion for the victim when they do not comply with prescribed or ideal victim behaviour, triggering victim-blame and 'an outpouring of hatred against them' (p. 18). Reactive victim scapegoating sacrifices the victim in order to resolve the conflict brought about by the wrong. Van Dijk shows reactive victim scapegoating at work in public responses to high profile crime victims. In the body of work I examine, the scapegoating action of reverse victimology is applied not so much to individuals as to entire political formations and collectives of progressive political actors who, by politicizing victimization and doing so collectively, have violated a cardinal rule of victimhood: the acceptance of compassion 'on condition of meekness' (p. 18).

As the feature of reverse victimology implies, neoliberal victim theory does not actually move beyond victim politics, instead articulating a new form of victim politics. Neoliberal victim theory self-presents as an effort to restore clarity about the nature of genuine victimization, intensifying the perception of victim identity as peculiarly susceptible to fraudulent uses and engaging in what Dean (2010) calls 'the fashioning of the exemplary victim' (p. 8), or the articulation of new, attenuated criteria of ideal victimhood. In this way neoliberal victim theory draws upon and updates the semantic heritage of the word 'victim' within Christian theology, which figures the ideal victim as forgiving and compliant, and the bad victim as angry, vengeful and politically threatening (Van Dijk, 2009).[7] Neoliberal victim theory remakes the distinction between victim and victimizer into a distinction between the ideal, genuine victim and the reviled figure of the 'power victim' – a subject who 'plays the victim' and blames others for their misfortune, undertaking activism and claiming unearned power on the basis of fraudulent victim identity. Progressive political projects, notably feminism and anti-racism, are blamed for the rise of the 'power victim', with progressive political actors and 'power victims' alike portrayed as perniciously oppressive, destructive and victimizing.

Somewhat paradoxically, then, the 'anti-victimist' orientation of neoliberal victim theory leads to a new form of victim politics: neoliberal victim theory impugns undeserving 'power victims' on behalf of deserving 'real victims' (for my early elaborations of this paradox, see Stringer, 2000, 2001). In the rhetoric of neoliberal victim theory, 'real victimization' takes place at the hands of progressives and power victims, for example through so-called 'reverse sexism' or 'reverse racism'. Apart from this, 'real victimization' is also re-defined as a form of injury, loss or misfortune that stands out clearly from everyday life, that can be construed as an isolated event rather than as a sign of embedded structure, with the victim ideally occupying a position of pure innocence. In tune with this rhetoric, victims of perceived political correctness and the 'nanny state', and victims of objectively unforeseeable and preferably spectacularly traumatic crime and disaster (see Nissim-Sabat, 2009) become the locus of legitimate victim talk in the neoliberal polity. 'Real victims' include subjects readily constructed as existing in an abject condition of absolute oppression, such as non-Western women; and subjects easily identified with worldless innocence, thus excusable non-responsibility, such as children (see Baird, 2008) and the unborn foetus (see Cole, 2007 and Stringer, 2006). Neoliberal victim theory does not in fact 'move beyond' or 'let go of' the category victim. Instead it redefines victimhood and reorganizes the perception of who can and cannot be seen as a real and legitimate victim.

The third primary feature of neoliberal victim theory is the motif of 'resentment', with progressive political actors and the figure of the 'bad victim' routinely depicted as being 'driven by resentment' or as having 'succumbed to resentment', and resentment itself construed as a form of toxic psychology that develops in response to suffering, real or imagined, one's own or that of others, that produces a will to politicize and complain about suffering. In texts that either strongly chorus or merely reflect the values of neoliberal victim theory, the 'victim problem' is repeatedly linked to the psychology of resentment, construed not only as an inability to let go of suffering, but as a pathological psychological attachment to suffering that, it is supposed, breeds a colourful variety of character traits and political tendencies, from wilful mendacity, perpetual other-blaming and toxic vengefulness, through to undemocratic moralism and frighteningly Manichean authoritarianism. The motif of resentment always appears in the vein of diagnosis, enabling neoliberal victim theory to adopt the appearance of clinical or quasi-clinical psychological knowledge, lending authority to its value-laden constructions of 'victim men-tality', the 'victim personality', and their political expression as 'victimism'. The motif of resentment powerfully supports the personalizing, psychologizing and pathologizing turn victim talk takes in the context of neoliberalism, and is in this way profoundly depoliticizing. This motif directs scepticism towards the inner feelings presumed to motivate collective and individual acts of politicizing victimization, sponsoring the problematic and rather narrow depiction of progressive political projects as grounded in toxic emotion rather than in a credible account of power relations in the social world. Of the features of neoliberal victim theory outlined here, the motif of resentment is the most pervasive, being strongly present on both sides of the permeable border between progressive and conservative depictions of 'the victim problem'.

In some of the texts I examine, namely critiques of feminism as a 'politics of *ressentiment*' in feminist political theory, Nietzsche's theory of *ressentiment* (resentment) is drawn on extensively to inform and authorize the diagnosis of feminists as negatively fixated on suffering and as harbouring 'toxic resentments parading as radical critique' (Brown, 1995, p. xi). My analysis closely examines this depiction of feminism and investigates Nietzsche's concept of *ressentiment*, weighing the way Nietzsche theorizes the politics of resentment against the diagnostic instrumentalization of Nietzsche's theory in feminist anti-victim discourse. I argue that Nietzsche's theory of *ressentiment* provides a way to conceptualize victim identity as a site of identificatory upheaval rather than fixity. My reading of Nietzsche foregrounds the theme of asceticism, or the way a political regime can preserve itself amidst counter-hegemonic threats, by popularizing a victim-blaming discourse that encourages subjective practices of 'self-discipline, self-surveillance, and self-overcoming' (GOM: III, 15, 16).[8] I observe that the operation of asceticism – the use of victim-blame to return complainers to compliance, quelling the threat their rebellion poses to the established order – bears a striking resemblance to the political tasks of neoliberal victim theory: to deprive certain kinds of political complaint of credibility and authority; to normalize and promote the victim-blaming values of 'personal responsibility'. I argue that it is Nietzsche's discussion of asceticism, and not the conception of *ressentiment* as toxic psychology, that provides the most useful Nietzschean resource for interpreting the dynamics of victim politics in the neoliberal era.

My analysis is critical of the way feminist theory has shown a lapse in theoretical caution in relation to the category 'victim', but it does not, however, suggest that this lapse is evident right across contemporary feminist engagement with the theme of victimhood. In contrast, I emphasize that feminist theorizations and politicizations of gendered violence in particular have been venues for a productive critique of the social construction of victimhood. Feminist theorizations and politicizations of violence and sexual harm have long been engaged in the kind of work that Van Dijk argues is necessary if the analysis of victimhood is to avoid supporting the depictions of victimhood essential to reactive victim scapegoating. Feminist work on gendered violence has led the way in the understanding of secondary victimization (see Anderson and Doherty, 2008), or the way prevailing definitions of victims, victimhood and victimization shape social, cultural, scholarly and legal responses to victims, and can do so in ways that are profoundly harmful and inequitable, thus constituting 'secondary' victimization – a further harm 'added' to the original harm, which takes place when recognition as a 'legitimate victim' is unjustly denied, or granted in a marginalizing way. Perhaps the most salient example of secondary victimization in feminist accounts is the way criminal justice responses to rape, from police response through rape trials, can stage a 'second rape', notably by permitting attacks on the complainant's credibility that frame them as the guilty party, eroding their authority and thereby neutralizing their complaint.

In my analysis I use Lyotard's (1988) theory of the differend to theorize secondary victimization, arguing that feminist politicizations of gendered violence and sexual victimization undertake the kind of work Lyotard describes as 'bearing witness to the *differend*' (No. 22, original emphasis): the theoretical work of examining the conditions under which a wrong cannot be signified as 'wrong' within a shared idiom, which enables the political work of attempting to ameliorate erasure of the wrong. In this light I interpret feminist efforts to reform criminal justice responses to rape, the theories and practices of rape crisis feminism, and the critique of victim-blame central to the current SlutWalk movement. Of course, in the body of work critiquing victim feminism, this kind of feminist work is constituted as 'victimism', by the popular press and postmodern feminists alike. Feminist theorizations and politicizations of gendered violence and sexual harm are depicted as 'myopically' focused on victimization and its aftermath and are criticized for not assuming a more positive focus on what women can do to prevent being victimized. My analysis observes the way this line of critique of 'victim feminism' conforms to a fundamental tenet in the neoliberal government of crime: the focus on crime 'before it occurs' (O'Malley, 1992, p. 262), or the shifting of the burden of prevention from the state to the individual.

The archive of progressive conceptions of the victim I marshal in my analysis thus includes Nietzsche's discussion of slave revolt and asceticism, Lyotard's conception of the differend and a range of feminist discourses that contribute to the analysis of the social construction of victimhood found within feminist theory, anti-racist and postcolonial feminist critique, rape crisis feminism and the SlutWalk movement. These resources help to direct feminist analysis away from diagnosing the victim problem in feminism, and towards analysis of the politics underpinning the now pervasive depiction of 'victimhood' as unquestionably problematic. Progressive conceptions of victimhood enable us to theorize victimization in ways that subvert the victim/agent dichotomy, to recognize and respond to the problem of secondary or effaced victimization and to reassert sociological approaches to victimization against approaches that individualize, psychologize and pathologize victimhood. As such, these conceptions give a different view of the role of the language of victimhood in the politics of emancipation, providing alternatives to the confines, prejudices and contradictions of neoliberal victim theory.

The structure of the book

The first three chapters of *Knowing Victims* examine the body of feminist work that seeks to move feminism 'beyond victimhood', beginning in Chapter 1 with the popular press critiques of 'victim feminism'. Challenging their construction of feminism as centred on a view of women as passive victims, I provide examples of the way feminists have tended to theorize the victim instead as an agentic bearer of knowledge. Identifying the key features of neoliberal victim theory in the popular press critiques, I show that they coopt rather than depart from victim politics, and do not affirm women's agency, instead situating Western women as standing in need of instruction in the ways of entrepreneurial agency. I argue they produce a new and subsequently highly influential articulation of feminism that reflects the core values of neoliberalism. The neoliberal feminist lens they elaborate recasts issues of gendered structural oppression as individual problems of personal responsibility, or as depoliticized social problems to be dealt with by criminal law, reflecting neoliberalism's rubric of personal responsibility and intensification of criminal law.

Chapter 2 then analyses scholarly feminist critiques of feminist anti-rape politicizations. A key claim in these critiques is that feminist efforts to improve legal recognition of rape merely strengthen rape law's patriarchal construction of femininity as embodied vulnerability. This leads to the further claim that feminist anti-rape politicizations should 'turn to agency', focusing instead on progressive representations of women as agents who are capable of resisting rape. Challenging the presumed progressiveness of woman-as-agent constructions, I use Lyotard's concept of the differend to explore the role of these constructions in legal forms of victim-blame. My analysis shows that rape law typically figures femininity not as embodied vulnerability, but as responsible agency, and never more so than in the current neoliberal era of privatized social risk, where women are expected to align with an ideal rape-preventing subject. Demonstrating that not all images of women as agents are progressive and liberating, I argue that the real ethical problem confronting feminist anti-rape politics, intensified in the era of neoliberalism, is that of finding a way to phrase women's agency without reinscribing patriarchal representations of women as the blameworthy agents of their own victimization. Rape crisis feminist discourses of survivorship, and the critique of victim-blame central to the current SlutWalk movement, provide my examples of how such phrasing is possible.

Chapter 3 analyses critiques in feminist political theory of feminism as a politics of *ressentiment* characterized by 'reiterative attachment' to feminine vulnerability. These critiques raise compelling questions about the way woman-as-victim constructions can erase differences among women, yet their psychologization of politics and pathologization of *ressentiment* strongly reflect the primary features of neoliberal victim theory. The diagnostic approach to *ressentiment* adopted in these critiques locates the source of resentment in individual character rather than in worldly power relations, continuing a long heritage of counter-revolutionary

Nietzscheanism. I argue, however, that Nietzsche's concept of *ressentiment* is valuable for understanding the dynamics of victim politics in neoliberal times, if we foreground Nietzsche's theme of asceticism. The chapter also examines critiques by anti-racist and postcolonial feminists that problematize the themes of victimhood and agency in Western feminism. Although these are said to have inspired corrective Western feminist movement away from 'victim feminism', my analysis points out that in this corrective movement, anti-racist and postcolonial feminists' explicit wariness of the racialized concept of 'agency' has disappeared.

Chapter 4 is the final chapter and focuses on Nietzsche's theory of *ressentiment*, slave morality and asceticism. The feminist political theorists discussed in Chapter 3 perpetuate the dominant understanding that the psychology of *ressentiment* serves to fix victims to victim identity, limiting their political action to resubordinative complaint against the oppressor. This narrow reading discards Nietzsche's equivocations about *ressentiment* and the complex evolution of this concept in his work. I argue that Nietzsche describes *ressentiment* as threateningly emancipative because it enables the victim to imagine a social world that will not depend on their victimization. Further, Nietzsche's vivid account of how the victim politics of the slave is disarmed by the asceticism of the priest captures, with surprising precision, the efforts to rhetorically and materially disarm progressive victim politics that are characteristic of neoliberal times. This interpretation of Nietzsche enables my critical conceptualization of neoliberal victim theory as a form of asceticism, and leads me to reconceptualize *ressentiment* as a generative force in the politics of progressive social change.

Notes

1   I draw this term 'victim talk' from Martha Minow (1993), who uses it to designate public and counter-public discourses of victimhood and victimization.

2   This kind of work is taken up in Berns (2004), Cole (2007), Naqvi (2007), Nissam-Sabat (2009) and Dean (2010).

3   In a recent example of how dis-identifying from 'victimhood' features prominently in the self-presentation of those who have suffered severe violence and trauma, Lani Brennan's (2013) autobiography begins with the words, 'I've suffered violence and abuse and degradation that no human being should suffer. But I am not a victim. I am a survivor' (p. 2).

4   Behavioural psychologist and talk show host Phillip C. McGraw ('Dr Phil') refers to the avoidance of 'victim mentality' as a 'life law', linking such avoidance to the proper uptake of personal responsibility: 'Don't play the role of victim, or use past events to build excuses ... You will never fix a problem by blaming someone else. Whether the cards you've been dealt are good or bad, you're in charge of yourself now' (www.drphil.com/articles/article/44, accessed 24 September 2012).

5   The term 'victocracy' comes from Larry Elder (2000), who 'coined the term "victicrats" for groups who blame all their ills, problems and concerns on other people' (Pizzey et al., 2000, p. ix).

6   Van Dijk (2009) observes that the original 'penal victimology', developed for purposes of criminal defence, gave criminological expression to 'the biases about victims of crime prevailing among many criminal lawyers at the time' (p. 19). The

later 'therapeutic victimology' which is focused on the impact of crime on the victim, similarly gave expression to biases about ideal victim behaviour (p. 22) – namely, a bias towards the forgiving, compliant victim and against the angry, activist victim. Contemporary discussions about victim's rights in the criminal justice system similarly promote the unfounded assumption that victims are bound to support 'tough on crime' policies, finding in them a reflection of their inner thirst for vengeance – even though, as Van Dijk observes, 'Empirical victimological research has consistently shown that crime victims are not more punitive than the public at large' (p. 20).

7   Van Dijk examines the history of 'the *victima* label' in European languages, producing the most thorough etymology of 'victim' to date. His etymology traces the changing meaning of '*victima*' (originally, 'beast for sacrifice') as it entered the language of Christian theology as 'a special name for Jesus Christ', the expiatory victim (Van Dijk, 2009, p. 4). This use of 'victim' 'will initially have impeded rather than facilitated a broadening of its meaning to ordinary human beings. Such usage would probably have struck religious people as blasphemous' (p. 4). Eventually 'victim' was generalized to others, initially through a Christian perspective that in suffering one experiences the 'passion of the Christ': the suffering brought by victimization brings one close to Christ, directing the sufferer to follow Christ into self-sacrificing forgiveness. Ostensibly, the category 'crime victim' is secular, but in fact our constructions of and reactions to crime victims continue to respect Christian precepts, offering 'compassion on condition of meekness' (p. 18).

8   In this book my references to Nietzsche's works are abbreviated in accord with the English title acronyms of his works (for example, *Beyond Good and Evil* is abbreviated as BGE). Roman numerals or abbreviated chapter titles are used to denote sections within single texts, and numbers denote aphorisms rather than pages. For example, aphorism number 21 in the Second Essay of *On the Genealogy of Morals* would be referenced as GOM: II, 21, and aphorism number 6 of the chapter entitled 'Why I Am So Wise' in *Ecce Homo* would be referenced as EH: Wise, 6. In all quotations from his works the emphasis is original.

1

VICTIMS LEFT, RIGHT AND CENTRE

Constructing 'victim feminism'

The relationship between feminism and victimhood has been widely problematized in recent decades, within and beyond popular and scholarly venues of feminist writing and debate. Of this diverse body of work, the best known and most visible contributions have been the critiques of 'victim feminism' produced by popular press feminist writers, including Camille Paglia (1994), Christina Hoff Sommers (1994), Katie Roiphe (1993), Naomi Wolf (1993), Rene Denfeld (1995) and Natasha Walter (1998) among others.[1] In the 1990s, these writers produced a spate of blockbuster books problematizing feminist representation of women as victims and arguing for a new agency-affirming feminism, designated with terms such as 'equity feminism' and 'power feminism'. Their books occupied a space previously held by an earlier generation of feminist blockbusters, by feminist writers like Betty Friedan (1963), Germaine Greer (1971), Marilyn French ([1978] 1992) and Susan Faludi (1992). Like these earlier blockbusters, the 1990s critiques of victim feminism are shaped as consciousness-raising texts and calls to action, aiming to profoundly alter women's perceptions of themselves and society. Yet where earlier feminist blockbusters all in some way agitate against the politico-economic status quo, the critiques of victim feminism vigorously reassert the status quo, often passionately defending it against further feminist incursion. Marking the 1990s as the decade of women's liberation from 'victim feminism', the popular press critiques of victim feminism problematize feminism rather than masculine dominance, calling upon readers to resist feminist victim identity and align instead with postfeminist agency and empowerment. Widely invoked by scholars and policy-makers as well as in the media, in the new century the critique of victim feminism has continued to be reiterated, sedimenting as a popular complaint against feminism. Rather than being exclusive to feminism, the derogation of victim politics has been a widespread theme in media and publishing since the late 1980s, voiced most stridently in critiques of 'political correctness' as spawning 'nations of victims' and 'cultures of complaint', to the detriment of personal agency.[2]

This chapter analyses a selection of popular press critiques of victim feminism, developing a critique of the way they conceptualize feminism, victimhood and agency, and tracking their legacy into the present. A number of commentators have already critically weighed the critiques of victim feminism, yielding important insights.[3] With few exceptions, however, existing feminist responses to these critiques have been surprisingly ready to accept their core constructions: their construction of feminism as plagued by a victim problem, of 'victimhood' itself as problematic, and their construction of 'agency' as coterminous with liberation. In this chapter I propose that these constructions, rather than assumed feminist victimhood, become the object of critical scrutiny, with due analytical attention given to the wider political context of critiques of victim feminism, namely, the growing ascendancy of neoliberalism and its efforts to replace the concept of structural oppression with the concept of personal responsibility. Popular press critiques of victim feminism are worthy of scrutiny not for what they might usefully tell us about feminism's 'victim problem', but for what their provocative and contestable constructions of this problem reveal about the terrain of feminist politics and gendered suffering in neoliberal times.

Identifying the key claims made in critiques of victim feminism and probing their conceptions of feminism, victimhood and agency, my analysis first of all defends feminism against the 'victim feminist' construct, pointing out that feminists have tended to conceptualize the victim subject as an agentic bearer of knowledge, rather than as passively victimized. This is the first of several conceptions of the victim explored in this book that I mark out as alternative conceptions, for they do not rest on the currently dominant binary of passive, innocent victimhood pitted against active, responsible agency. Thereafter, my analysis focuses on the way critiques of victim feminism reflect the core values of neoliberalism. Existing responses to these critiques have tended to recognize their conservative political entanglements, while seeing these entanglements as separable from the true problems with victimhood revealed in the critiques. I contend, however, that their very problematization of victimhood is profoundly reflective of neoliberalism and requires scrutiny.

Rather than move beyond 'victim feminism' and towards 'agency feminism', these critiques problematize and redefine victim politics, victimhood and agency in ways amenable to the entrenchment of neoliberalism as a political imaginary and mode of governance. While it is tempting to view critiques of victim feminism as backlash texts, they are more 'productive' than this term implies. Co-opting and reversing the politics of 'victim feminism', they contributed powerfully to the creation of a new and distinctly neoliberal version of feminism that has since become pervasive. Current discussions of feminism and neoliberalism perceptively analyse the blending of neoliberal ideals of self and citizen with feminist values of women's empowerment in contemporary 'postfeminist' ideals of femininity.[4] Complementing this work, I focus on the related phenomenon of *neoliberal feminism*, and analyse the version of feminism produced when the categories and issues of feminist politics are rearticulated through the values and worldview of neoliberalism. The critiques of victim feminism provide a powerful example of the way feminist discourse is co-opted and transformed in the context of neoliberalism, and as such they are relevant to the questions Nina Power (2009) and Nancy Fraser (2009) have raised about the meaning of 'feminism' in neoliberal times.

As Nina Power (2009) observes in *One Dimensional Woman*, a key feature of current geopolitical discourse is the co-opting of the language of feminism by substantively anti-feminist political figures: 'As a political term, "feminism" has become so broad that it can be used to justify almost anything, even the invasion of other countries' (p. 12). Also addressing contemporary shifts in the meaning of 'feminism', Nancy Fraser (2009) makes the argument that 'the rise of neoliberalism dramatically changed the terrain on which second-wave feminism operated. The effect . . . was to resignify feminist ideals' (p. 108). Power's and Fraser's analyses suggest that in neoliberal times anti-feminism does not necessarily assume the form of a rejection of feminism as such, but instead assumes the form of a discursive *resignification* of 'feminism' – the production of new, neoliberal 'feminist' discourses, or 'uncanny doubles' as Fraser terms them.

Fraser refers to Boltanksi and Chiapello's ([1999] 2005) argument that 'capital-ism periodically remakes itself in moments of historical rupture, in part by recuperating strands of critique directed against it' (Fraser, 2009, p. 109). Fraser's analysis identifies the way, on neoliberal terrain, second-wave feminism's 'best ideas' (p. 117) – the critiques of economism, androcentrism, étatism, and Westphalianism – have been recuperated and resignified. Second-wave feminism's critique of the family wage was 'once the centrepiece of a radical analysis of capitalism's androcentrism', but 'serves today to intensify capitalism's valorization of waged labour' (p. 111), while the second-wave feminist critique of welfare-state paternalism leads a 'perverse afterlife' (p. 111) in the legitimation of neoliberal welfare reform. On neoliberal terrain, Fraser argues, 'feminism' has two meanings: the usual meaning that refers to a social movement; and a new meaning in which 'feminism' operates as a general discursive construct that social movement feminists no longer own or control. In this second meaning 'feminism' becomes 'an empty signifier of the good (akin, perhaps, to "democracy"), which can and will be invoked to legitimate a variety of different scenarios, not all of which promote gender justice' (p. 114). As a result of this second meaning of feminism, where feminism operates as a general discursive construct, feminists encounter their 'uncanny double' in the political sphere: 'As the discourse becomes independent of the movement, the latter is increasingly confronted with a strange shadowy version of itself, an uncanny double that it can neither simply embrace nor wholly disavow' (p. 144).

Fraser's concept of feminism's 'uncanny double' provides a useful way to frame the critiques of victim feminism, which visibly perform the resignification of feminism she describes, while also constituting a different kind of example. Power and Fraser identify several 'uncanny doubles' in the terrain of neoliberal politics and the state, discerning resignifications of feminism in the US wars on terror and in European neo-racism (Power, 2009), in Thatcher's critique of the 'nanny state' and in the political rhetoric of Hillary Clinton and Sarah Palin (Fraser, 2009). In comparison with these examples, in which the political signs of feminism and women's liberation are invoked at a level of generality, the critiques of 'victim feminism' stage a very deliberate, systematic and explicit resignification of 'feminism' – a carefully wrought rearticulation of feminist theory and politics around the categories of neoliberal philosophy, framed as a sweeping away of 'victim feminism' and as the dawn of 'agency feminism'.

The critiques of victim feminism I focus on in this chapter – Sommers' (1994) *Who Stole Feminism? How Women Have Betrayed Women*, Roiphe's (1993) *The Morning After: Sex, Fear and Feminism* and Wolf's (1993) *Fire with Fire: The New Female Power and How it Will Change the Twenty-first Century* – collectively reveal the character and ethos of neoliberal feminism, as well as its operative contradictions. My analysis underlines the importance of recognizing that, contrary to their self-presentation, critiques of victim feminism *do not* move beyond victim politics, and *do not* affirm women's agency. Rather than move beyond victim politics, these critiques produce a revised version of victim politics that reflects the victim-blaming structure of neoliberalism's personal responsibility system. Creating new distinctions between genuine and false victims of gendered suffering, they influentially recast a spectrum of feminist issues – spanning victimization through violence, discrimination and inequality – as individual problems of personal responsibility, or as social problems to be dealt with by criminal law. Gendered suffering is blamed on 'victims' and 'criminals', displacing the concepts of collective responsibility and structural oppression in the explanation of social suffering, and promoting the neoliberal conception of genuine victimhood as notionally limited to the perfect abrogation of political right. Rather than affirm women's agency, critiques of victim feminism actually problematize women's capacity for agency, announcing a crisis of personal responsibility among women, who are seen as being particularly at risk of forfeiting personal responsibility in favour of passive victimhood. This updates a timeworn liberal construction of women as of questionable fitness for the rigours of citizenship, in this case, the market individualism of the neoliberal polis.

Identifying and analysing these depoliticizing transformations in the phrasing and framing of gendered suffering are valuable for an understanding of the fraught terrain now confronted by ongoing feminist efforts to politicize gendered suffering. Although dubious, the constructions of feminism, victimhood and agency in the critiques of victim feminism have proven to be influential, dovetailing with neoliberal transformations in the government of social problems, responsibility and crime. In the context of neoliberalism, feminist politicizations of gendered suffering face the difficult situation of being substantively countered and discursively co-opted by the rival discourses of their uncanny double: neoliberal feminism.

The story of victim feminism

Is 'victim feminism' a worthy and coherent description of feminism? Have feminists by and large, or in waves, conceived of women as passive victims of male domination rather than as agents capable of controlling their own fate? These are the first questions raised by the 1990s critiques of victim feminism, which mark that decade as dominated by victim feminists espousing passive victimhood. In order to address these questions, in this section I explore the way Sommers, Roiphe and Wolf tell the story of victim feminism, identifying their key claims and differences. What is 'victim feminism', and what do these writers see as problematic in it? As we will see, these authors define victim feminism as a form of feminism that sees women as passive victims of male domination, a view they regard as false, destructive and obsolete, particularly when applied to the West in the 1990s, where, they contend, the feminist work of ending male domination is complete or nearly so. As I will analyse in greater depth in Chapter 3, this rejection of the idea that women in Western liberal democracies are 'victims' operates as a displacement of the victim label onto non-Western women, providing a potent example of the emancipated/emaciated binary characteristic of Western feminist universalism in its closest resemblance to and complicity with imperialism. The critiques of victim feminism make the same representations Christina Scharff (2011) found in her recent analysis of young British and German women's views on feminism: '[t]he construction of Muslim women as powerless victims of patriarchy facilitates the repudiation of feminism as unnecessary in western countries' (p. 128).

Sommers, Roiphe and Wolf all tell the story of victim feminism in broadly the same way. They organize modern feminism into a dichotomy between a bad feminism that persists with a false and obsolete theory of women as victims, and a good feminism that is cognisant of Western women's present agency. This ur-narrative of modern feminism structures each critique, even as they locate 'victim feminism' and rationalize the need for its demise in different and at times conflicting ways. The political tenor of this ur-narrative is consistent and brazen, with each critic using 'the victim problem in current feminism' as a venue for derogating feminism's politically radical variants (Wolf, 1993, p. 148). Differences and debates among feminism's radical variants (gynocentric, cultural, anti-rape, poststructuralist, socialist, materialist) disappear as these feminisms are gathered together and constructed as a resentful, anti-democratic ethos of passive victimhood, positioning the alternative feminist view promoted in these texts as a progressive, properly democratic ethos of powerful agency. Their concern with the question of how feminists should regard women – as 'capable agents' or 'passive victims' – is expressed as a concern with the kind of political agency feminists should assume within the politico-economic arrangements of the 'post-socialist' 1990s. In this regard their ur-narrative of modern feminism is accompanied by an ur-narrative of modern patriarchy. They describe modern patriarchy as dead or dying, discrediting the feminist view of social reality as still characterized by masculine dominance. In this postfeminist context, feminism no longer needs to be a radical politics oriented to structural change, except where applied beyond the West, where women are *truly* oppressed.

Sommers: liberation and the 'feminist establishment'

In Sommers' version of the ur-narrative in her book *Who Stole Feminism?* (1994), the good feminism in the dichotomy is classical liberal feminism, which she calls 'equity feminism'. In Sommers' telling, equity feminism originated with the 1848 Seneca Falls Convention and was the mainstream feminism until the New Left emerged in the 1960s. Led by Enlightenment liberal philosophy, equity feminism ascribes to 'traditional, classically liberal, humanistic' values (Sommers, 1994, p. 22), and is guided by belief in women's and men's shared humanity, thus equality. Narrowing the variety of forms liberal feminism has assumed historically down to one conservative position, Sommers defines equity feminism as a limited programme of reform oriented to equitable opportunity. Equity feminists work with rather than against liberal capitalism, purging gender bias from written law in order to grant women the opportunity to take up the rights and responsibilities of liberal citizenship. In Sommers' view, New Left radical feminism has usurped equity feminism as the mainstream feminist position, and her aim is to restore equity feminism to mainstream status. She refers to New Left radical feminism as 'gender feminism' and, at times, 'resenter feminism', arguing that feminists who see women as victims are motivated by resentment, diminishing their capacity for reason. These terms 'gender feminism' and 'resenter feminism' are interchangeable with the term 'victim feminism', which comes from Wolf's critique.

According to Sommers, gender feminism emerged in the 1960s as an anti-establishment critique of liberal-capitalist patriarchy and has since become the new 'feminist establishment', wielding inordinate influence 'in the schools, in the feminist centres, in the workplaces' (p. 274). Gender feminism is misandrist (man-hating) as well as misogynist (disapproving of traditional femininities). It demands special treatment rather than legal equality for women as an oppressed group, and esteems femaleness as a source of alternative moral values such as nurturance and pacifism. Sommers refers to gender feminism as 'transformationist' (it is revolutionary rather than reformist) and 'ideological', with 'ideology' denoting an interpretation of social reality that is widely believed but fictional (p. 257). Sommers frames gender feminism as a self-contained industry. It appropriates public monies from government and educational institutions to fund biased research that will attest to victimization experienced by women; this biased research in turn furnishes gender feminists with moral authority, professional longevity, reason for being and more funding. Women and the US nation-state need to be liberated from the fraudulent labours of gender feminism. 'Getting out from under the stifling, condescending ministrations of the ideologues is a bracing cause and an exhilarating necessary step for the truly liberated women to take. When enough women take it . . . their power structure will not survive' (p. 274).

Sommers' mapping of the gender feminist power structure includes a wide array of forms of feminist organization. Feminist theory, particularly theory influenced by Marx and Foucault, the discipline of Women's Studies and on-campus feminist organizations are said to dominate universities, while feminist organizations such as rape crisis and women's shelters, and feminist politicizations of issues such as date rape, sexual harassment, pornography, spousal violence, pay parity and the gender pay gap, dominate the public sphere. She does not specify how or why, but Sommers observes that equity feminism's agenda for reform is 'not yet fully achieved' (p. 22). Nonetheless, she argues, it has enjoyed sufficient success to discredit gender feminism: 'Women today can no longer be regarded as the victims of an undemocratic domination' (p. 260).

Sommers' campaign against gender feminism is ongoing (see Sommers, 2013). In the body of work she has produced since *Who Stole Feminism?*, Sommers continues to invoke the tyrannical dominance of gender feminism in education and politics, latterly characterizing gender feminism as a threat to the economy. Her follow-up book, *The War Against Boys: How Misguided Feminism Is Harming Our Young Men* (Sommers, 2000) argues that victim feminism has commandeered the education system, empowering girls at boys' expense. In the lead-up to the US invasion of Iraq, Sommers (2002) recast her critique of victim feminism as a legitimating argument for the wars on terror, dovetailing with wider representation of these wars as taking place in the name of Islamic women's liberation. In her 2002 testimony to the US Senate Foreign Relations Committee advising non-ratification of CEDAW, and her subsequent article 'The Subjection of Islamic Women' (2007), Sommers chastises 'establishment feminists' for ignoring the oppression of Islamic women while portraying American women as victims of oppression. Sommers (2002) argues that the next historical task of equity feminism lies abroad rather than at home, supporting US foreign policy efforts to liberate Islamic women: 'American women have achieved virtual equality with men . . . we have to help women in other parts of the world secure the freedoms we now take for granted' (p. 16). In her recent work on the gender pay gap, Sommers reiterates the argument she developed in *Who Stole Feminism?* refuting the victim feminist view that women's lesser earnings from paid work reflect gendered structural oppression.

Roiphe: sex, lies and meritocracy

Where Sommers' critique of victim feminism is wide-ranging in scope, Katie Roiphe's *The Morning After* is focused more narrowly on university-based feminist politicizations of sexual harm, taking the controversial stance that sexual harassment and date rape are bogus concepts. Sommers cites Roiphe's critique appreciatively (Sommers, 1994, p. 222). But the New Left radical feminism Sommers impugns as gender feminism, Roiphe renders as a powerful and worthy ethos of female strength, agency and liberation. According to Roiphe, victim feminism came along *after* the second wave of feminism, in the 1980s, when feminism took a neo-Victorian turn. Where 1960s and 1970s second-wave feminists threw off prudish stereotypes and asserted sexual agency, neo-Victorian feminists of the 1980s revived those stereotypes by focusing on sexual victimization. As a result, second-wave feminist emphasis on sexual liberation was supplanted by neo-Victorian emphasis on sexual regulation, or the making of rules specifying correct sexual conduct with the aim of protecting women from sexual harm. Sommers and Roiphe locate the period before victim feminism in very different moments in feminist history – for Sommers, the second wave is the dawn of victim feminism, for Roiphe, it was the shining moment before victim feminism emerged. Yet they revise these historical moments in similar ways. Both are rendered as moments in which strong individualism and personal agency, as opposed to collective struggle and politicization of victimization, were the reigning feminist values.

Roiphe otherwise characterizes victim feminism similarly to Sommers. Having usurped a more worthy feminism, its oppressive political correctness reigns supreme on college campuses and in public life, fed by public monies funding biased research attesting to problems that do not exist. Roiphe does not describe a scenario in which feminism's goals are nearly achieved. Instead she suggests that feminism's goals have been fully realized, but that neo-Victorian feminists are creating a backlash against feminist success, to ensure feminism is still needed:

> Feminists are closer to their backlash than they'd like to think. The image that emerges from feminist preoccupation with rape and sexual harassment is that of women as victims . . . This image of a delicate woman bears a striking resemblance to that fifties ideal my mother and the other women of her generation fought so hard to get away from.
>
> (Roiphe, 1993, p. 6)

Like Sommers, Roiphe continues to voice her critique of feminism, and periodically revisits her argument about the 'capricious' concept of sexual harassment in newspaper columns and blog sites (Roiphe, 2011, 2013). Her stance has been strongly critiqued by feminists, yet Roiphe's concern with a shift in feminism from a politics of sexual liberation to a politics of sexual regulation is strongly reflected in scholarly feminist problematizations of feminism and victimhood (see Chapters 2 and 3).

Wolf: feminism at the end of history

Compared to those of Sommers and Roiphe, Naomi Wolf's critique of victim feminism occupies an ambivalent position in the debate. Sommers (1994, p. 232) and Roiphe (1993, p. 125) both mark Wolf as a victim feminist, arguing that her book *The Beauty Myth* (Wolf, 1990) renders women as passive victims and weaves a mythology of patriarchal backlash against feminism. Yet in her follow-up to *The Beauty Myth*, *Fire with Fire*, Wolf enjoins the critique of victim feminism. Wolf differentiates her position from those of other critics. Wolf will 'confront the growing voices of critics who are charging that *all* feminism is puritanical, man-hating, and obsessed with defining women as "victims"' while also separating 'the nugget of truth in those charges from the destructive, categorical hype' (Wolf, 1993, p. xvii, original emphasis). *Fire with Fire* will identify feminism's true victim problem, distinguishing it from false accounts of the problem. Accordingly, there are differences between Wolf and the other critics of victim feminism, particularly in terms of how they handle issues of sexual victimization. There is also, however, a substantial ground of agreement, with Wolf's narrative of victim feminism following the same broad arc as those of Sommers and Roiphe, albeit by way of a different set of political markers.

Wolf conceptualizes the pair 'victim feminism' and 'power feminism' as feminist 'traditions' that express 'two different ways by which women can approach power' (p. 148) which have coexisted throughout feminism's modern history. Despite this more flexible conception of co-existence, Wolf's account of victim feminism in feminist history does not differ significantly from those of Sommers and Roiphe. Wolf argues that victim feminism has become the reigning feminism of the era – a dominant and dangerous 'maladaptive attitude' (p. xvi) that, in an era of near-equality, stands as the last obstacle to full gender equality. Reflecting Sommers' and Roiphe's respective claims that feminists use violence against women as a 'band-wagon' (Sommers, 1994, p. 188) and 'trump card' (Roiphe, 1993, p. 56), Wolf observes that victim feminism is characterized by 'misuse of the reality of women's victimization' (Wolf, 1993, p. 147). Where power feminism emphasizes 'strong individuals' and is 'without resentment', victim feminism emphasizes 'collective identity' and 'fosters resentment' (pp. 149–150). Like Sommers, Wolf identifies power feminism with the first wave, singling out Emmeline Pankhurst and Lucretia Mott as 'early champions of power feminism' (p. 157). Similarly, Wolf identifies victim feminism with the New Left of the 1960s, arguing that victim feminism's signature 'reflexes' ('anti-capitalism, and insider–outsider mentality, and an aversion to the "system"') find their genesis in the New Left (p. xvi). The only difference is that where Sommers presents radical left politics as perfectly and always untenable, Wolf allows that victim feminism's left reflexes once were 'necessary and even effective [but] are now getting in our way' (p. xvi).

Wolf's equivocal view sees victim feminism alternately as bad in itself (it is an underhanded and dishonourable approach to life and politics) and as bad only insofar as it is currently obsolete. Two historical events spelled victim feminism's obsolescence: the 'genderquake' that took place in the wake of the Thomas–Hill hearings in 1991, and the fall of the Berlin Wall in 1989 (pp. 29–39). The sexual harassment case Anita Hill brought against Clarence Thomas sparked mass female support for Hill.[5] According to Wolf, in this moment 'something critical to the sustenance of patriarchy died' and 'conditions . . . shifted to put much of the attainment of equality in women's own grasp' (p. xv). Collective feminist politicization of victimization became outmoded and obstructive as paths to individual empowerment opened up en masse, signalling the need for 'a third wave of power feminism' (p. 323). In an 'end of history' argument common in the 1990s, Wolf takes the fall of the Berlin Wall and subsequent collapse of Stalinism in the Second World as a sign of liberal-capitalism's historical inevitability, marking the end of a productive alliance between feminism and left politics.[6] Wolf adopts a centre-left or 'Third Way' position, which acknow-ledges the exploitative nature of capitalism while affirming its inevitability, charting a path between the state-centric social democracy of the old left and the free market neoliberalism of the new right.[7] According to Wolf, with the loss of any genuine historical alternative to capitalism, victim feminism is rendered 'archaic' (p. 263), making way for power feminism's 'use of *realpolitik* and capitalism' (p. 336), which better befit the age.

Unlike Sommers and Roiphe, Wolf's subsequent work has not reiterated the critique of victim feminism. Ironically, since *Fire with Fire*, in the media reception of her 2004 article, 'The Silent Treatment', about sexual harassment at Yale University, Wolf is again characterized as a victim feminist. New binaries that *Fire with Fire* helped to entrench – between victim feminism and power feminism, between false and genuine victims – greeted Wolf's revelation in the article that she had experienced sexual harassment as a student at Yale. Wolf (2004) describes her experience and those of other women, problematizing the way the university deals with, or fails to deal with, complaints of sexual harassment. Under the headline 'Crying Wolf belittles plight of real victims', Miranda Devine (2004), a conservative Sydney journalist and long-standing critic of victim feminism, framed Wolf's account as an example of fraudulent victim identity:

> We can thank feminists such as Naomi Wolf for helping blur the line between sexual assault and the clumsy grope, for crying wolf so often they have exhausted the sympathy that might be reserved for genuine victims of sexual violence. The latest contribution to the victimification of women is Wolf's 21-year-old allegation . . . [Wolf has] trivialized the pain of every woman with a genuine claim to victimhood.
>
> (p. 15)

Wolf's discussion of victimhood in *Fire with Fire* never assumes the scathing tone of this conservative journalist, yet the logic of Devine's rebuttal is the same as that espoused across the critiques of victim feminism: feminist claims about gendered victimization are destructive, inspiring false complaints, 'victimifying' women and obscuring 'genuine' gendered suffering.

The ur-narratives that appear across these texts – the story of victim feminism's dominance, falsity and obsolescence, the story of dying or near-dead patriarchy – rest on two key claims. First, there is the claim that feminists theorize that women are passive victims and refuse to acknowledge women's agency. In order for the 'victim feminism' construct to hold water, it must be shown that feminists participate in the passive victim theory Sommers, Roiphe and Wolf malign. In the following section I argue that the 'victim feminism' construct is sustained through a tailored telling of feminist theory and politics, with feminist conceptions of agency taken out of the picture. I also observe that, in a paradox worthy of careful scrutiny, these critics participate in the very theoretical position they are challenging. Second, the ur-narratives of these critiques rest on the empirical claim that, in view of an apparent decline of patriarchal gender relations within liberal-capitalist settings, feminists are wrong to continue to regard women as an oppressed group (a view that may or may not involve seeing women as 'passive victims'). Targeted here are feminist accounts of structural oppression: systems of gender segregation, discrimination, inequality and violence embedded within the economic, political

26

and social institutions of liberal-capitalism. As my later discussion will show, rather than meet feminist accounts of structural oppression with data on declines in reported rapes or bridged pay gaps, the critics of victim feminism call upon a variety of techniques through which to diffuse, downplay and depoliticize even the strongest indicators of gendered inequality and violence in liberal-capitalist settings. In so doing they demonstrate clearly what the terrain of feminist politics looks like when viewed through the lens of neoliberal philosophy, based as it is on the premise that structural oppression exists only in the eyes of the left.

Feminist theory and the victim subject

Critics of victim feminism make the very particular claim that much feminist thought and activism turns on a theory of women as *passive* victims, failing to recognize and value women's capacities for agency and responsibility. As a matter of orthodoxy, feminists identify women with a particular kind of victim subject: a passive, helpless, innocent victim subject who lacks strength, self-knowledge and the capacities for self-reliance and personal responsibility. As Sommers (1994) puts it, victim feminism regards women as 'benighted' (p. 257), or 'helpless, possessed and robotic' (p. 232). As Roiphe (1993) puts it, victim feminism robs women of agency by presenting 'a portrait of the cowering woman, knocked on her back by the barest feather of peer pressure' (pp. 67–68). As Wolf puts it (1993), victim feminism emphasizes 'female victimization at the expense of female agency' (p. 154) resulting in a distorted imagining of women as powerless non-agents. They characterize feminism's theory of women as passive victims variously as insulting, infantilizing, harmful, sexist, disempowering, alienating and substantially untrue. For women individually, this theory is existentially disabling – it revives old scripts of feminine passivity that stymie women's 'will to power' and inhibit the proper assumption of personal responsibility. For feminism generally, it is politically regressive – the passive victim theory alienates women, exaggerates and potentially exacerbates actual victimization and its dogmas threaten the liberty of individuals and groups in a variety of ways.

Existing critical responses to the critiques of victim feminism have pointed out that when it comes to the task of providing concrete examples of feminists espousing a theory of passive victimhood, the critics of victim feminism engage in legerdemain. To substantiate their claims they employ a particular representational technique, dubbed the 'zoom lens effect' by Shane Rowlands and Margaret Henderson (1996). This technique involves focusing on an instance in which the victim feminism accusation can be seen to ring true, and elaborating this into a story about feminism in general: 'an event, a tendency, a version, a current, a localized practice becomes magnified and distorted into the current condition of feminist politics and activism everywhere' (Rowlands and Henderson, 1996, p. 12). Similarly, in her book *Outlaw Culture* (1999), bell hooks discusses the way Roiphe's polemical critique maintains a narrow focus on examples of 'feminist excess' which are made to stand in for feminism in general: 'When Roiphe turns her powerful critical spotlight on these feminist excesses she does so in a manner that completely overshadows and erases that which is meaningful in feminist critiques of and resistance to sexism, patriarchy, and male domination' (pp. 103–104). Further, Roiphe's polemic erases 'the many feminist thinkers who have warned against these excesses' (p. 104), particularly thinkers who challenge feminist universalism and expose the politics of race-ethnicity and class in feminist theories of the victim and formulations of victim politics.

Rowlands, Henderson and hooks suggest that genuine examples of 'victim feminism' do exist, but are either unrepresentative or already being challenged within feminist debates. Taking a different tack, the examples I discuss expose a different form of legerdemain to that described by Rowlands, Henderson and hooks. I want to show that even in examples where one may expect to find clear feminist commitment to a theory of women as passive victims, there is always more going on. The critics of victim feminism not only generalize on the basis of unrepresentative examples and elide existing challenges to feminist victimhood. They also strategically omit the discourses of agency *within* feminist accounts of victimization, fully collapsing the distinction between politicizing victimization and espousing a theory of women as passive victims. Such is the case with Sommers' discussion of Sandra Lee Bartky's second-wave theory of feminist consciousness, and Wolf's discussion of rape crisis feminism as an exemplar of victim feminism.

To illustrate her argument that the gender feminist establishment is committed to a view of women as passive victims, Sommers (1994, p. 42) discusses Bartky's 1976 essay 'Towards a Phenomenology of Feminist Consciousness', quoting the following statement: 'Feminist consciousness is a consciousness of *victimization* . . . to come to see oneself as a victim' (Bartky, 1990, p. 15, original emphasis). This quote clearly implies that Bartky regards victim identity as central to feminism, and gives no reason to doubt that by 'victim' Bartky means to identify women as *passive* victims, or subjects who are unable or unwilling to exert control over their circumstances. But Bartky's victim theory is more complex than this. In her essay she actually goes on to describe a 'divided consciousness':

> But at the same time, feminist consciousness is a joyous consciousness of one's own power, of the possibility of unprecedented personal growth and the release of energy long suppressed. Thus, feminist consciousness is both a consciousness of weakness and a consciousness of strength . . . Many women do not develop a consciousness divided in this way at all: they see themselves, to be sure, as victims of an unjust system of social power, but they remain blind to the extent to which they themselves are implicated in the victimization of others.
>
> (p. 42)

Instead of a theory that women are passive victims, we find in Bartky's essay a theory of the victim as a complexly responsible actor for whom consciousness of victimization can operate as a vehicle of knowledge and agency. For Bartky, victimization does not prohibit power, strength, self-knowledge and, in view of embedded structures of ethnic hierarchy and class privilege, victim subjects are likely to be implicated in the victimization of others, occupying complex non-innocent positions in relations of power. Bartky's theory is concerned with the consciousness or knowledge women can develop about sexist injustice. She draws what may appear to be an esoteric distinction between benighted victims, who do not recognize that they or others are being victimized, and knowing victims, who recognize the workings of injustice in their own lives and in the world. Yet this distinction is compelling as it situates experiences of victimization as sources of knowledge about power and ethics, rather than as mere individual episodes that are best downplayed or forgotten, yielding nothing of value for political and ethical reflection. Overall, Bartky's theory disrupts the passive victim/free agent binary, providing an alternative way to think about victimhood. Sommers was obliged to omit these aspects of Bartky's theorizing of the victim, in order to make way for the construction of 'establishment feminists' as committed to a view of women as passive victims.

Showing a tendency to shift positions to the point of self-contradiction in order to maintain an unflinchingly negative stance against victim feminism, at another point in her book, Sommers directly contradicts her complaint that feminists regard women as benighted rather than as knowing subjects. In her discussion of feminist interventions in the field of philosophy of science, Sommers attacks feminist standpoint theory (see Hartsock, 1983 and Harding, 1986), not because it regards women as benighted, but because it does the opposite: it attaches epistemic value to subjugated knowledges, or the perspectives on society, economy and polity arising from subjugated groups, such as working-class women, the poor, indigenous peoples and peoples of colour. Rather than affirm this feminist effort to recognize the status of subjugated groups as agentic bearers of knowledge, as would be consistent with her agency-affirming position, Sommers (1994) renders subjugated groups as benighted by virtue of their subjugation: 'The oppressed and socially marginalized often have little access to the information and education needed to excel in science, which on the whole puts them at a serious "epistemic *dis*advantage"' (p. 75, original emphasis).

In the same way that Sommers omits agency from Bartky's theory of the victim, Wolf's case study of victim feminism omits the discourses of agency espoused within rape crisis feminist approaches to sexual victimization. In *Fire with Fire*, Wolf (1993, pp. 165–169) develops a case study of victim feminism focussed on her experience as a volunteer in a rape crisis centre, detailing her concerns about the centre's internal political climate and leftist use of consensus decision-making. In the context of *Fire with Fire*, the case study moves from the particular to the general, its window onto one rape crisis centre telling a wider story about rape crisis feminism and feminist politics more generally. As such, the case study forms part of a finely crafted legerdemain. Rape crisis feminists reject the term 'victim' to describe women who have experienced rape, preferring the alternative term, 'survivor'. As Dawn McCaffrey (1998) observes, rape crisis feminists are centrally concerned to 'redefine what it means to be victimised by sexual violence', and regard 'victim' as a stigmatized and disempowering identity (p. 278). Rape crisis feminism's ethos of survivorship is designed to counter the negativity and stigma of victim identity by encouraging rape survivors to identify with their capacities for self-definition, strength and resistance. As McCaffrey describes, survivors of sexual violence 'strive to minimise feelings of weakness and vulnerability by emphasising strength and agency in the definition of survivorship' (p. 273). Yet in Wolf's case study of rape crisis feminism as 'victim feminism', the ethos of survivorship is not mentioned at all. Instead, the values of this ethos – its critical stance on 'victim' as a social marker, its emphasis on agency, strength and resistance – are co-opted and redefined in *Fire with Fire* as 'power feminism'.

Echoing rape crisis feminism, Wolf treats victim identity as a disabling malaise. 'A person who identifies chiefly as a victim will do less well than someone who sees herself chiefly as powerful and effective' (Wolf, 1993, p. 228). Rape crisis feminists distinguish between victimization as an experience and victim as a social identity arising out of this experience, encouraging victims to ensure victimization does not define who they are. Wolf draws the same distinction between 'identifying one's victimisation' and 'moulding it into an identity', cautioning that 'victim identity is bad for women' (p. 148). Rape crisis feminism and Wolf's power feminism share the same broad valorization of a positive self-identity as capable, powerful and resistant, a self whose self-relation is not determined by the experience of victimization by another. Yet Wolf disavows the likeness and, in a predicament similar to that of Sommers, was more or less obliged to omit rape crisis feminist discourses of agency from her case study, in order to erase the obvious barrier to her rendering of rape crisis feminism as a prime exemplar of 'victim feminism'.

Probing Wolf's construction of rape crisis feminism as victim feminism also shows that Wolf ignores an important aspect of victim identity that rape crisis feminists acknowledge centrally. Namely, the much-examined tendency of victims of rape to engage in self-blame and 'experience only self-directed anger' (Alcoff and Gray, 1993, p. 284). Wolf espouses a version of survivorship called power feminism, without carrying through rape crisis feminism's cautions about forms of agency that centrally involve self-blame. A core argument of Wolf is that victims are peculiarly at risk of failing to assume personal responsibility – this is what is so disabling about victim identity. Rape crisis feminists put the problem very differently: victims often assume *excessive* responsibility, for their own actions and for the actions of others. In fact, for rape crisis feminists, 'victim identity' primarily consists of this self-blaming consciousness. The self-blaming victim is a counter-intuitive figure in the sense that, in accusing and blaming themselves, they confound the expectation that victims desire recognition as victims and will naturally blame the victimizer. Rather than seek the 'rewards' of victim recognition, the self-blaming victim situates themselves as the agent of their own victimization. In *Fire with Fire*, Wolf sidesteps the complexities posed by the self-blaming victim, whose readiness to assume responsibility for themselves and for others suggests that Wolf's call for victims to 'take responsibility' is profoundly misdirected.

In order to fit Bartky's theory of feminist consciousness and rape crisis feminism into the 'victim feminism' construct, Sommers and Wolf discuss them in ways that ensure we do not hear about their conceptions of agency. In their texts we meet feminists dogmatically committed to a theory of women as passive victims, rather than theorists and activists who in their challenges to victimization are critically concerned with the forms of agency available to those who experience victimization in any of its forms. This kind of legerdemain effectively blurs the distinction between politicizing victimization and espousing a theory of women as passive victims, such that anyone engaged in feminist victim politics is seen to eschew agency and participate in this theory. Yet, as Zillah Eisenstein (1997) observes, 'Feminism theorises the fact that where there is a victim, there is a struggle over power; that there is always at least the potential for resistance' (p. 40). Eisenstein suggests that the victim subject in feminist theory is more likely to be conceptualized as an agent in the sense of being an active subject – a resistant subject engaged in power struggle – than as a victim who is perfectly dispossessed of agency. For Eisenstein, feminist victim theory and victim politics are not in any necessary sense tied to a theory of women as *passive* victims, and in fact tend not to be tied to such a view. Similarly, as Carine Mardorossian (2002) has clarified, in the context of second-wave feminist anti-rape and anti-violence politicizations, 'being a victim did not mean being incapacitated and powerless. It meant being a determined and angry (although not pathologically resentful) agent of change' (p. 767). In other words, erasure of feminist discourses of agency is required if one is to provide albeit specious evidence of broad feminist commitment to a theory of women as 'passive victims'. In order for the 'victim feminism' construct to hold water, a tailored telling of feminist victim theory must take place.

As with feminist theories of the victim subject, the critics of victim feminism erase the complexity of feminist theories of oppression. In their texts, 'oppression' is used in its classical and narrow sense of 'the exercise of tyranny by a ruling group' (Young, 1990, p. 40). They presume that when feminists use the term 'oppression' to describe gendered power relations, they mean to posit a totalizing view that women as a group are directly tyrannized by men as a group. As Sommers (1994) puts it, the concept of oppression feeds the feminist accusation 'that men are collectively engaged in keeping women down' (p. 21). Erased here are feminist accounts of *structural oppression*, a form of oppression that does not rely on a dyadic relation of ruler and ruled and, as such, does not lead to a totalizing feminist view of women as passively enslaved by tyrannical men. As Iris Marion Young (1990) elucidates, new left social movements including feminism shifted the meaning of the concept of oppression:

> In its new usage, oppression designates the disadvantage and injustice some people suffer not because a tyrannical power coerces them, but because of the everyday practices of a well-intentioned liberal society

31

... in this extended structural sense oppression refers to the vast and deep injustices some groups suffer as a consequence of often unconscious assumptions and reactions of well-meaning people in ordinary inter-actions, media and cultural stereotypes, and structural features of bureaucratic hierarchies and market mechanisms – in short, the normal processes of everyday life ... While structural oppression involves relations among groups, these relations do not always fit the paradigm of conscious and intentional oppression of one group by another.

(p. 41)

Feminist accounts of structural oppression highlight the ways in which the interests and life chances of men in general, or certain groups of men, typically are *privileged* in relation to those of women in general, or certain groups of women. Such privileging is evident, for example, in the paid workforce, where becoming a parent tends to have markedly different consequences for women compared with men, with women facing wage, status and career progress penalties men either do not face, or tend to face on significantly different terms. This arrangement does not affect individual women or men in identical ways, perfectly withdrawing or bestowing advantage. But its aggregate effect is to distance women as a group from economic independence and relative wealth, perpetuating the historical link between femaleness and what are in liberal terms negative states of economic dependence and relative devaluation. Rather than regard women's position of comparative disadvantage within the sphere of paid work as the result of a patriarchal tyrant's evil intentions, the concept of structural oppression asks that we examine the array of institutionalized norms, beliefs, values and processes that serve to organize work in ways that produce, sustain and depend upon gendered inequality.

Critics of victim feminism avoid recognizing the distinction between tyrannical and structural oppression, participating in a form of political discourse that Young argues is common in liberal-capitalist contexts such as the USA:

Dominant political discourse may use the term oppression to describe societies other than our own, usually Communist or purportedly Communist societies ... In dominant political discourse it is not legiti-mate to use the term oppression to describe our society, because oppres-sion is the evil perpetrated by the Others.

(p. 41)

In this discourse, Stalinist Communism and more recently Islamic despotism symbolize true and genuine oppression and, accordingly, structural oppressions in liberal-capitalist contexts are protected from critique. Reflecting this discourse, the critics of victim feminism are ready to regard women in earlier periods of history and in non-Western contexts as genuinely oppressed, while rejecting use of the term 'oppression' to describe gendered systems of segregation, inequality and violence in contemporary liberal-capitalist contexts. Roiphe and Wolf argue that feminist characterization of the USA as patriarchal is questionable in view of more severe sexisms suffered by 'veiled women' (Roiphe, 1993, p. 72) and 'third world women' (Wolf, 1993, p. 317), while in her later work Sommers fully adopts the imperial feminist position, situating the wars on terror as 'feminist' (Sommers, 2002, p. 16). I return to and examine the racialist dimension of their anti-victim critique in Chapter 3.

Apart from the need to engage in legerdemain in order to convincingly construct feminism as 'victim feminism', there is a further and less obvious reason why these critics would refuse to acknowledge the complexity at play in their own examples of victim feminism. For in their books they themselves articulate a victim politics – a politics that would be stripped of its sentimentality and dramatic force if it were to picture the 'victims of victim feminism' as complexly responsible actors rather than as passively victimized.

Reversing victimology: the victims of victim feminism

A theory of the victim as passive and benighted turns out to be more germane to the critiques of victim feminism than to the feminisms they impugn. As bell hooks (1999) has observed, these critiques 'seem to exploit the very notion of victimhood' (p. 99) that they decry. In the course of these critiques, 'victim feminism' receives a kind of double treatment: it is politically invalidated and, at the same time, discursively co-opted. Rather than point the way beyond the passive victim theory, this theory is placed in the service of new narratives in which victim feminism is presented not just as obsolete or wrong-minded, but as perniciously victimizing. 'Victim feminist' narratives of female victimization are reversed and replaced with narratives of victimization by feminism, with rival populations of victims cast as passively victimized by feminist domination. This reverse movement is strongly evident in the way Sommers and Roiphe portray women who participate in victim feminism.

Sommers presents victim feminism as the predilection of a small but powerful minority, conforming to her argument that its view of women as passive victims alienates a majority of women. This presents a conundrum, however, since Sommers also portrays victim feminism as an alarming epidemic, the exigency of which her book is acting upon. Although alienating, victim feminism's persuasiveness has reached epidemic proportions: it has become a majority view and is shaping a new generation of 'impressionable' youth in US educational institutions (Sommers, 1994, p. 106). In order to account for victim feminism's epidemic popularity while also sustaining her argument that women find it alienating, Sommers adopts the very theory she maligns, casting women who participate in victim feminism as passive victims of ideological indoctrination. Sommers refers to women's studies departments as 'reeducation camps' in which students are '"converted" to a view of the society they inhabit as a patriarchal system of oppression' (pp. 116, 47). The brainwashing action of victim feminism's 'ideologically correct censorious revisionism' produces 'new crops of young feminist ideologues' to take over the public sphere (p. 269). Here Sommers traffics in the imagery she associates with victim feminism, with junior proponents of victim feminism cast as benighted dupes – passive victims of victim feminist ideology.

Roiphe similarly portrays women as easily swayed by victim feminism's training in victimhood. She argues that victim feminism teaches women to fear sexual victimization and to regard themselves as vulnerable to an array of dubiously defined sexual harms. This training 'transforms perfectly stable women into hysterical, sobbing victims' (Roiphe, 1993, p. 112). Roiphe and Sommers credit victim feminism with a strong capacity to dictate women's beliefs and behaviours, crediting women not with self-reliance, but with special susceptibility to victim identities promulgated by feminism. In the process, they represent women as benighted dupes and passive victims, reversing the victim feminist claim. In their narratives, victim feminism has replaced patriarchy as that which dupes and victimizes women.

Women who participate in victim feminism are complexly also presented as victimizers. This can be seen when we probe the true nature of the critics' objection to victim feminism. Their manifesta is that feminists ought to recognize women as capable agents rather than as passive victims, yet their true objection to victim feminism seems to be that it concretely bestows upon women the wrong kind of agency – a bad form of agency best described as the cultural capital of victimhood. They disapprove of victim feminism not because it is disempowering, but because it empowers women to become the wrong kind of agent: *an agent who claims power on the basis of an identity as a powerless victim.* Ostensibly, the political intervention made by critics of victim feminism is about arguing for a timely transition from victim-focused feminism to agency-affirming feminism. But the real task they undertake is that of discriminating between legitimate and illegitimate forms of agency in the context of liberal meritocracy. Complaining, in effect, that victim feminism grants women excessive scope to contest the gendered victimizations they may experience, the critics cast women as untrustworthy bearers of the right to contest victimization, raising fears of widespread fraudulent victim identity among women.

Women who participate in victim feminism alternately are presented as passive victims of victim feminist ideology *and* as consciously self-maximizing beneficiaries of victim feminism's regime of political correctness, which 'rewards them for being oppressed' (Roiphe, 1993, p. 125). Victim feminism alternately is accused of undermining women's agency *and* of shoring up too powerful a form of agency, which they term 'the power of the powerless' (p. 35). Although self-presenting as advocates of women's power, they consider that victim feminism grants women *excessive power*. They present the power of the powerless as a potent form of moral authority that translates into a rich currency for self-identified victims, who win undeserved sympathy, belonging, prominence and the ability to victimize others with impunity, when they draw on the cultural capital of victimhood. This essentially fraudulent arrangement – special treatment for self-identified victims within a regime of political correctness – violates the proper workings of liberal meritocracy, creating confusion about who the genuine victims are and who is truly worthy of the 'advantages' of being publicly recognized as a victim. In this feminist version of an anti-affirmative action position, the terms of feminist victim politics are fully reversed. Women who participate in victim feminism are marked as excessively empowered victimizers, while those subject to their fraudulent wiles (falsely accused men, well-meaning officials, institutions and public funding bodies) emerge as the new victims – powerless, innocent, benighted subjects whose liberty is under siege. Sommers' critique is shaped as an anti-establishment act of apostasy aiming to inspire victim consciousness in the victims of feminist domination. Yet the theme of women's dangerous and excessive empowerment is most prominent in the critiques of Roiphe and Wolf.

The worry that victim feminism grants women too much power animates Roiphe's discussions of rape and sexual harassment. These discussions waver between two different arguments against feminist efforts to politicize sexual harm. Roiphe's first argument is that such efforts operate as self-fulfilling prophecies. Feminists falsely depict social reality as a zone of sexual danger and risk; this false depiction inspires fear of sexual victimization, training women to surrender agency and expect victimization; this feeling of fear in turn 'substantiates' the false depictions, lending them an aura of truth and mandating feminist authority. Thus feminism 'creates the problem' it claims to redress (p. 110). With this argument Roiphe contends that genuine sexual harm does not really exist independently of feminist campaigns against it or, if it does, is far rarer than feminists claim. Roiphe's second argument about feminist politics and sexual harm is very different to the first. Roiphe contends that victim feminism does not so much undermine women's agency by training them in passive victimhood, as provide them with a new form of agency through this training – the cultural capital of victimhood. Victim feminists have built politically correct environs in which women stand to gain kudos if they identify as 'innocent', 'fragile', 'passive', 'gullible' and 'sensitive' victims (pp. 60, 66, 172, 69, 172). When women 'embrace the mantle of victim status', they are relieved of self-responsibility and accorded undeserved power and authority: 'There is power to be drawn from declaring one's victimhood and oppression' (p. 44). Roiphe contends that her generation has invested in the victim mantle for its easy purchase on power, positioning herself as the sole resisting witness to this vast moral fraud.

These two arguments are powerful in combination. With the first, Roiphe identifies the problem of sexual harm with those mobilized against it; with the second, she renders those who claim to have experienced sexual harm as false victims hoping to cash in on the cultural capital of victimhood.[8] Accordingly, rape and sexual harassment evaporate as social problems, and are replaced with a new social problem: a crisis of personal responsibility among women, brought on by feminism. As Roiphe has it, feminism arranges for women to exchange healthy, self-responsible agency for the corrupt agency of victimhood, enabling them to claim power and status within a public sphere bent on ameliorating their albeit non-existent sufferings. A multitude of women are posing as powerless victims, in exchange for inordinate institutional and interpersonal powers. Emphasizing that men stand to be victimized by this corrupt form of empowerment, Roiphe reads David Mamet's play *Oleanna* as a sign of men's new vulnerability to false accusations of sexual harm. In the play a student claims power over her professor by falsely accusing him of sexual harassment. Angered by his inability to prove his innocence, the professor finally does assault the student, who thereby becomes 'the victim she never was' (p. 107). The innocent professor emerges as the real victim, while the mendacious student emerges as the real victimizer – the one who is possessed of excessive power, the one we ought to fear and doubt, the one who literally 'asked for it'.

Although fictional, *Oleanna* stands among Roiphe's emblems of victim feminism's excessive empowerment of women and victimization of men. Roiphe also describes her own victimization by victim feminism. It has served to minoritize and silence her values and worldview. Accordingly, her authorial identity is that of a victim finally breaking the silence about her victimization: 'This book comes out of frustration, out of anger, out of the names I've been called, out of all the times I didn't say something because it might offend current feminist sensibility' (p. 7). Roiphe's view of empirical reality mirrors that of victim feminism – it replicates and reverses it. Reversing the victim feminist truth-claim that women are victimized in contexts of masculine dominance, Roiphe's truth-claim is that men, and Roiphe, are victimized by feminism and its false victims. Feminist efforts to foster public recognition of sexual victimization are manufacturing a multitude of false claims to victim status, and those targeted, minoritized or otherwise oppressed by such claims are the real victims of the scenario – the ones who must now rise up and contest their victimization.

In *Fire with Fire*, Wolf (1993) effectively rebuffs Roiphe's view that complaints of sexual harm are manufactured by feminism.

> Roiphe . . . paints an impressionistic picture of hysterical 'date-rape victims' who have made it all up, but she never looks squarely at the epidemic of sex crimes that has been all too indelibly documented by police forces the world over.
>
> (pp. 147–148)

Wolf defends feminist politicizations of rape and sexual harassment, making an observation about feminist politics similar to that made by Eisenstein:

> The act of documenting the way others are trying to victimize women is the very opposite of treating women as natural victims. The premise of such documentation is that women are not natural victims. . . . There is no way around it: women are not natural victims, but they certainly *are* victimized.
>
> (pp. 147–148, 153, original emphasis)

36

Wolf emphasizes that sexual victimization exists independently of feminist campaigns against it, and that such campaigns do not rely on a theory of women as 'natural victims'. Yet Wolf also shares Roiphe's worry that victim feminism confers upon women an excessive form of empowerment, observing that some claims to victim status 'strike a false note' (p. 207) and that the politically correct left encourages fraudulent claims to victim status.[9]

Like Roiphe, Wolf advances two distinct arguments about victim feminism and women's agency: victim feminism disempowers women *and* empowers them in the wrong way. Rather than encourage women to 'take responsibility for the power they do possess', victim feminism 'urges women to identify with powerlessness' and 'turns suffering into a virtue', asking women to seek power 'on the basis of feminine specialness instead of human worth, and to fight underhandedly rather than honourably' (pp. 161, xvii, 147).[10] Power feminism, in contrast, 'seeks power and uses it responsibly' (p. 149). As in Roiphe's critique, the locus of Wolf's concern with victim feminism lies with its promulgation of an unhealthy form of agency, unhealthy because its victim posturing results in an inability or unwillingness to assume personal responsibility. Rather than encourage women to enjoin men in the full exercise of citizenship rights and responsibilities, victim feminism grants women the power of the powerless: moral authority and special treatment as 'victims', unfettered by the rigours of personal responsibility.

Roiphe and Wolf associate victim feminism's underhanded mode of empowerment with Victorian morality, where ideals of feminine virtue and goodness are at once the seat of female power and its disguise. Yet they invoke this heritage only to effect a sharp reversal of victim feminism's purported morality. A new morality centred on the virtues of personal responsibility is pitted against an original morality promulgating the vices of victim identity, setting the crooked beneficiary of 'victim feminist political correctness' against a new heroine of exemplary feminist virtue: the robustly autonomous and self-responsible woman who remains unenticed by the 'advantages' of feminine victimhood. Rather than foster overdue recognition of women's agency, or supplant a theory of women as passive victims with a theory of women as agents, Roiphe and Wolf impart ethical lessons about the proper conduct of personal agency, lessons in which the crooked beneficiary of victim feminism is present in order to underline the virtues of personal responsibility. Their construction and derogation of victim feminism as morally fraudulent express an anxiety that women easily stray from the proper practice of personal responsibility, requiring the clear instruction of pastoral care, as in Wolf's programme of workshops oriented to transforming women into psychologically robust entrepreneurial citizens (p. 263). In this way their delineations of feminism's 'victim problem' devolve into the problematization of women's fitness for the responsibilities of citizenship in the 'post-socialist' age.

Although the critiques of victim feminism promise to enact a shift from victim-focused feminism to agency-affirming feminism, this is not what takes place in their texts. They call for movement beyond victim politics, but end up articulating a new and different victim politics. Where we expect to find affirmations of women's agency, we find instead problematizations of women's agency, with focus on victimization maintained as feminist narratives of female victimization are reversed and replaced by narratives of victimization by feminism and its false victims, creating an opposite emancipatory politics in which 'victim feminism' replaces patriarchy as the overarching coercive power that women must now resist. I call this critique of victim politics that is also a victim politics a *reverse victimology*. Reverse victimology involves mirroring in order to directly rival the politics of a foe. In reverse victimology 'victim' and 'victimizer' exchange places. Those claiming victim status for themselves or for others are recast as non-credible victimizers, while those formerly marked as victimizers are deemed the Real Victims.

According to Thomas Frank's mapping of US political discourse, what I am calling reverse victimology is a signature feature of conservative posturing in the culture wars. Frank provides an incisive analysis of conservative discourses in which left victim politics in general, and certain figurations of the resentful, complaining victim in particular, are mobilized as derogated political signs in a culture war against a conjured enemy: 'political correctness', or the purported ascendance of left-liberalism in American public life. Frank's analysis helps to explain the contradictions that take shape in critiques of victim feminism, and I locate these texts as belonging to the broad discursive movement he discerns, constituting its feminist wing. Of particular interest is Frank's (2006) discernment of how, in this movement against political correctness, right-wing political discourse takes on the shape and style of left-wing political discourse, but 'with the economics drained out' (p. 119). Focusing on the US Republican Party, Frank describes the way, in the era of neoliberalism, the right mimes in order to rival the left:

> Liberalism is beyond politics, a tyrant that dominates our lives in countless ways great and small, and which is virtually incapable of being overthrown. Conservatism, on the other hand, is the doctrine of the oppressed majority . . . While liberals use their control of the airwaves, newspapers, and schools to persecute average Americans . . . the Republicans are the party of the disrespected, the downtrodden, the forgotten. They are always the underdog, always in rebellion against a haughty establishment, always rising up from below. All claims on the right, in other words, advance from victimhood. This is another trick the backlash has picked up from the left.
>
> (p. 119)

Mimicking the rhetorical style of left-wing political argument, right-wing complaint against left-wing political correctness is couched as an emancipatory challenge to established orthodoxy that breaks the silence about effaced suffering, raising consciousness in the name of liberation. Invoking the language of the left, right-wing discourses resemble left-wing discourses, but continue to represent elite interests, obfuscating the really existing socio-economic inequalities brought to light in left analyses, inequalities which have actually intensified with the implementation of neoliberal programmes of structural adjustment. Rather than acknowledge the reality of these inequalities, conservative political discourses represent the social body as under siege by politically correct claims that inequalities exist. This style of representation very clearly marks the critiques of victim feminism, which also 'drain out the economics', failing to accord reality to the growth and intensification of gendered economic inequality in the era of neoliberalism.

One aspect Frank's analysis does not track, however, is the altered set of meanings 'victimhood' carries when left victim politics is mimed and rivalled on the right. Conservative discourses borrow the rhetorical shape of left-wing discourses, draining out the economics, while also draining out the complex non-binary conceptions of victimhood, agency, power and oppression found in left-wing discourses. In their place stands a redefinition of victimhood. In the following section I argue that critiques of victim feminism *redefine* victimhood against left feminist conceptions of the victim, invoking a strong victim/agent dichotomy and producing new, radically attenuated criteria for distinguishing between genuine and false gendered suffering. As Frank would lead us to expect, their redefinition of victimhood directly reflects the politics of neoliberalism.

Erasing oppression, re-defining victimhood: the neoliberal feminist lens

As I observed earlier, the ur-narratives in the critiques of victim feminism rest on two key claims, the second of these being the empirical claim that in the twilight of Western patriarchy, feminists are wrong to regard women in liberal-capitalist settings as an oppressed group. We have seen that critics of victim feminism avoid recognizing the concept of structural oppression, using 'oppression' in the classical sense of tyrannical oppression, arguing that, far from Western women being tyrannically oppressed by men, the West is tyrannically oppressed by feminism. One of the consequences of erasing the concept of structural oppression, however, is it requires that the critics of victim feminism provide alternative explanations for the forms of gender segregation and inequality that evidently do exist in liberal-capitalist settings, such as women's overrepresentation as victims of rape and spousal violence, underrepresentation in the upper echelons of the paid workforce and in parliament, and lesser share of wealth and income within national economies across the liberal-capitalist bloc. How do the critics of victim feminism explain these enduring forms of gendered segregation and inequality, if not as forms of structural oppression?

We have seen that Roiphe responds to feminist claims about sexual victimization by dismissing them as largely fictional. Also, Sommers' and Wolf's idea that patriarchy is *nearly* dead allows for some remaining inequalities. Beyond these, however, the critics of victim feminism use a particular set of techniques through which to recast and depoliticize ongoing issues of structural oppression. Through these techniques the critics meet feminist claims about structural oppression with new and radically attenuated criteria for judging genuine gendered victimhood – criteria that redefine what it means to be a victim by posing new limits on the forms of victimization that are able to be regarded as genuine and worthy of public attention and redress. In so doing they elaborate what I call the neoliberal feminist lens, resignifying gendered suffering and feminist politics through the categories and logics of neoliberal philosophy, ultimately producing a neoliberal version of feminism. In this final section of the chapter I identify these techniques, first describing the wider neoliberal transformation in the meaning of victimhood enjoined by the critics of victim feminism.

Neoliberal victim theory

Central to neoliberalism as a form of governance is the establishment of a personal responsibility system, by which the sphere of state responsibility contracts in the same measure as personal responsibility expands, privatizing social risk.[11] In a riposte to Keynesian and radical left conceptions of public responsibility in the amelioration of socio-economic inequality, neoliberal programmes of structural adjustment pursue a philosophy of individual responsibility for individual socio-economic fate, encapsulated in Margaret Thatcher's famous assertion, 'There is no such thing as society' (Keay, 1987, p. 9).[12] This philosophy marks a significant shift in the liberal discourse of citizenship, supplanting the historical emphasis on *rights* with new emphasis on citizens' *responsibilities*. In this philosophy 'victim' is a derogated identity and the subject position 'victim' is rendered impossible, pathological, suspect or exceptional. Victims are presented as *self-made*: victimization is not the result of embedded systems of violence, inequality and discrimination, but of bad choices, irresponsibility or pathology on the victim's part; and victims are solely responsible for ameliorating the negative conditions of life. The individual is reckoned as a fully autonomous agent who exists in a condition of radical freedom; this presentation of the subject as a perfect non-victim pre-empts recognition of socially made unfreedom. Accordingly, the privatization of social risk is accompanied by a proliferation of victim-blaming discourses in which victims of poverty, inequality, discrimination and violence are presented as the authors of their own suffering.[13] As Kathy Laster and Edna Erez (2000) observe, 'In the neoliberal world, victim status must be avoided at all costs since to require assistance and support suggests a lack of enterprise and application' (p. 247).

In his *Brief History of Neoliberalism*, David Harvey (2005) demonstrates that, discretely and cumulatively, neoliberal programmes of structural adjustment have overseen a vast redistribution of wealth from labour to capital, creating a global context of 'rising inequality everywhere' (p. 119): 'The main achievement of neoliberalism has been to redistribute rather than generate wealth and income' (p. 159; see also Duménil and Lévy, 2004). Discourses of victim-blame operate to disguise this condition of rising inequality: 'Personal failure is generally attributed to personal failings, and the victim is all too often blamed' (Harvey, 2005, p. 76).

In the victim-blaming discourses of neoliberalism, the social foundations of particular forms of suffering and social exile disappear, and with them the means to explain suffering sociologically. The meaning of victimhood is transformed, from the conception that victimhood can be explained sociologically, to the conception that victimhood finds its explanation in the subjectivity of the victim. Reversing Judith Shklar's (1984) dictum that 'Victimhood happens to us. It is not a quality' (p. 17), suffering is seen to arise out of the sufferer's inner world, rather than out of worldly power relations. Victimhood becomes a *quality of the sufferer*, rather than something that happened to them. As Mardorossian (2002) astutely observes, 'The meaning of the term *victimization* itself has . . . changed from an external reality imposed on someone to a psychologised inner state that itself triggers crises' (p. 770).

When the meaning of victimhood is altered in this way, new lines are drawn between genuine and false, worthy and unworthy, legitimate and illegitimate claims to victim status. The idea that victimization includes structural oppressions that are collectively experienced and embedded in everyday practices is supplanted by the idea that genuine victimization is limited to events of spectacularly traumatic suffering and boldly direct discrimination – events that stand out clearly from everyday life, even if they are acknowledged as happening every day. Thus, as Kristin Bumiller (2008) observes, the mass circulation of spectacular images of violence against women in neoliberal polities suggests cultural sensitivity to the violence women endure, yet the violence itself is represented as random and incomprehensible rather than as 'arising from long-term oppressive relationships' (p. 17), or is made comprehensible only through a language of social pathology, with violence against women cast as a problem of criminality brought about by diseased individuals, pathologizing victims and perpetrators alike.[14] In this conception of the victim, some victims will be granted blamelessness and legitimacy, their claim to victim status rendered 'genuine'. Even genuine victims, however, will be exhorted not to 'hold on' to victim identity, which is seen as being at odds with the proper uptake of personal responsibility: if the victim is not responsible for their suffering, they are responsible for overcoming it. Victimhood becomes a valueless experience that is to be expunged – a construction that provides a potent counter to left theories of subjugated knowledges, which situate the victim's perspective as a worthy source of knowledge about worldly power relations, politics and ethics.

Neoliberal philosophy encourages a conception of victimization as an event and not a structure, while also co-opting the notion of structural victimization. In a double standard identical to that which plays out in critiques of victim feminism, neoliberal philosophy turns the category 'victim' to its own uses, setting groups of worthy victims, whose claims to victim status are beyond question, against the unworthy victims championed in Keynesian social policy and left politics. Poverty, inequality, discrimination and violence are able to be cast as matters of individual pathology or will, while a particular array of structural sufferings is always rendered genuine and exigent: free markets are victims of nanny states, capital is vulnerable to organized labour, states are captured by politically correct special interest groups, order and security are permanently threatened by rapacious criminality. Reflecting the bolstered role of criminal law and incarceration in the neoliberal polity, the category 'crime victim', and the conservative politics of the victims' rights movement, become the locus of legitimate victim talk in the neoliberal polity. At first sight, the victims' rights movement appears to be at odds with the victim-blaming orientation of neoliberal philosophy: this movement champions the victim's perspective, while neoliberal philosophy derogates victimhood as a failure of personal responsibility. Yet the victims' rights movement (and neoconservatism more broadly) is an important companion to neoliberalism, supporting rather than challenging the anti-sociological heuristics of neoliberal victim theory.[15]

As Harvey observes, despite its theoretical emphasis on individual freedom and minimal state intervention, neoliberal reform strengthens the coercive arm of the state, extending the range and reach of the punitive powers. Incarceration becomes 'a key state strategy to deal with problems arising among discarded workers and marginalised populations' (Harvey, 2005, p. 77). Accordingly the numbers of criminally convicted and detained persons in the West, notably in the USA, have soared in the era of neoliberalism.[16] In the USA the neoliberal war on crime has been a gendered and racialized class war noticeably aimed at African-American men as well as African-American women (Roberts, 1997). Vindicating Angela Y. Davis' radical critique of the US criminal justice system as slavery's historical replacement in the maintenance of white supremacy (see Mendieta, 2005), the resulting scenario of mass criminalization and incarceration of minority men has given rise to what Pettit and Western (2004) describe as 'the emergence of incarceration as a new stage in the life course of young low-skill black men' (p. 151).

Reflecting this aspect of neoliberal state reform – the intensification of the carceral state and development of the prison-industrial complex despite the rhetoric of the small state – victims' rights movements channel the horror and distress of criminal victimization towards an array of political claims (for stronger policing, longer gaol terms, the death penalty) that support extension of the punitive powers and legitimate the punitive model of justice. The victims' rights movement champions 'victims' perspectives', but only where those perspectives appear to align with the will to strengthen and extend the power of criminal law to police, convict and incarcerate.[17]

Crime victims are notionally promoted as Real Victims, their rights pitted against the rights of the correctional population, who are seen as inordinately protected by current law, which has succumbed to political correctness in the administration of justice. The privileging of crime victims – specifically those whose stories do not disrupt the valuing of punitive justice[18] – in turn legitimates the 'tough on crime' policies characteristic of neoliberal governance, helping them to appear less contradictory and defending them against the variety of movements that challenge the punitive model of justice and the practice of incarceration.[19]

The neoliberal emphasis on blamelessness in genuine victimhood is not critiqued but instead taken to its extreme in some versions of the victims' rights position. A strong example of this is the victims' rights position adopted by the pro-life movement which champions the 'unborn victim' as the purest and most genuine victim, in whose 'preborn' status is figured perfect vulnerability. In an important victory for the US pro-life movement, the *Unborn Victims of Violence Act* (UVVA) was passed in 2004. The Act codifies the pregnancy/foetus as an individual person and potential crime victim, rendering violence against pregnant women as violence against the unborn.[20] The UVVA is an example of Fraser's 'uncanny double' – it was supported largely by conservative politicians who had previously opposed legislative measures pertaining to violence against women, yet these supporters mobilized feminist political signs, invoking feminist anti-violence discourses and arguing that the UVVA would extend women's right to freedom from violence and exclude pregnant women from prosecution. In practice, this law has contributed to the climate of increased surveillance and criminalization of women's conduct while pregnant and fertile, and pregnant women have been prosecuted directly under the UVVA (Paltrow, 2008). From a feminist perspective, the UVVA is highly contentious because, by conferring legal status and certain rights upon foetuses, it furthers and extends the pro-life attack on women's reproductive rights, in particular the right to choose whether or not to continue a pregnancy. As I have argued elsewhere (Stringer, 2006), the UVVA is also problematic in terms of its rather improbable depiction and subsequent codification of violence against pregnant women as violence that is not experienced by pregnant women.

The UVVA individualizes the foetus as the sole victim of violence against the pregnant woman's person, eliding the fact that violence against a pregnancy/foetus is necessarily enacted upon the body of the pregnant woman. The UVVA upholds law's individualism against the complexities the maternal subject poses, and addresses violence against pregnant women by presuming the absence of pregnancy. To make the pregnant woman analogous to legal norms, maternity and foetality are absented and 'she' becomes two separate legal subjects: the 'intended victim' (who avoided 'actual' victimization) and the 'actual victim' (her pregnancy/ foetus, conceived here as a separate legal person and directly analogous to a non-foetal 'born person'). This mode of address to pregnant women ensures that, while the violence they experience will not be recognized, they may be perceived as potential perpetrators or accessories to violence against their own person – guilty parties in 'violence against the unborn'. Perceiving the dubious logic of a law that elides women's experiences of violence in order to elevate foetal personhood and negate women's reproductive rights, in 2005, the New South Wales parliament pursued the more promising approach of extending the legal meaning of 'person' to include 'pregnant woman', remedying the law's neglect of violence against pregnant women but in a manner that effectively blocked the anti-abortion movement's politicization of the NSW legislation. The amendments made in 2005 show the existence of a strong and more cogent alternative to the way this form of violence is codified in the UVVA, though they have since been challenged. As the example of the UVVA demonstrates, allied with social conservatism, the neoliberal logic of genuine victimhood has serious consequences for the understanding and adjudication of violence against women. Feminism's 'uncanny doubles' are also feminism's new political opponents.

The characteristics of neoliberal victim theory traced here – the victim-blaming derogation of victimhood as a failure of personal responsibility, the positing of victimhood as subjective rather than social, and the discourse of genuine victimhood, including its elaboration in the victims' rights position – all appear in the critiques of victim feminism, most visibly in their techniques for depoliticizing ongoing issues of structural oppression. Beginning with the accusation of resentment, used to pathologize sociological thinking, these techniques 'apply' neoliberal victim theory to feminist politics, giving rise to a specifically neoliberal feminist perspective on gendered violence, discrimination and inequality.

The accusation of resentment

In Sommers' *Who Stole Feminism?*, the accusation of resentment is an important instrument for setting up a concept of genuine victimhood designed to discredit feminist accounts of gendered violence and inequality. The theme of resentment and the figure of the resentful feminist appear right across the spectrum of critiques of victim feminism, from popular press to poststructuralist. In this body of work, resentment is cast as a toxic, consuming and undemocratic emotion, with feminist fixation on victimhood 'diagnosed' as symptomatic of personal affliction with resentment. Scholarly feminist critiques of the theme of victimhood in feminism draw on Nietzsche's theory of *ressentiment* (resentment) to conceptualize feminism's problem with victimhood, identifying feminism with what Nietzsche calls 'slave morality', or the elaboration of values from the victim's perspective, to the disadvantage of the strong (see Chapter 3). Of the texts addressed in this chapter, Wolf's *Fire with Fire* also draws on Nietzsche's theory, but the theme of resentment is most pronounced in Sommers' critique, where the accusation of resentment is used to pathologize sociological explanation of gendered victimization.

Sommers meets feminist accounts of gendered violence and inequality with the claim that these accounts have sprung from the feeling of resentment, and cannot therefore be trusted. Distinguishing between healthy indignation and unhealthy resentment, Sommers contrasts the feeling of resentment ('not a wholesome passion') with the scientific reason and ethically oriented sense of indignation equity feminism possesses on account of its Enlightenment liberalism (Sommers, 1994, p. 43). Where the indignant yet ethical liberal feminist can perceive 'real injustice' (p. 42) with clarity and reason, the gender feminist afflicted with resentment has a distorted perception of injustice: her resentment leads to the view that injustice is an effect of embedded systems and structures of oppression. In a pathologizing account of political feelings, Sommers casts resentment as a disease of the will that is hostile to truth and beyond the reach of reason:

> Resentment is 'harboured' or 'nurtured'; it 'takes root' in a subject (the victim) and remains directed at another (the culprit). It can be vicarious –

you need not have harmed me personally, but if I identify with someone you *have* harmed, I may resent you. Such resentment is very common and may easily be as strong and intense as resentment occasioned by direct injury. In a way it is stronger, for by enlarging the class of victims to include others, it magnifies the villainy as well. Having demarcated a victimised 'us' with whom I now feel solidarity, I can point to one victim and say . . . 'Anyone who harms a woman harms us all' . . . The next step is to regard the individual who wronged 'us' as himself representative of a group, giving our animus a larger project . . . My social reality has now been dichotomised into two groups politically at odds, one of whom dominates and exploits the other.

(p. 42, original emphasis)

According to Sommers, it is through the vicarious will of resentment that individual instances of 'direct injury', or genuine victimization, are elaborated into a collective politics waged on behalf of women as a group. In the politics of resentment, genuine victimization is 'enlarged' and 'magnified', creating the false impression that gendered relations of oppression actually exist. The unwholesome passion of resentment acts on its host as does a disease, impairing their social vision and political judgement. Having lost perspective on the realities of genuine victimization, the feminist afflicted by resentment acquires 'the habit of regarding women as a subjugated gender' and, moreover, 'may even be ready to fabricate atrocities' (p. 42) to match her distorted view.

For Sommers, the distorted view of victimization generated by the feeling of resentment is itself victimizing, it is an 'injuriously divisive' source of social conflict. Here, the accusation of resentment enacts a transference and reversal of blame for social conflict concerning gender. According to Sommers, feminist resentment is divisive because it creates a gendered 'us and them', an 'ontology of a society divided against itself along the fault line of gender' (p. 224). Feminist claims about gender segregation and inequality, rather than really existing gender segregation and inequality, set women and men against each other in a 'gender war' (p. 41). In reality, the divisive ontology Sommers describes *belongs* to liberalism: it reflects, rather than falsifies, liberal democratic social formations, based as they are on symbolically and materially gendered divisions between the public and private spheres. The public/private dichotomy is liberalism's primary fault line of gender, a divisive ontology that is not, as Sommers insists, fabricated by feminism, but instead continues to complexly interpellate feminist politics. Sommers disavows liberalism's status as a gendered politics, neatly transferring and reversing blame for social conflict concerning gender: feminist resentment, rather than readily discernible patterns of gender segregation and inequality in liberal-capitalist settings, is located as the 'source' of feminist complaint. Through the accusation of resentment, Sommers stigmatizes talk of structural oppression – forms of victimization beyond 'direct injury' – as purely self-referential, arising out of the personal pathology of resentment.

Depoliticizing conceptual makeovers

The accusation of resentment sets the frame for Sommers' subsequent discussion of key issues in feminist politics – the examples I will discuss are spousal violence, rape and the gender pay gap – each of which is rendered as a 'fabricated atrocity' attesting to emotional disease among feminists rather than systemic violence and structural oppression within society. These atrocities have been fabricated by using 'exaggerated' and 'overblown' statistics (Sommers, 1994, p. 220), and inserting 'gender-specific analysis' (p. 225) where it is not warranted, in order to promote 'the belief that American culture is sexist and misogynist' (p. 222). In her discussion of these issues, Sommers downplays indicators of gendered asymmetries of privilege and power by offering a series of conceptual makeovers that serve to displace the gendered aspects of each issue: domestic violence is recast as privately dys-functional intimacy; rape narrows to a symptom of criminal pathology; and the gender pay gap is rendered, first, as an effect of natural sex differences and, second, as a reflection of free and private choices made by women individually. These ministrations lay bare the overall dynamic of Sommers' critique: it contracts, where feminism's radical variants have expanded, the public parameters of victim recognition and the grounds on which feminist claims about systemic violence and structural oppression might be made.

Sommers argues feminists are mistaken when they treat spousal violence as a gender issue because 'it appears that battery may have very little to do with patriarchy or gender bias' (p. 200). Against the feminist view that spousal violence forms part of a gender order in which violence against women is common and normalized, Sommers proposes an alternative conception of genuine spousal violence as pathological, exceptional and gender-neutral. Sommers reconcep-tualizes spousal violence as a 'pathology of intimacy' (p. 200), an anti-social abnormality for which the women and men involved bear equal responsibility, suffering and committing violence in broadly equal measure. Genuine cases of this pathology are rare, and Sommers warns against 'counting all acts of violence as acts of abuse' (p. 197) to avoid inflated statistics. In Sommers' account of this pathology, spousal violence comes to appear as a quality of those affected by it, with the language of diseased individuals replacing talk of socially embedded victimization through violence.

Sommers' reconceptualization of spousal violence as a gender-neutral pathology is designed to counter the distortions of victim feminism's 'gender-specific analysis'. In order to portray spousal violence as gender-neutral, however, Sommers omits the gender differences that are in evidence. Sommers draws on *Physical Violence in American Families* by Gelles and Straus (1990) and participates in an interpretation of their data that these authors have since rejected emphatically (see Berns, 2004).[21] Using their work to spotlight women's violence and downplay violence against women, Sommers (1994) reports that their study found 'women assault their partners at about the same rate as men assault their partners' (p. 194). As Gelles and Straus have since clarified, this ignores the crucial finding that 'nearly three fourths of the violence committed by women is done in self-defence' (cited in Berns, 2004, p. 123). As Nancy Berns (2004) documents in her book, *Framing the Victim*:

> Even though Gelles and Straus say that women may be violent in the home, they agree that women sustain more physical injury, lose more time from work, and require more medical care. Furthermore, Gelles and Straus's survey data focus on counting acts of violence and do not consider other strategies of control and intimidation such as psychological, sexual and verbal abuse and the use of threats against children, relatives, and pets.
>
> (p. 123)

Sommers' (1994) technique for countering the distortions of gender-specific analysis is to narrow the definition of 'what counts as battery' (p. 195) while ignoring the gender differences that are in evidence. Her equity feminist reconceptualization of spousal violence is a feminist example of what Berns calls the 'antifeminist frame', a counter-discourse to feminist anti-violence work that simultaneously degenders the violence and genders the blame. Discussion is focused on either 'women being violent to men' or 'women victims who are responsible for bringing violence upon themselves' (Berns, 2004, p. 122), situating women as the blameworthy agents of spousal violence.

Sommers (1994) extends the effort to represent violence against women as gender-neutral into her discussion of rape, setting out to prove that rape 'is not caused by gender bias, misogyny, or "patriarchy"' (p. 225). Because the evidence attesting to women's overrepresentation as victims of rape is overwhelming, the option of presenting men as equally victimized by rape is not available. Rather than acknowledge men's vulnerability to rape and in this way attempt to produce a 'gender-netural' account of rape, Sommers pursues the different move of framing men as acutely vulnerable to false accusations of rape, and framing rape itself as a rare criminal act, rather than a common social practice, as feminists claim. Sommers attacks feminist definitions of rape, setting up a genuine victim/false victim binary that serves to redefine 'real rape' and minimize rape statistically. Like Roiphe, Sommers argues that feminists have manufactured false evidence of a 'rape epidemic' (p. 220). The 'device' enabling feminists to exaggerate rape statistics is an 'expanded definition of rape': a definition that recognizes that rape can occur between people known or related to one another and establishes that 'any sexual intercourse without mutual desire is a form of rape' (p. 220). As in Roiphe's critique, Sommers argues this definition is unduly broad, inspires false rape claims that victimize men, and serves to obscure genuine victimization. 'By such definition, privileged young women in our nation's colleges gain moral parity with the real victims in the community at large' (p. 220). Genuine rape victims, she suggests, can be found 'on the streets of downtown Trenton' not in 'an office in Princeton' (p. 220). Roiphe (1993) similarly argues that the word 'rape' be 'reserved' to describe 'instances of physical violence or the threat of physical violence' (pp. 81–82). This way, the experiences of women 'raped by a stranger at knife point' would not be falsely equated with the experiences of women 'raped by their former boyfriend' (p. 82). This 'corrective' view of rape is designed to protect men and the courts from the flood of false rape claims victim feminism purportedly inspires.

Seeking to counter feminist interventions in the area of rape law, Sommers and Roiphe will a return to traditional rape law, in which physically brutal stranger rape sets the benchmark for reckoning genuine law-worthy rape. Presumptively, they identify genuine sexual victimization with maximum physical trauma, and their concept of genuine sexual victimization conspicuously excludes women who knew their rapist. Sommers and Roiphe position themselves as working on behalf of genuine rape victims, whose experiences, they argue, are trivialized in the context of feminist politicizations of rape. Having set up this binary between genuine and false rape, Sommers further explains that when genuine rape does occur, it is gender-neutral. In an effort to counter the feminist 'rape culture' critique of hegemonic masculinity and the normalization of sexual violence, Sommers casts rape as a problem of criminal pathology rather than gender politics. Sommers (1994) observes that rape is caused by 'criminal violence, not patriarchal misogyny' (p. 223) and is 'perpetrated by people who are wont to gratify themselves in criminal ways' (p. 225). Asking that we understand rape not as an event that transpires most commonly between men and women, but between criminals and crime victims, Sommers proposes that gender politics be erased from rape law, with rape legally codified as 'just one subvariety [of] crime against the person' (p. 226). This recasting of rape as a gender-neutral problem caused by criminal pathology situates the criminal justice system as the appropriate arbiter of individual cases of genuine rape, against the feminist critique of rape law as complicit in rape culture and the normalization of violence against women.

When it comes to discussing the gender pay gap Sommers abruptly desists in the idea of gender-neutrality, turning instead to talk of natural sex differences. As with the issue of rape, in relation to gender pay gaps, Sommers is unable to dispute women's overall unequal position at the level of empirical reality. It is well established that, despite the fact that many countries of the world have incorporated goals of gender equity and anti-discrimination into their labour legislation while female labour participation rates have risen substantially, the world remains bereft of a national economy in which women as a group earn as much income from paid employment as men as a group. Labour markets within liberal-capitalist settings are still vertically and horizontally segregated by gender, with women typically concentrated in low-paid and low-status work, and occupational 'women's work' typically underpaid. Parenthood still has a markedly differential impact upon the economic status of women compared with men, and solo parents, the majority of them women, tend to be peculiarly disadvantaged in the economy. Feminists view the gender pay gap's tenacity as an indication that gender discrimination is institutionalized within rather than incidental to the current organization of work – the labour market's ideal competitors remain modelled on the lives of a majority of men, lives in which a comparatively lesser amount of unpaid domestic responsibility typically facilitates greater access to paid public participation (Rose and Hartmann, 2004).

To dispute the idea that labour markets perpetuate and depend upon systemic gender discrimination, Sommers (1994) develops the alternative explanation that women's comparative devaluation in the sphere of work 'naturally results' (p. 188) from their childbearing role, and cannot therefore be regarded as 'discriminatory' (p. 241). Redrawing a classic anti-feminist argument, responsibility for women's unequal status rests with Nature, which is impervious to political intervention. The female reproductive body, rather than the sphere of paid work's aggregate failure to fully and equitably accommodate women who have dependent children, becomes the locus of the problem, suggesting an inevitable distance between female sexual specificity and successful liberal individuality. In effect, women own and earn less than men *because they are women*. With this explanation, Sommers loses sight of equity feminism's emphasis on women and men's shared humanity, thus equality. Rather than deny sexual difference, she calls upon it to provide the justifying explanation that gender pay gaps are 'caused' by childbearing.

Sommers further presents unequal economic status as freely chosen by women, arguing that the situation is simply that women 'choose to move into and out of the workforce during childbearing and child-rearing years', bringing less 'experience' (p. 241) to the workplace and accruing less remunerative merit. Importantly, in her attempt to recast the gender pay gap as a question of individual work/life preference rather than as an eliminable collective inequality, Sommers distorts social reality to the same extent she claims victim feminists do. At her time of writing, women were the sole, primary or co-equal earners in more than half of American families (Galinsky and Friedman, 1995). With the decline since 1970 of the breadwinning wage, women have emerged as the new providers: their income from paid work is indispensable rather than disposable family income. In the absence of assured government income support such as childcare subsidies and paid parental leave, and since the transition from welfare to workfare, many women cannot afford the freedom to choose between paid work and childrearing that Sommers implies is available to all women. If they do not work in paid employment, or fail to manage the competing demands of paid work, housework and childcare amidst rising living costs and declining real wages, they are punished with poverty – the main reason why over 30 per cent of all female-headed house-holds in the USA currently live in poverty.[22] Given these arrangements the freedom of choice Sommers describes is desired by many but available to few – an affluent and typically partnered minority for whom leaving the paid workforce will not mean entering or nearing poverty, and who can afford quality replacement childcare if need be.

In her recent work Sommers not only denies these realities; she presents the policies that might ameliorate them – paid parental leave, publicly subsidized childcare and gender pay parity – as 'harmful' and 'unjust' (Sommers, 2002, p. 2) threats to the economy. Fully reversing the feminist view that women as a group are unjustly burdened by gendered economic inequality, Sommers argues that such policies 'undermine economic prosperity' and 'burden a country's economy' (p. 2). In Sommers' view, women are not victims of gendered economic inequality. Rather, governments and free markets are victims of feminist efforts to ameliorate gendered inequality.

Individual transformation versus structural change

Where Sommers denies, downplays and naturalizes gendered inequalities, Wolf pursues the different move of acknowledging that gendered inequalities do exist, while arguing it is victim feminism that ensures their continued existence. If one goes to *Fire with Fire* asking 'Why do women own and earn less than men?', the answer given is that feminism has failed to equip women, and women have failed to equip themselves, with an appropriate 'psychology of power' (Wolf, 1993, p. 323). Victim feminism not only encourages women to 'cling to an outdated image of ourselves as powerless'; further to this, it has actively 'discouraged women from appropriating the power of the political and financial world to make that power at last their own' (p. 160). Operative here is a transference of blame similar to that found in Sommers' critique. Conforming with her view that victim feminism is the last remaining barrier to female empowerment, Wolf links feminism's radical variants, notably socialist feminism, with an active desire that women remain poor and underrepresented. Women's oppression appears as a perverse gift to feminism. Victim feminism's desires are blamed for the feminization of poverty, while the norms and processes that serve to structure labour markets in ways that marginalize women and undervalue their labours, are protected from critique. Where Sommers casts feminists who politicize structural oppression as resentful people who generate social conflict, Wolf casts those same feminists as desiring and perpetuating the very oppressions they are politicizing.

This transference of blame also sees Wolf recast questions of political and economic status as matters of individual psychology and agency, resulting in a further displacement of the concept of structural oppression. In an argument strongly reminiscent of the positive thinking movement's linking of mental attitude to economic status,[23] Wolf contends that women suffer from particular psychological problems – 'fear of money' (p. 175) and a negative tendency to undervalue their own skills and capacities – that serve to perpetuate gendered socio-economic inequality, resulting in the feminization of poverty. Directly reflecting the neoliberal project of entrepreneurial professionalization, Wolf proposes to counter women's psychological problems, and hence the gendered inequalities they perpetuate, through a programme of empowerment workshops oriented to enabling women to realize their capacity to become suitably self-esteeming and assertive wage labourers and entrepreneurs. Sending the right messages to women about the proper conduct of personal agency, these workshops will provide venues for 'the masculine, potent act of putting the means to generate profits in women's own hands' (p. 263). As Engin Isin (2002) explains, entrepreneurial professionalization is the prevailing form of disciplinary power in the context of neoliberalism: 'While disciplinary professionalization was oriented toward various groups as objects of cure, correction, and rehabilitation, entrepreneurial professionalization aims for neither reformation, nor salvation, but for interpellating these subjects as responsible agents of their destiny' (pp. 271–272). In an apparently non-interventionist gesture of empowerment, the neoliberal state 'steps away' from the subject, governing them by 'ungoverning' them, constituting them as 'active subjects of their own making' (p. 272), rather than as right-bearing subjects able to make claims and demands. Exactly this responsibilization of the subject – as Isin puts it, 'to enable or empower them to constitute themselves as active citizens . . . under terms and conditions that they may not have articulated' (p. 272) – forms the objective of Wolf's empowerment workshops.

For Wolf, the answer to the feminization of poverty is not structural change, but individual transformation – specifically, women's realization of the capacity and responsibility to practise entrepreneurial selfhood, signalling proper adaptation to neoliberalism's personal responsibility system, its privatization of risk and ready conception of victimization as personal failure.[24] With gendered economic inequality thus tied to women's capacity to be entrepreneurial, inequality is depoliticized and explained in reference to the absence or presence of this capacity, rather than in reference to the gendered forces of economic distribution and social opportunity circumscribing an individual's material situation, and without recognition of their existing efforts to adapt to the economy. As we saw earlier, the self-blaming victim is blind spotted in Wolf's critique of victim feminism, with Wolf failing to acknowledge the problem of self-blame in rape survival. This is explained when Wolf's orientation to neoliberalism is exposed. Exhorted to 'take responsibility', the ideal neoliberal citizen is by definition self-blaming, their capacity for self-blame valued rather than problematized. Accordingly, self-blame is not problematized by Wolf. Wolf presents the power feminist solution to the feminization of poverty as a way to grant women the form of agency that victim feminism has denied them: the agency of market individualism. Yet, as a proposal that serves to displace feminist efforts to bring about structural change, it actually withdraws from women in general, and feminists most certainly, a particular form of *political* agency: that of exerting influence over the character and shape of the world's political and economic structures.

Conclusion

Collectively, the techniques I have identified radically downsize and revise the terrain of feminist politics, articulating a specifically neoliberal version of feminism and defending the neoliberal status quo against the socio-political transformations and economic redistributions called for in radical feminist theses of systemic violence and structural oppression. The accusation of resentment pathologizes sociological explanation of gendered victimization, giving only the most conservative articulations of feminism monopoly on reason and legitimacy. The depoliticizing conceptual makeovers of key issues in feminist politics follow the logic of genuine victimhood, introducing new criteria for discerning genuine victimization against suspect claims to victim status, elaborating new grounds for regarding victims as blameworthy and responsible for the violence and inequality they experience. Reflecting the victim-blaming structure of neoliberalism's personal responsibility system, these makeovers, as Bern suggests, 'de-gender the violence while gendering the blame', spotlighting women as responsible for violence. Finally, the emphasis on individual transformation over structural change applies the logic of entrepreneurial professionalization, locating women themselves, their individual psychology and practice of agency, as the source of gendered inequality, in this way updating liberalism's historical problematization of women as of questionable fitness for the rights and responsibilities of citizenship. Over the course of these ministrations, feminists and women are multiply stigmatized, while the populations of victims the critics represent – the victims of victim feminism – are spared these various aspersions.

The relationship between critiques of victim feminism and neoliberal politics has been mutually beneficial: these critiques supply a spectrum of ways to depoliticize and recast issues of feminist politics and, in return, these critiques are resuscitated in contexts of neoliberal government, actualizing the revenge of 'mainstream' feminist values they call for. In the period since the first circulation of these critiques, the victim feminist construct has been invoked in a wide array of contexts, in places where one would expect to find strong critique of feminism, such as fathers' rights groups, but also in key sites of neoliberal governance, informing policy change.[25] In Australia, for example, the idea that victim feminism must be overcome operated as a justifying explanation for the Howard government's disestablishment of the key federal agency for monitoring and actualizing gender equality, the Office For the Status of Women. As a government spokesperson put it, consigning this office to history meant liberation from 'the left wing ideology of victimhood that once claimed the women's movement' (Goward, cited in Humphries, 2006). Similarly, the World Bank's shift towards focusing on men in analyses of gender and development has been cast not as a new legacy of feminist analyses of gender, but as a liberating departure from the 'oppositional and two-dimensional "women as victim, men as a problem" attitude' (Bannon and Correia, 2006, p. 253) enforced by victim feminists. In these examples the critique of victim feminism is reiterated by key agents of neoliberal reform, informing the Howard government's and the World Bank's self-presentation as forces of liberation, rather than as purveyors of social conservatism and inequality.

That the critiques of victim feminism participate in the normalization and generalization of neoliberal victim theory would be less significant if it were not for the fact that in both developed and developing countries women as a group have borne the brunt of neoliberalism's inequality-generating programmes of structural adjustment. They betray little indication of having been produced in a time of rising inequality, yet the narrative of patriarchal decline in these texts runs counter to the measurable impact of neoliberal reform upon women as a group. The feminization of poverty and overrepresentation of women in low-paid, minimum condition work have intensified rather than subsided in neoliberal times. Neoliberal welfare reform has had an inordinately detrimental impact upon women, who form the majority of welfare beneficiaries across the West. With the steady withdrawal of state support from the domain of social reproduction, survival itself has become acutely feminized, with households increasingly reliant on women's unpaid labours, and the lowly paid labours of migrant women workers, to survive.[26] In the period since their first circulation, it has become increasingly evident that the critiques of victim feminism participate in a pernicious contradiction: the stigmatization of victim subjects and victim politics on behalf of a philosophy and economic programme that has been, for many people of the world, distinctly victimizing.

Notes

1 See also Garner (1995) and Bail (1996). Recent critiques of victim feminism include Coulter (2009) and Maushart (2007).
2 See Hughes (1993), Sykes (1992), D'Souza (1991), Bloom (1987) and Green (2006). The broad archive of work critiquing victim politics in the USA is perceptively analysed in Cole (2007).
3 See Abrams (1995), Smith (1997), Walters (1998), Atmore (1999) and Davis (1997).
4 See McRobbie (2004), Gill (2007b), Gill and Scharff (2011), Radner (2011), Sherman (2011) and Zaslow (2009).
5 For alternative readings of the historical and political significance of the Thomas–Hill hearings, see Morrison (1992).
6 For the 'end of history' argument, or the view that the collapse of Stalinism signalled the historical victory of liberal-capitalism over its rival political forms, see Fukuyama (1992).
7 Adopting the Third Way approach, Wolf (1993) argues that while capitalism cannot be countered, it can be tamed:

> Capitalism is innately exploitative. It does oppress the many for the benefit of the few; its excesses must be tempered by compassionate policies. But the collapse of communism in Europe suggests that the left in Britain or the United States should not hold its breath waiting for the socialist revolution. The progressive community serves its values better by engaging with capitalism to fund social change than it does by professing an aversion to it.
>
> (p. 263)

For articulations of the Third Way position, see Giddens (2001) and Blair (1996). As Pollin (2000) and Callinicos (2001) have argued, in practice, the Third Way approach fully maintains the neoliberal policy agenda.
8 In a particularly strong example of this, Roiphe (1993) observes of a Take Back the Night march that 'students are willing to lie' (p. 39) about experiences of sexual harm so they can assume the power of the powerless. Roiphe depicts 'truth' as victimized by rape survivors:

> The line between fact and fiction is a delicate one when it comes to survivor stories . . . the truth may be stretched, battered, or utterly abandoned. It's impossible to tell how many of these stories are authentic, faithful accounts of what actually happened. They sound tinny, staged.
>
> (p. 42)

9 As Wolf (1993) elaborates, 'The fashionable lapse in logic among the left right now is that you can't identify *with* victims of oppression unless you identify *as* a victim' (p. 217, original emphasis).

10 The form of empowerment Wolf describes is dubbed 'professional victimhood' by Diane Long Hoeveler (1998). Elaborating on Wolf's account of feminism and bad agency, Hoeveler (1998) identifies the historical inception of 'victim feminism' – 'an ideology of female power through pretended and staged weakness' (p. 7) – with eighteenth-century women Gothic novelists, whose heroines are 'professional victims' (p. xiii). The professional victim's social mask of acquiescent innocence is a form of passive aggression, by which she ritually manipulates and victimizes others in order to enjoin bourgeois status and win the master and his house. The professional victim converts patriarchal scripts of feminine virtue, weakness and passivity into a subversive means of attaining socio-economic empowerment within a patriarchal context. Hoeveler's discussion contributes to the analysis of tropes in the historical articulation of white femininity. The 'professional victimhood' she depicts, however, does not transpose neatly onto the forms of radical left feminism Wolf identifies as 'victim feminism'. The non-radicalism and individualism of Hoeveler's 'professional victimhood' seem more akin to the (neo)liberal feminist strategy Wolf advocates in *Fire with Fire*.

11 The privatization of social risk is a central and generic feature of neoliberal programmes of structural adjustment, yet the 'rolling out' of this process and the discourses surrounding it differ according to context. As Harvey (2005) observes, there are tensions between neoliberal theory and actual processes of neoliberalization, between the 'Utopian' schemes of neoliberal philosophy and on-the-ground neoliberal politics.

12 Thatcher's full statement, made in a 1987 interview with Douglas Keay for the British women's magazine *Woman's Own*, is as follows:

> And, you know, there is no such thing as society. There are individual men and women, and there are families. And no government can do anything except through people, and people must look to themselves first. It's our duty to look after ourselves and then, also, to look after our neighbour. People have got the entitlements too much in mind, without the obligations, because there is no such thing as an entitlement unless someone has first met an obligation.
>
> (Keay, 1987, p. 9)

13 On victim-blame and the moral symbolism mobilized in neoliberal welfare reform, see Handler and Hasenfeld (2007) and Schram (2000).

14 Bumiller (2008) elaborates:

> The representation of sexual violence as ever present and cataclysmic grips the social imagination with images often primed to provoke deep-seated animosities and stimulate incomprehensibility rather than foster a compassionate understanding of the situations of either perpetrators or victims.
>
> (p. 17)

15 Harvey (2005) argues neoconservatism is complexly aligned with neoliberalism, and I would locate the victims' rights movement as an important vector in this alliance. As a theory of human liberty and the market economy, neoliberalism is not obviously kindred with the religious, moral and cultural values promoted by neoconservative special interest groups, such as the pro-life and family values movements of the Christian Right. Harvey argues, however, that the apparent opposition between neoconservatism and neoliberalism is superficial. Neoconservatism shares the pro-business orientation of neoliberalism while also attempting to answer its consequences

and contradictions through a galvanizing moral unity and certainty, redirecting and diffusing the anomie and revolt generated by neoliberal reform. See Harvey (2005, pp. 81–86).

16 Since the late 1970s the US prison population has increased sixfold (US Census Bureau, 2009). With the roll-out of federal and state 'tough on crime' policies since the early 1990s, between 1990 and 2008, the prison population more than doubled. The current total correctional population (in prison or on parole) exceeds 7 million, excluding approximately 4.3 million ex-convicts. Approximately 1 in every 100 adults is incarcerated.

17 For a discussion of the victims' rights position in relation to the conservative figure of the vigilante in film, see Stringer (2011).

18 Van Dijk observes that the construction of crime victims as vengeful and punitive is questionable. There is 'overwhelming evidence' demonstrating that 'crime victims are not more punitive than the public at large' (Van Dijk, 2009, p. 20).

19 For a discussion of the challenges to punitive justice and incarceration, see the interviews with Angela Y. Davis in Mendieta (2005).

20 Violent assault by a current or ex-partner is the leading cause of death of pregnant women in the USA. Under the UVVA violence against a pregnant woman resulting in loss of or damage to pregnancy can be legally tried as murder of a foetus and given a life sentence (but not the death penalty). If the pregnant woman dies in the assault, her murder is tried separately. For full analysis of the category 'unborn victim' as figured in the UVVA and similar legislation proposed in Australia, see Stringer (2006). Also relevant here is the trend Barbara Baird (2008) has called 'child fundamentalism', or the steady replacement of women with the figure of the vulnerable child as the primary focus of anti-violence efforts and public discourses of risk; the demotion and rearticulation of the issue of violence against women as issues of child abuse assume greater public prominence.

21 As Berns (2004) observes, in the following statement Gelles and Straus reject the use of their data to downplay violence against women:

> Unfortunately, the data on wife-to-husband violence has been misreported, misinterpreted and misunderstood . . . [some] have used the data on violence by wives to minimise the need for services for battered women. Such arguments do a great injustice to the victimisation of women.
>
> (p. 123)

22 The percentage figure for 2010 is 31.7, or 4.7 million 'female-householder-with-no-husband-present families' (US Census Bureau, 2011) living in poverty, up from 4.4 million in 2009. By comparison, 'male householder no wife present' families make up 15.8 per cent, or 880,000 living in poverty. In 2010, the poverty rate climbed to its highest level since 1993. Women are overrepresented across all poverty measures. Sharon Hays' (2003) book *Flat Broke with Children: Women in the Age of Welfare Reform* provides indispensable insight into the impact of welfare reform on US women, particularly mothers, in the era of neoliberalism.

23 See Donald Meyer's (1980) history of the American positive thinking movement, which traces its roots in Christian evangelism and presence in the New Right rhetoric of the Reagan era; and Ehrenreich's critique of contemporary positive thinking, which highlights the way positive thinking works on behalf of neoliberal capitalism by providing 'an apology for the crueler aspects of the market economy' (Ehrenreich, 2009, p. 8). A practice of forced optimism, positive thinking reinforces the neoliberal conception of personal responsibility and derogation of 'victimhood' and 'resentment':

> The flipside of positivity is . . . a harsh insistence on personal responsibility: if your business fails or your job is eliminated, it must be because you didn't try

hard enough, didn't believe firmly enough in the inevitability of your success. As the economy has brought more lay-offs and financial turbulence to the middle class, the promoters of positive thinking have increasingly emphasised this negative judgement: to be disappointed, resentful, or downcast is to be a 'victim' and a 'whiner'.

(pp. 8–9)

24 Joanne Baker's important research attests to the effectiveness of neoliberal philosophy in shaping women's self-perceptions. Baker (2008, 2010) conducted in-depth interviews with a sample of young Australian women, investigating their responses to the post-feminist discourse that exhorts women to be self-responsible, avoiding victim identity. Baker found the women in her sample had very strongly internalized popular discourses critiquing victim identity in women, organizing their personal values and actions around an idealized identity of self-responsible agency.

25 On fathers' rights groups, the critique of victim feminism and presentation of men as the 'new victims', see Kaye and Tolmie (1998).

26 These and other trends of gendered economic inequality in the era of neoliberalism are perceptively analysed in the following sources: Scott, Crompton and Lyonette (2010), Brodie (2005), Ehrenreich and Hochschild (2004), Hays (2003) and Abramovitz (2002).

2

VULNERABILITY
AFTER WOUNDING

Feminism, rape law and the differend

'I was portrayed as endowed with a type of terrifying sexual power that once unleashed was capable of annihilating a man' (XX [Anonymous], 1997, p. 53). These words come from a woman whose experience of sexual harassment served as a catalyst for the 'victim feminism' debate in Australia.[1] In 1991, she and a fellow student lodged a complaint against the Master of Ormond College at the University of Melbourne following his sexual harassment of them at the college valedictory dinner. The university ignored their initial and subsequent complaints, so they approached police and filed criminal charges of indecent assault. The charges were upheld in the Melbourne magistrate's court. The case attracted intense media scrutiny, with the lion's share of public sympathy swaying against the complainants. Following the pattern of reverse victimology I described in Chapter 1, the complainants' actions and the court's decision were narrated as politically correct attacks upon a fine upstanding man. This narration was articulated most vehemently by noted Australian feminist Helen Garner (1995), whose book *The First Stone: Some Questions about Sex and Power* investigates the Ormond case and portrays the Ormond College women as pernicious victimizers while rendering the Master as their unassuming prey. Drawn from a reply to Garner's book and to mass media representations of her case, the statement quoted above captures the particular aspect of victim politics I examine in this chapter: the role women-as-agent constructions play in victim-blame, in the context of sexual harm. As the statement indicates, woman-as-agent imagery did not empower the Ormond complainants, instead operating as a kind of secondary victimization. References to their 'terrifying sexual power' served to deny, compound and prolong their experience of victimization, enacting the dramatic withdrawal of compassion for the victim Jan Van Dijk (2009) describes as 'reactive victim scapegoating' (p. 13). Critiques of victim feminism generally do not acknowledge that woman-as-agent imagery can operate in this negative way, instead positing woman-as-agent imagery as an empowering alternative to the woman-as-victim theme. As we saw in Chapter 1, this very clearly takes place in the popular press critiques of victim feminism. In this chapter, I point out, however, that it also takes place in certain scholarly feminist critiques of the theme of victimhood in feminist politicizations of sexual harm, which similarly treat women-as-agent imagery as coterminous with liberation.

The statement from XX (Anonymous) draws our attention to secondary victimization, or the additional and adjacent forms of victimization that take place after or amidst primary victimization, such as when a victim is blamed, not believed, depicted as the 'real' perpetrator, or in a range of other ways finds they cannot attest the wrong they have suffered. In this regard, the second statement I want to cite is from Lyotard's book *The Differend*, which I situate in this chapter as an important text for thinking about feminism and the politics of sexual victimization. Lyotard (1988) writes, 'It is in the nature of a victim not to be able to prove that one has been done a wrong' (No. 9).[2] In his book Lyotard proposes a unique theory of the victim as one who has suffered a wrong that is not presently recognized in law and exists instead as a 'differend', or a form of suffering that cannot be phrased in a shared idiom. Where 'vulnerability' refers to the ability to be wounded, Lyotard's theory of the victim points up a second-order vulnerability: the ability to be wounded and to then have that wounding effaced, in language, by others, by the law. In this chapter I draw on Lyotard's theory to think about feminist efforts to reform rape law and ameliorate its effacement of various forms of rape. Though Lyotard does not discuss rape law, its notoriously attenuated codifications of 'real rape', which serve to exclude certain forms of rape from law-worthiness and recognition, provide powerful examples of the scenario of effaced suffering Lyotard sought to illuminate in *The Differend*. Rape law is replete with differends, and, accordingly, feminist efforts to reform rape law correspond to the kind of political work Lyotard describes as 'bearing witness to the *differend*' (No. 22, original emphasis) – political work that endeavours to counter the linguistic, cultural and legal effacement of particular forms of suffering, through the invention of new idioms that give suffering visibility.

In using Lyotard's theory to think about feminist anti-rape politicizations, my aim is to challenge the criticism that these politicizations are excessively and counter-productively focused on women's vulnerability to rape. Since Sharon Marcus' landmark essay 'Fighting Bodies, Fighting Words: A Theory and Politics of Rape Prevention' (1992), a prominent strand of postmodern feminist critique has followed Marcus' argument that feminist efforts to improve criminal justice responses to rape are counter-productive, because, in the effort to make various forms of rape socially and legally visible as wrong, they merely reinscribe patriarchal constructions of femininity as embodied vulnerability, perpetuating a sexist linking of femininity with victimhood rather than agency.[3] As Lisa Vetten (2011) has recently summarized, 'Emphasizing only the aftermath of rape, Marcus argued, is not an effective political strategy because it accepts that women will be raped and are rapeable' (p. 269). Marcus' alternative 'rape prevention' approach suggests that a better answer to the problem of rape lies in positive counter-images of women as agents who are capable of preventing rape. In Vetten's words: 'An emphasis on prevention . . . declares that women are not for raping—particularly when women themselves take preventive action' (p. 269). This focus on prevention is pitched against a focus on victimization established by 'dominance feminists' Catharine MacKinnon and Andrea Dworkin, who are regularly summoned in anti-victimist texts as extreme examples of feminist victimism, despite contrary evidence (Atmore, 1999) and Dworkin's stated anti-victim stance – her calling upon women to practise 'the revolutionary refusal to be a victim' (Dworkin, 1976, p. 72; see also Talbot, 2005).[4]

Questioning the progressiveness of this shift towards woman-as-agent constructions in postmodern feminist accounts of rape, in this chapter I use Lyotard's theory of the differend to clarify that modern rape law has typically represented women as capable of resisting rape, invoking images of women as agents in order to deny that sexual victimization has taken place. Rather than being new to history or loaded with nascent feminist promise, woman-as-agent constructions have been essential to the patriarchal differends of modern rape law, underpinning its use of victim-blame to efface various forms of rape. My analysis shows that rape law typically figures femininity not as embodied vulnerability but as responsible agency, and never more so than in the current neoliberal era of privatized social risk, where women are expected to align with an ideal rape-preventing subject. In the body of work that takes its bearings in Marcus' critique, some contributors raise important questions about the relationship between feminism and neoliberalism, arguing that feminist efforts to reform rape law and criminal justice responses to rape aid and abet the growing carceral powers of the neoliberal state.[5] I point out, however, that the agency-oriented feminism that emerges from Marcus' critique supports neoliberalism's equally problematic responsibilization of would-be crime victims and reflects the central theme of prevention in neoliberalism's distinctive approach to governing crime: the targeting of crime 'before it occurs' (O'Malley, 1992, p. 262) by disciplining the self-protective practices of the would-be victim. Demonstrating that not all images of women as agents are progressive and liberating, my analysis suggests that the real ethical problem confronted by feminist anti-rape politicizations, a problem that is intensified in the era of neoliberalism, is that of finding a way to phrase women's agency without reinscribing the patriarchal differends of rape law, which construct women as the blameworthy agents of their own victimization, reducing 'agency' to the ability to be blamed for suffering a wrong. In the final section of the chapter, I locate rape crisis feminism's ethos of survivorship and the SlutWalk movement as examples of progressive negotiation with this ethical problem.

Victim-bad/agent-good

In the previous chapter we saw that, though their treatment of themes of victimhood and agency is deeply paradoxical, the popular press critiques of victim feminism voice an ostensibly simple message: to regard women as victims is disabling, regressive and harmful, while to recognize women as agents is enabling, progressive and liberating. I call this the 'victim-bad/agent-good' formulation. My discussion in this chapter demonstrates the twofold problem with this formulation: its emphasis upon the negativity of 'victim' blinds us to instances in which victim recognition is progressive, while its emphasis upon the positivity of 'agent' blinds us to the workings of victim-blame, in particular, the way victim-blame in the context of sexual harm draws upon constructions of women as self-responsible agents. As I hope to show in this chapter, Lyotard's theory of the differend is illuminating where the victim-bad/agent-good formulation is blinding. Before honing in on this discussion, I want to first address the point that the victim-bad/agent-good formulation is not particular to the popular press critiques of victim feminism, but also appears in venues of scholarly feminist writing where the concept of victimhood is similarly rejected in favour of agency-affirming feminism. Here my argument is kindred with Carine Mardorossian's (2002) view that postmodern feminist accounts of rape, led by Marcus' influential account, share much in common with the popular press critics of victim feminism, or 'backlashers' as Mardorossian terms them.

Comparing the way postmodern feminists and popular press feminists critique feminist anti-rape activism, Mardorossian (2002) writes, 'There is paradoxically more continuity between contemporary postmodern feminists and the "back-lashers" than between postmodern and activist feminism' (p. 746). An objection to Mardorossian's view could be that it gives little visibility to scholarly feminist work that had, by the time of writing, already offered a robust critical response to the backlashers.[6] It is true perhaps that Mardorossian does not give due acknow-ledgement to feminists before her who framed the popular press critiques of victim feminism as backlash texts, clearly discerning the political conservatism at play in their language of choice and unconstrained individual agency. It is also true, however, that much of this critical work has focused exclusively on the problematic formulations of backlash texts, protecting similar formulations in postmodern feminist texts from critique. An important exception to this can be found in the work of Nicola Gavey, whose book *Just Sex? The Cultural Scaffolding of Rape* (2005) critiques the way the popular press critics handle themes of victimhood and agency, while also marking cautions around the agency-affirming, prevention-oriented approach proposed by Marcus:

> [T]he potential cost of this strategy is that it may do violence to the experience of women who are victimized and traumatized by rape; that is, by conveying disrespect for their experience or even implicitly blaming them for not having been able to avoid rape. Sensitivity to this possibility is necessary so that stories of particular kinds of resistance don't come to be privileged in ways that contribute once again to a silencing of women's experiences of victimization.

> (p. 188)

Whereas Gavey's discussion opens up a space for questioning both popular and postmodern critiques of victim feminism, other scholarly responses have tended to affirm the victim-bad/agent-good formulation, defending feminism against the charge of 'victim feminism' on the basis that feminist scholars are already invested in this formulation and indeed originated it. For example, Bonnie Dow's (1996) response to the critiques of victim feminism is to argue that feminists are 'already aware of "the dangers of victim ideology"' (p. 216, citing McDermott, 1995, p. 670): feminists have already rejected the notion of 'victim' and made the progressive shift to 'agency'. Similarly, amidst an otherwise trenchant critique, bell hooks (1999) writes, 'I do not believe that Roiphe's critiques are all wrong-minded . . . [Roiphe's] book draws heavily upon and restates critiques that have been continually voiced within feminist circles' (pp. 104–105).

Dow and hooks are correct of course. It is the case that the critics of victim feminism elide existing scholarly feminist critiques of victimhood, borrowing insights from this critical work and presenting them as novel apostasies. Arguably, however, this scenario of borrowed insight implies the need to also scrutinize the scholarly critiques of victimhood located 'within feminist circles' – as Mardorossian and Gavey, in their different ways, suggest. In view of this, in the following passages I consider an argument made in bell hooks' essay 'Sisterhood: Political Solidarity Between Women' (1984). This essay provides one of the earliest systematic critiques of the theme of victimhood in feminism and raised the question of victimhood in the context of a highly significant intervention upon racist sexism in the women's liberation movement. hooks (1984) argued that women's liberationists had created a political framework in which the respective categories 'woman' and 'man' are sharply drawn as 'victim' and 'enemy' – a framework set up to marginalize rather than interlock with anti-racist politics and class struggle, and which disguises 'the fact that many women exploit and oppress other women' (p. 44). While I do not doubt the argument hooks makes here (see Chapter 3), her further and in some ways more influential argument that feminism's woman-as-victim theme 'directly reflects male supremacist thinking' (p. 44) requires scrutiny.

The détente between postmodern and popular press critiques of victim feminism takes place around the idea that the woman-as-victim theme is existentially disabling, in itself and with respect to feminist politics. The key point of agreement is that the feminist representation of women as victims occurs within a cultural context already well prepared to see women in this way. Feminism's woman-as-victim theme, it is supposed, merely reflects and further cements existing patriarchal constructions of women as powerless, vulnerable, violable and passive. This feeds the further supposition that constructions of women as powerful, active, surviving, resistant agents necessarily constitute liberating and progressive feminist counter-imagery. The first supposition is strongly present in hooks' essay. hooks observes, 'Sexist ideology teaches women that to be female is to be a victim. Rather than repudiate this equation . . . women's liberationists embraced it' (p. 45). Here hooks posits a more or less seamless relation between patriarchal and feminist representations of women as victims, arguing that feminist politics waged in the name of woman as a victim subject merely redraws patriarchal scripts of female weakness and passivity, following the patriarchal logic that 'to be female is to be a victim'. The postmodern critiques of feminist anti-rape politics advance the same argument. As Rachel Hall (2004) puts it, following Marcus,

61

feminist politicizations of sexual victimization reflect and revive 'the paternalistic myth of women's vulnerability' (p. 1). But is it really the case that there are no substantive differences between patriarchal and feminist representations of women as victims? Is it true that 'sexist ideology' and 'paternalistic myth' only operate through images of female victimhood, and not through images of female agency?

In response to the first question, two substantive differences spring to mind. First, the patriarchal logic that hooks describes – 'to be female is to be a victim' – presents victimization as woman's inevitable destiny, thus as elemental and ultimately benign, or as a necessary sacrifice, thus as incontestable. It is questionable whether, by this logic, women are situated as victims at all, if by 'victim' we mean one who not merely suffers but who has been wronged, and if by 'victimization', we refer to practices, acts or relations that can feasibly be rendered as unjust. Rather than reflect the sexist ideology that women are bound for sacrifice as 'natural victims', feminist politicizations of sexual victimization have attacked the normalization of gendered sacrifice, proceeding on the assumption that rape culture, though pernicious and pervasive, is unjust and eliminable. Patriarchal and feminist representations of women as 'victims' thus mobilize different meanings of the term 'victim': the destined or sacrificial victim whose victimization cannot legitimately be contested, versus the victim of a wrong whose victimization is able to be framed as unjust. The second substantive difference between patriarchal and feminist representations of women as victims is that feminist anti-rape politicizations advance a critique of socially constructed binary sexual difference in rape culture, complemented by strong critique of victim-blame; whereas the patriarchal logic 'to be female is to be a victim' locates femaleness – not sexist gendering – as the causative agent of victimization experienced by women. By this patriarchal logic, perpetrators of normalized practices of violence against women acquire innocence, because women are blamed for their own victimization: it is the self-referential effect of a property that belongs to them, 'femaleness'.

It is clear why hooks identifies as 'sexist' and 'male supremacist' a logic that inscribes women as inevitable victims and as self-referential victims of femaleness. These representations actually serve to *withhold* rather than accord recognition of women who are victimized as victims of a wrong – they suggest natural destiny has taken its course or a necessary sacrifice has been made, not that wrongs have been enabled by sexist gendering in rape culture. There are no doubt tensions and contradictions in feminist anti-rape politics, the discourses of which cannot be said to stand clean of the patriarchal constructions interpellating them. But the feminist commitment to imagining a world without sexual violence stands as a clear obstacle to the reading of anti-rape feminism as mere patriarchal mimesis. Patriarchal logic does, as hooks suggests, attempt to prepare women for victimization – by inscribing some or all women as the weaker sex, by casting female sexual agency as a powerful force some or all men cannot resist, by rendering some or all women as desirous or deserving of rape and so forth. Yet patriarchal logic does not in so doing hold that victimization – a wrong, an injustice – is what takes place. Patriarchal logic militates *against* the invention of idioms by which victimization experienced by women can be articulated as wrongs done to women – feminists have had to invent those idioms, embattled as they are.

The second question I asked above – concerning whether 'sexist ideology' and 'paternalistic myth' only operate through images of female victimhood, and not through images of female agency – finds its answer in my later discussion. Although feminist rape law reform efforts are routinely called upon to exemplify the way victim feminism revives 'the paternalistic myth of women's vulnerability', it is by no means clear that rape law neatly figures femininity as embodied vulnerability in the first instance. Sexist constructions can serve to inscribe women as vulnerable and passive but also, and just as problematically, as powerful and agentic. As my discussion of rape law's 'resistance requirement' (see Estrich, 1987) and the concept of victim precipitation will demonstrate, this area of law continues to be strongly oriented to a perception of women as actively resistant agents who bear responsibility for preventing rape. Rather than teach a male supremacist lesson that 'to be female is to be a victim', rape law mobilizes constructions of women as agents in order to *withhold* victim recognition from certain kinds of rape complainants. hooks' argument that there is a more or less seamless relation between patriarchal and feminist representations of women as victims is questionable because it obscures important distinctions between these different representations, directing analysis away from the repertoire of images of women as agents to be found in 'male supremacist thinking'. As we will see in Chapter 3, however, no such challenge can be raised in relation to the other primary argument hooks makes in her essay: that feminist articulations of the theme of victimhood are shaped around the politics of race-ethnicity and class.

Other texts that bring the popular press critiques of victim feminism together with postmodern critiques of feminist anti-rape politics express the view that the postmodern critiques differ from their popular press counterparts in being more complex, sophisticated and politically progressive. In this vein, Aya Gruber organizes popular and scholarly critiques of victim feminism into a conservative/ progressive binary. Gruber marks critiques by authors such as Naomi Wolf and Katie Roiphe as simplistic and politically conservative, contrasting these with postmodern feminist critiques of victimhood led by Marcus, which Gruber situates as politically progressive for two key reasons. First, unlike their counterparts in the popular press, their interrogation of anti-rape feminism's 'myopic focus on women as victims' (Gruber, 2009, p. 607) does not devolve into strong individualism and the abandonment of sociological explanation. An example of the difference Gruber is pointing to here can be found in Pamela Haag's (1996) article 'Putting Your Body on the Line: The Question of Violence, Victims, and the Legacies of Second-Wave Feminism'. Following Marcus, Haag (1996) critiques the theme of victimhood in anti-rape feminism, but she also actively interrogates the way the popular press critiques of victim feminism promote a discourse of women as 'John-Wayne-like individuals, fully self-determining nonvictims' (p. 61). Visibly disaffiliating from strong individualism, Haag's anti-victim critique takes a deconstructive approach to the victim/agent dichotomy, arguing that the shift from 'victim' to 'nonvictim' is problematic because this pair of figures, 'insofar as they require full abjection or full self-determination, respectively, are both distortive models of subjectivity and social roles' (p. 61).

It cannot be said, however, that Haag's deconstructive approach to the victim/agent dichotomy constitutes a departure from the victim-bad/agent-good formulation, the values of which are affirmed in Haag's critique. Arguing that 'The feminists of identity politics . . . stylize the victim, exaggerating her vulnerabilities and indignities to enshrine her as a singularly damaged subject who deserves cultural and legal redress' (p. 61), Haag treats 'victim' as a wholly negative and disabling identity while affirming Marcus' agency-oriented rape prevention approach, seeing in it a revival of second-wave feminist strategies that emphasize women's positive capacities for directly combative resistance to male violence. As Gruber (2009) describes, the postmodern critiques of anti-rape feminism advocate a 'thick view of female autonomy' (p. 607) underpinned, as the example of Haag shows, by an active critique of strong individualism. Yet their analyses still treat agency and victimhood as mutually exclusive terms and reject one over the other, leaving unexamined the complex interweaving of the categories 'victim' and 'agent' in legal and popular apportionments of blame and responsibility in relation to sexual harm.

The second contrast Gruber draws between popular and postmodern critiques of victim feminism is that the latter interrogate anti-rape feminism's attachment to the theme of feminine vulnerability in order to launch a more radical critique of the way feminist anti-rape politics has 'moved off the streets and into the state' (Halley, 2006, p. 20), aiding and abetting the latest incarnation of masculinist state power: the carceral politics of neoliberal capitalism and its wars against crime. For Gruber, anti-rape feminism's focus on reforming rape law and criminal justice responses to rape show the inherently philosophical tensions one expects 'when a sub-ordinated group turns to state police power to achieve equality' (Gruber, 2009, p. 604). Seeking group justice through increased criminal penalties conflicts 'philosophically and practically with the goal of antisubordination' (p. 605). As Gruber describes the North American situation, feminist efforts to eliminate sexual violence have devolved into the resubordinative political form Janet Halley calls 'governance feminism', indicated by 'the "noticeable installation of feminists and feminist ideas in actual legal-institutional power"' (Gruber, 2009, p. 604, citing Halley, Kotiswaran, Shamir and Thomas, 2006, p. 340).[7] Subsumed within the neoliberal state's practical strategies of criminalization and law enforcement, anti-rape feminism's focus on sexual victimization and pursuit of law reform has served only to further the punitive powers of the state. Gruber (2009) advises that feminist anti-rape activists 'leave the halls of criminal power and return to the streets' (p. 657), abandoning the strategy of law reform. Gruber writes:

As the United States became more and more punitive, feminists hopped on the bandwagon by vigorously advocating reforms to strengthen the operation of criminal law to combat gendered crimes. Today, many associate feminism more with efforts to expand the penal laws of rape and domestic violence than with calls for equal pay and abortion rights. The zealous, well-groomed female prosecutor who throws the book at 'sicko' sex offenders has replaced the 1970s bra-burner as the icon of women's empowerment . . . feminism is now publicly and politically associated with gender crime control.

(pp. 583–606)

As Kristen Bumiller (2008) reminds us, 'only a small percentage of [rape] cases lead to the actual punishment of the defendant' and 'law reform has brought about limited change in regard to increasing the likelihood that a victim will be vindicated by the courts' (p. 159). Notwithstanding this, Gruber's line of critique raises compelling questions about whether and how feminist anti-rape efforts have ceded ground to the 'tough on crime' policies of carceral neoliberalism. Clinton's 'three-strikes' policy of mandatory sentencing and the concurrent war on drugs have been the primary contributors to the boom in the US correctional population, though a growing rate of rape and sexual assault convictions (particularly the latter) have also made some contribution.[8] Beyond the question of conviction rates, according to Bumiller, feminist law reform has provided occasion for giving criminal justice authorities greater powers of surveillance and control 'over juveniles, homosexuals, and those with prior convictions for sexual offenses', in a context where 'the rampant occurrence of sexual abuse within prisons is given little attention or priority as a social problem' (p. 162). As I observed in Chapter 1, neoliberalism's prison-industrial complex is a site of acute and continued racist violence and discrimination, which feminists need to contest rather than reinforce.

Gruber's and Halley's critiques of feminist legalism appear to be a form of anti-legalism or extra-legalism, in the sense that they are urging feminists away from the political strategy of 'capturing' the power of law, and towards a presumably more radical positioning 'on the streets', where it is possible to assume a more confrontational positioning in relation to law and the state. In a sense, however, this appearance of anti- or extra-legalism is specious because Gruber's and Halley's critiques of feminist legalism seem very much embedded in the context of the law school and can be said to reflect the law school left's privileging of criminal defence. When reading Gruber and Halley, it is important to bear in mind the way the left and the right play out in the political sensibilities of the law school in relation to criminal law, where the pursuit of criminal defence is often an expression of progressive, left-wing political commitments and a humanitarian orientation to the rights of the accused to fairness in the dispensation of justice, while pursuing criminal conviction (and the more lucrative legal work of prosecuting for the state or Crown) is associated with a more conservative, right-wing orientation to the punitive politics of law-and-order. This configuration of the left and the right immediately puts feminist efforts to reform criminal justice responses to rape in alignment with the conservative 'prosecutorial attitude' of law enforcement

(Gruber, 2009, p. 585). Gruber and Halley are scrutinizing feminist criminal justice reform from the perspective of the law school left. Halley (2006) critiques contemporary feminism as always 'carrying a brief' for 'something F' (i.e. working against the subordination of women) (p. 45). To adapt Halley's phrase, in their discussions of feminism, these critical legal theorists are 'carrying a brief for the defence'.[9] In the neoliberal era of mass incarceration, the perspective of the law school left is indispensable as a check on the abuse of legal power. In terms of social and criminal justice responses to rape, however, the perspective of the law school left is often inappropriate in the sense that the victim, and not the accused, typically stands unofficially as the defendant. Historically, the unfair positioning of the victim in the context of criminal justice responses to rape owes something to the law school left, which in an earlier era served as the crucible for the first victimology, 'penal victimology', which instructed defence attorneys in the ways of victim-blaming and scapegoating (Van Dijk, 2009), notably in the context of rape law (Amir, 1971).

In Gruber's analysis, the perspective of the law school left also sponsors an unduly narrow account of the scope and character of feminist anti-rape activism, reducing a multi-directional spectrum of forms of activism down to one project of gaining 'prosecutorial power'. Gruber situates feminist law reform efforts within the bloc of conservative victim's rights movements, discounting the way feminists have not simply argued for increased convictions and incarceration, but for formal shifts in the adjudication of rape, such as displacing the adversarial trial by creating a spectrum of responses to rape including the different model of restorative justice and 'options within and outside the criminal justice process' (MacDonald and Tinsley, 2011, p. 379). In these and other ways, feminist anti-rape activism has been a site for critiquing and reimagining conceptions and practices of justice, rather than simply an exercise in capturing and strengthening law's criminal power. Gruber's notion of conscious feminist *complicity* with the neoliberal war on crime also needs to be considered against the different scenario Nancy Fraser (2009) draws of neoliberal resignifications of 'feminism', and what Bumiller (2008) describes as a neoliberal 'appropriation' of the feminist movement against sexual violence.

But the main problem with the analysis Gruber makes is that it suggests the postmodern critiques of anti-rape feminism, unlike their popular counterparts and the feminist activists they are criticizing, somehow stand free of entanglement with the categories and logics of neoliberalism, alone occupying the truly radical position. While the postmodern feminist critiques raise important questions about feminism and the law-and-order agenda, their move against 'vulnerability-victimhood' and towards 'agency-prevention' reflects the way neoliberal strategies of crime control address the would-be victim. As I later describe, neoliberal crime control strategies combine intensified use of the prosecutorial and carceral powers of the state with prevention-oriented discourses that exhort citizens to assume responsibility for making themselves invulnerable to crime. The postmodern call to reject victimism in the feminist politicization of rape – to reimagine the 'female body as an "object of fear and agent of violence", rather than as a wounded and violable space' (Vetten, 2011, p. 269, citing Marcus, 1992, p. 400) – echoes these prevention-oriented discourses, discursively supporting the neoliberal story of good citizenship as consisting in individual readiness to combat and prevent crime.

Feminism, rape law and the differend

Feminist interventions in the area of rape law have sought to transform its parameters of victim recognition. These interventions have sought to place events formerly not characterized as rape or not seen as law-worthy rape, and persons formerly not recognized as law-worthy if they experience rape, within the purview of victim recognition and have sought as well to shift juridical vision away from a primary focus on the traits, behaviours and histories of rape complainants, in order to reverse a distinctive feature of modern rape law: its positioning of victim behaviour as heuristically central in the explanation of rape. These efforts took shape in a context where forms of sexual victimization were not recognized as victimization (as in, for example, child sexual abuse and marital rape), were recognized but in ways that blame the victim, or were only likely to be recognized if certain traits were present, such as the victim's being virginal, white, of means or unknown to the accused. As efforts to transform the way sexual victimization is adjudicated and understood, feminist anti-rape politicizations have the character of what Lyotard (1988) calls 'bearing witness to the *differend*' (No. 22, original emphasis).

Lyotard's theory of the differend distinguishes between plaintiff and victim, and this can also be seen as a distinction between two kinds of victim. First, there is the plaintiff, who has the means to establish that they have been done a wrong and is therefore in principle able to be recognized as a victim in the sense of being recognized as one who has suffered a wrong. Second, there is the 'victim' in Lyotard's particular sense of that word, who finds that 'no presentation is possible of the wrong he or she says he or she suffered' (No. 9). Paradoxically, the victim in Lyotard's sense is one from whom legibility as a victim, in the established legal and extra-legal sense of that word, is *withheld*. For Lyotard, one is a victim not in the moment of suffering a wrong but in the moment of being divested of the means to prove a wrong occurred, a moment in which one is *not* seen (by others, in language, by the law) as a 'victim' in the sense of being regarded as the wronged party: 'I would like to call a *differend* the case where the plaintiff is divested of the means to argue and becomes for that reason a victim' (No. 12, original emphasis).

To the extent that established law operates on the principle of innocent until proven guilty, all plaintiffs may become victims in Lyotard's sense. The legal genre makes it incumbent upon the plaintiff to establish the reality of the wrong, and one may lose the means to do so in a variety of ways. Lyotard describes a range of circumstances in which the plaintiff may become a victim:

> This is the case if the victim is deprived of life, or of all his or her liberties, or of the freedom to make his or her ideas or opinions public, or simply of the right to testify to the damage, or even more simply if the testifying

phrase is itself deprived of authority. In all of these cases, to the privation constituted by the damage there is added the impossibility of bringing it to the knowledge of others, and in particular to the knowledge of a tribunal . . . the 'perfect crime' does not consist in killing the victim or the witnesses . . . but rather in obtaining the silence of the witnesses, the deafness of the judges, and the inconsistency (insanity) of the testimony. You neutralise the addressor, the addressee, and the sense of the testimony; then everything is as if there was no referent (no damages) . . . then the plaintiff is dismissed, the wrong he or she complains of cannot be attested. He or she becomes a victim.

(No. 7–No. 9)

The victim Lyotard theorizes cannot signify the wrong. This circumscribed relationship to signification is a wrong 'added' to the wrong that cannot be signified. This added or second-order wrong cannot be signified but can be felt. The differend is disclosed as a feeling that '"asks" to be put into phrases, and suffers from the wrong of not being able to be put into phrases right away' (No. 9):

The *differend* is the unstable state and instant of language wherein something which must be able to be put into phrases cannot yet be. This state includes silence, which is a negative phrase, but it also calls upon phrases which are in principle possible . . . What is at stake in a literature, in a philosophy, in a politics perhaps, is to bear witness to *differends* by finding idioms for them.

(No. 22, original emphasis)

From the feeling of the differend arises the possibility of bearing witness to it. Lyotard's theory invokes a terrain of creative struggle to invent new idioms:

This is when the human beings who thought they could use language as an instrument of communication learn through the feeling of pain that accompanies silence (and of pleasure which accompanies the invention of a new idiom), that they are summoned by language . . . to recognise that what remains to be phrased exceeds what can presently be phrased, and that they must be allowed to institute idioms which do not yet exist.

(No. 23)

Feminist anti-rape and anti-violence politicizations are replete with examples of idioms brought into being by differends. Our current ability to regard an array of forms of sexual harm *as* victimization is not given but rather has been forged through creative struggle in the feminist social movement.

Feminist terms such as 'marital rape', 'date rape', 'acquaintance rape', 'sex-worker rape', 'child sexual abuse' and 'sexual harassment' refer to forms of sexual harm that until recently were not dominantly recognized as 'wrong' within and beyond the legal genre. Developing these terms has predominantly involved challenging victim-blaming constructions in legal and social perceptions of victims of sexual harm. For example, as Stephen Angelides (2005) observes, prior to feminist politicizations of child sexual abuse,

> [A]dult child molesters were rendered as pathetic and innocuous, [while] children were routinely rendered sexually flirtatious, precocious and even seductive . . . so prominent was this view that even adult offenders were themselves sometimes portrayed as the victims.

> (p. 278)

In a different example, before the 1980s in most jurisdictions of the West, the law did not recognize that it was possible for a husband to rape his wife. In a historical vestige of the legal doctrine of coverture, sexual coercion among spouses was regarded not as a form of challengeable victimization – a wrong, an injustice – but as an exercise of conjugal right, a private and benign aspect of normal spousal relations. What is now recognized as marital rape existed, in Lyotard's terms, as the feeling of the differend: a form of suffering that exceeded what could be phrased in a shared idiom.

Just as Lyotard enumerates a range of ways in which the plaintiff can become a victim by losing the means to establish the reality of the wrong, so too is there a range of differends in rape law. Differends inhere when the law does not recognize certain forms of rape as rape *at all*. Differends inhere when, officially or tacitly, the law arbitrarily excludes certain kinds of rape victims from the possibility of recognition as such. Differends inhere in the general orientation of rape law to call upon the agency of the victim in order to explain individual events of rape. Differends inhere in the continuing interconnections of rape law with gender segregation, class stratification and ethnic hierarchy. The differends in rape law are inseparable from wider social perceptions of sexual victimization. Rape myths circulating beyond law can reinforce and be reinforced by rape myths in written law. Accordingly, feminist anti-rape politicizations have always combined law reform efforts with extra-legal activism, education and service provision, notably the development of networks of rape crisis centres and their ethos of survivorship.

In critiques of victim feminism the political work I have described as the work of bearing witness to the differend is not seen as a progressive effort to give suffering visibility. Rather, the effort to broaden and deepen rape's visibility in law is seen as a regressive extension of patriarchal scripts of female vulnerability and violability: political work that ends up re-victimizing women by further constituting them as vulnerable victims rather than as capable agents, normalizing rather than eliminating sexual harm while contributing to the adjacent harm of growing incarceration. As Gruber suggests, feminist anti-rape politicizations are diagnosed as a failed success. They have succeeded in making a series of reforms that alter legal perceptions of rape and compel the law to take rape seriously, leading to feminist capture of 'prosecutorial power' (Gruber, 2009, p. 585). Yet in their multiplication of new idioms, they have merely re-dressed femininity in vulnerability and masculinity in agency, committing the reformist wrong of complicity with the masculinist powers of the state and the law and failing ultimately to eliminate the problem of sexual violence. Before testing this argument against dominant configurations of gender, vulnerability and agency in rape law, I will outline the way this argument unfolds in Marcus' essay 'Fighting Bodies, Fighting Words' (1992) and subsequently in the work of Heberle (1996), which adopts Marcus' agency-oriented paradigm for theorizing rape.

In her critique of feminist anti-rape politicizations, Marcus (1992) argues that these politicizations have concentrated attention on the 'post-rape' phase, neglecting the 'pre-rape' phase in which rape can be resisted, thus securing on behalf of patriarchal power an impression that rape can 'only be feared or legally repaired, not fought' (p. 347). Marcus situates rape not as a biologically ordained event but as a socially scripted interaction informed by a process of sexist gendering in which women are cast as always already rapeable and men as always already capable of rape. She argues that the 'apocalyptic tone' (p. 347) of feminist discussions of rape, combined with exclusive focus on the post-rape remedies of law and criminal justice reform, serves merely to confirm the sexist gendering of the rape script, helping to render rape as inevitable rather than preventable. Marcus' argument makes an important contribution to the theorization of gender and power, challenging the view that male domination is total and unflinching with a conception of masculine dominance as unstable and dependent upon repeated practical renewal. On this reading, men do not attempt rape because they simply possess the power to do so; instead, an attempt to rape is a bid to accord reality to this otherwise theoretical power, a bid that is vulnerable to failure. Marcus proposes an alternative theory and politics of rape prevention focused on women's capacities to disrupt the rape script and 'take the ability to rape completely out of men's hands' (p. 388). By refusing the victim role, the would-be-victim can deny the would-be rapist power in the moment:

> To take male violence or female vulnerability as the first and last instances in any explanation of rape is to make the identities of rapist and raped preexist the rape itself. If we eschew this view and consider rape as a scripted interaction in which one person auditions for the role of rapist and strives to maneuver another person into the role of victim, we can see rape as a process of sexist gendering which we can attempt to disrupt.
>
> (p. 332)

Drawing on Marcus' account, Renee Heberle (1996) similarly argues that counter-images of female agency and resistance are lacking in anti-rape feminist politics. In their efforts to accord recognition to a greater array of sexual harms and to shift how sexual harms are perceived, feminists have revived patriarchal protectionism, according masculine dominance the sense of political stability it actually lacks. For Heberle, counter-images of female agency will serve to remedy the malaise of victim-focused feminism as well as the forms of sexual harm it presses against. Such counter-images will conjure 'increased possibilities for prevention and resistance in the moment' and enable anti-rape feminism to exceed the limited 'protectionist' project of defending, by way of the agency of the law, 'vulnerable bodies against sexual aggression' (Heberle, 1996, pp. 72–73).

Although this critical work makes an important contribution to the theorization of gender and power, there are problems with the argument advanced in it, especially with respect to the themes of vulnerability, victimhood, agency and resistance.[10] First, the argument discounts the idea that feminist efforts to expand the parameters of victim recognition can work also to expand the parameters for resistance to victimization. As Lyotard's (1988) theory implies, a wrong that is recognized as wrong within a shared idiom may be more readily resisted than a wrong that has the character of a differend, a wrong that is a 'perfect crime' (No. 7) because the wrongdoer's impunity is guaranteed. Rather than cast women as inevitably vulnerable, feminist rape law reform efforts have sought to cast victimization as non-inevitable. This they do by casting victimization as 'victimization' in the sense that it is a wrong that is contestable, in a legal and social context where a variety of forms of sexual victimization have not been recognized as such but rather have been rendered invisible, benign, normal, natural and thus incontestable.

Second, it is highly questionable whether women are, as the postmodern critics contend, uniformly regarded as 'always already rapeable'. As Mardorossian (2002) argues, 'It is extremely problematic to assume that women share a similar psychological makeup or relation to the social script before the rape' (p. 752). In rape law and in social scripts of rape, there are hierarchies of harms as well as hierarchies of victims, with particular categories of women in particular contexts and historical moments – such as wives, sex workers, Indigenous women, poor women, homeless women – arbitrarily distanced or barred from the possibility of being recognized as the victim of a wrong if they experience rape, thus regarded in a certain sense as *unrapeable*. This can be seen, for example, in the way sex workers struggle to be recognized as vulnerable to rape by a client. Though feminists are sharply opposed on the question of whether sex work should be decriminalized, the typical consignment of sex workers to the category 'unrapeable' has been continuously contested in feminist anti-rape politicizations. Feminist efforts to accord reality to the wrong of sex worker rape not only target the post-rape context of police response and the rape trial. They work more broadly to interrupt a dominant assumption that the rape of a sex worker is not rape but rather a benign act that is 'only to be expected', *not* by identifying sex workers with inevitably vulnerable embodiment, but rather by disseminating the unexpected view that the rape of a sex worker is a wrong and, as such, contestable: vulnerable to resistance in the moment as well as to legal redress.

But the more serious problem with the line of argument advanced initially by Marcus is that it beckons counter-images of female agency without questioning their status *as* counter-images. This line of argument is situated as an emancipatory

71

feminist departure from patriarchal scripts of feminine victimage, yet its emphasis on women's agency is reminiscent of (and not meaningfully distinguished from) the sexist logic of victim-blame embedded in modern rape law: a logic in which women are regarded less as vulnerable victims than as agents who bear responsibility for preventing rape; a logic by which the agency of plaintiffs is scrutinized in ways that serve to protect the agency of defendants from similar scrutiny. Heberle (1996) argues that feminist anti-rape politicizations have so far failed to contribute to 'the general deconstruction of identifications of women with real sexual vulnerability and men with real sexual power' (p. 72). She argues further that a deconstructive approach to these identifications would not be of use 'in the legal context' (p. 75 n. 18) for this context is in no way amenable to identifications of women as capable of resistance:

> The law demands that victims be victims through and through before rendering its limited forms of justice. Because the law needs victims in order to render justice, it perpetuates the very gender arrangements that create the terms that make sexual violence possible in the first place.
>
> (p. 75 n. 18)

That the law demands 'victims be victims through and through' is correct in the sense that rape laws specify criteria of ideal victimhood that rape complainants have to fulfil in order to be regarded in law as rape victims. What is not acknowledged here, however, is that the ideal victim in rape law is *an agent who actively resists rape*, an agent whose identification as a victim will hinge on their ability to prove that they possess and did exercise resistant agency. Far from discouraging images of women as agents, rape law is one venue in which women have consistently been viewed as self-responsible, resistant agents.

Victims as agents: resistant and precipitant victims

The tradition in rape law has been that for an event to be legally described as rape, for the event to be distinguished from consensual sex, and for a plaintiff to conform to the law's figuration of the rape victim, a victim must prove that they met the wrongdoer's use of physical force with utmost resistance, demonstrating nonconsent. To qualify as a victim in this idiom, one must be able to render oneself as an agent whose agentic capacity was expressed as physical resistance and whose momentary deprivation of agency was physically enforced by the wrongdoer. Rape law's resistance requirement (in either its original formal uses or now more common informal usage in the criminal defence of rape) narrows the legal response to rape down to a choice between two judgements of the plaintiff: 'she resisted, thus is a blameless victim', or 'she failed to resist, thus is a blameworthy non-victim'. Writing in the late 1980s, Kristin Bumiller (1987) points out the key problem with the resistance requirement: 'Women who are sexually attacked are concerned with their survival, not with the demonstration of nonconsent' (p. 77;

see also Bumiller, 1990). In the resistance requirement, women who do not physically resist or are unable to corroborate their resistance are rendered as blameworthy non-victims, with rape that proceeds without physical coercion or in the absence of a weapon rendered as consensual sex. In this way the resistance requirement set up evidently brutal stranger rape as the benchmark for reckoning 'real' law-worthy rape (Estrich, 1987). Feminist efforts to counter the resistance requirement – by arguing, for example, that the law recognize verbal coercion as a form of force and verbal nonconsent as a sign of nonconsent, and by attempting to counter juridical focus on victim behaviour – have not sought to identify women as *incapable* of resisting rape. Rather, these efforts have sought to ensure that the forms of resistant agency available to women are not used to establish them as blameworthy if they experience rape.

As the example of the resistance requirement illustrates, rape law is intimately concerned with female agency. As Bumiller (1987) puts it, rape law has tended to focus adjudicatory attention centrally on 'the image of the rape victim as a reactive agent' (p. 84). In addition to the good agency ascribed to the ideal victim by the resistance requirement, there is the bad agency ascribed to the pseudo-victim by the concept of victim precipitation. The victimological concept of victim precipitation was developed in the late 1950s by the criminologist Marvin Wolfgang (1958) and subsequently adapted for use in the litigation of rape cases by Menachim Amir in his book *Patterns in Forcible Rape* (1971). In the context of popular no less than legal understanding of rape, the concept of victim precipitation performs a particular labour: it serves to recast the victim as the agent of her own victimization in a bid to neutralize her complaint. The concept of victim precipitation enables two judgements of the victim: 'she actively guarded her own safety, thus is a blameless victim', or 'she failed to secure her own safety, thus is a blameworthy non-victim'.

Like the resistance requirement, the concept of victim precipitation takes as given the status of rape victims as self-responsible agents. This presumption of agency provides the pretext for examining the manner in which the victim has conducted her agency, with the aim of spotlighting actions and behaviours that can be cast as directly precipitous, irresponsibly negligent or insufficiently resistant. Where these ministrations prove effective, the victim emerges as a self-assailing pseudo-victim, one who in some way 'asked for it' and so may be regarded as having actively visited the passivity of victimization upon themselves. Thus the rape victim who knew her rapist, who wore revealing clothing, who hitchhiked or went out at night alone, who allowed someone to buy her a drink, gift or meal, who opened the door to a stranger, whose 'no' was not sufficiently clear or fervent (Amir, 1971) or who failed to guard her drink, may be construed not as a victim of rape but as the causative agent of what is now regarded as non-victimization. Just as in the resistance requirement, the concept of victim precipitation deploys an identification of women as agents as the basis for establishing rape victims as the blameworthy agents of rape. Where plaintiffs are seen to have enacted their agency appropriately – through active resistance, through adequate guarding of personal safety – they are able to be regarded as victims; where they are seen to have failed on that count –

lack of resistance, apparent neglect of personal safety – they are seen not as victims but as the blameworthy agents of the victimization they claim to have experienced. In both cases, victim recognition centrally involves identification with a particular script of agency: the victim who is a victim 'through and through' (Herberle, 1996, p. 75 n. 18) is, in essence, an actively resistant and self-responsible agent. Contrary to expectations, then, there is no clean victim/agent dichotomy in rape law. When victims are recognized as victims, it is because they are seen to have deployed their agency appropriately (the true victim is a good agent); when victims are denied recognition as victims, they are seen instead as the blameworthy agents of the victimization they claim to have experienced (the false victim is a bad agent). The 'false victim' is a victim in Lyotard's unique sense of that term. Their complaint is met by a regime of victim-blame and they lose the means to prove a wrong occurred.

The resistance requirement and the concept of victim precipitation have been thoroughly contested by feminists, and the differends that inhere in rape law's regime of victim-blame have been just as thoroughly challenged. Yet these ways of understanding rape have intensified rather than abated in neoliberal times. The feminist work of bearing witness to the differends of rape law and critiques of this work as 'victim feminism' have coincided historically with the rise of neoliberalism's distinctive approach to the government of crime, which Pat O'Malley (1992) has called the 'situational' approach (p. 262). Marking a depar-ture from earlier approaches that focused on the causes and aftermath of crime, the situational approach to crime control is centrally focused on prevention, on crime 'before it occurs' (p. 262). In tune with the neoliberal rubric of individual responsibility for individual socio-economic fate, in the situational approach the onus for crime prevention shifts from the state to the individual, privatizing risk and responsibilizing individuals in particular and gendered ways. The situational approach generates 'the rudiments of a user pays system of policing security', with the categories of wrongdoer and victim simultaneously depoliticized:

> Just as the offenders are disconnected from the political dimensions of their existence, so too are the victims, for victims like offenders are to be understood as rational choice actors, responsible and free individuals. Prevention now becomes the responsibility of the victim.
>
> (p. 266)

Would-be victims are exhorted to cultivate knowledges and engage in practices appropriate for the management of risks to personal safety and well-being: lifestyle changes, purchase of insurance and security, self-defence training, everyday and life course practices of vigilance and risk calculation (Laster and Erez, 2000). As Laster and Erez observe, 'The ideal reasonable victim . . . actively resists becoming a victim altogether, according to neoliberal ideology' (p. 249). Reflecting the neoliberal conception of victimhood as self-made, the situational approach to crime control displaces theses of systemic violence and structural oppression. Explanations of crime that stress structural factors such as economic inequality, ethnic hierarchy and masculine dominance cede ground to explanations that stress individuals' acumen, or lack thereof, in the management of risk. Laster and Erez highlight the gendered ramifications of this shift: 'For women, such individually based precautionary measures are touted at the expense of social solutions such as improved transport, adequate childcare, decent education and, more generally, cultural change to equalise women's position in a gendered world' (p. 249).

As Lise Gotell (2008; see also Gotell, 2010, 2012) has shown, these individually based precautionary measures produce revised distinctions between ideal and deviant femininities, distinctions that carry particular ramifications for the adjudication of rape, shoring up new forms of victim-blame. Gotell (2008) observes in her analysis of discourses of risk in contemporary Canadian sexual assault law,

> Within a universe of rape management constituted in and through discourses of risk, the performance of diligent and cautious femininity grants some women access to good citizenship, while women who fail to follow the rules of safekeeping can be denied recognition . . . The new 'ideal' and valourised victim is a responsibilised, security conscious, crime-preventing subject who acts to minimise her own sexual risk . . . victim-blaming constructions emerge repeatedly in judicial discourses when complainants fail to behave as responsible risk managers.
>
> (pp. 878–879)

Gotell describes the emergence of a new binary in which the ideal rape-preventing subject is set against the figure of the 'risky woman', an identification largely reserved for socially marginalized women, whose vulnerability to violence is seen not as an effect of power relations but as a result of their having chosen 'high-risk lifestyles' (p. 891). Gotell discusses sexual assault cases in which homeless women, Aboriginal women, and drug-addicted women become the 'risky woman': an untrustworthy pseudo-victim who is seen to have brought victimization upon herself (p. 891). She says, 'Just as neoliberal discourse pathologises welfare recipients and constructs the poor as individually blameworthy for their poverty, so too is the violence enacted on the bodies of vulnerable women personalised and individualised' (p. 884). In the context Gotell describes, the resistance requirement has become the risk-management requirement, and the concept of victim precipitation comes into its own. The forms of agency available to women – the agency of resistance, the capacity to guard personal safety – continue to provide grounds on which women can be construed as blameworthy agents if they experience rape.

Rape law's consistent attentiveness to women's agency indicates the need to rethink the claim that feminists have reinforced rather than deconstructed existing 'identifications of women with real sexual vulnerability and men with real sexual power' (Heberle, 1996, p. 72). This claim misapprehends the encounter between feminist politics and rape law, as regards the issue of agency. In tune with the victim-bad/agent-good formulation, postmodern critiques of feminist anti-rape politicizations present women's agency as a hitherto neglected fund of counter-imagery that is coterminous with liberation inasmuch as it promises to cut against conceptions of women as always already vulnerable to rape. But rape law is replete with images of women as capable agents and a defining feature of rape law has been its recourse to this imagery to establish women as always already responsible for rape. Thus the primary objects of feminist deconstructive work within and beyond rape law have been identifications of women with real agency and men with real vulnerability to accusation of rape. To the extent that rape law has been skewed towards indicting the victim and protecting the accused, it has been more prepared to see men as victims of agentic women than it has women as victims of agentic men. Critics of victim feminism reserve the term 'protectionism' to describe feminist rape law reform efforts, arguing that such efforts merely recast women as helpless victims who stand in need of masculine protection. Yet this term is more appropriate as a descriptor of rape law itself. Protectionism aptly names the victim-blaming discourses by which images of women as agents provide systematic and reliable protection for those who may stand accused of rape. At the same time, rape law's gendered system of distributing blame and protection carries on the work of maintaining ethnic hierarchy and class stratification, with victim-blaming discourses and protectionism applying selectively and unevenly across the spectrum of social difference, as they have done historically.

While I do not contend that images of women as powerful, agentic and resistant entirely lack emancipatory promise because they dovetail with established forms of victim-blame, I question how, in view of the problem of victim-blame, such images can arrive at emancipatory promise. Ignoring existing amenability to woman-as-agent constructions within and beyond rape law, critics of victim feminism locate the emancipatory promise of this imagery with the element of cultural surprise: to contradict pervasive representations of women as vulnerable victims, feminists should surprise the culture with counter-intuitive representations of women as capable, resistant, preventive agents. But this recommendation for how feminist politics should rekindle its progressive edge is in a certain sense regressive, for it discounts the more powerfully counter-intuitive idiom feminists have sought to disseminate through their efforts to expand the parameters of victim recognition within and beyond rape law. That idiom is: women have the potential capacity to prevent and resist rape, *yet are not responsible for rape on account of this potential capacity.* In feminist anti-rape politicizations, the counter to rape law's regime of victim-blame has not been 'Women are not capable agents, they are vulnerable victims.' Rather, the counter has been 'Just because it is possible for women to resist rape does not make them responsible for rape if it takes place.' In relation to sexual harm and in response to a regime of victim-blame, an emancipatory feminist discourse cannot simply rest on the assertion of women's capacity for agency; rather, it needs to work publicly and assiduously to de-link women's agency from victim-blame, in order to counter the powerful role victim-blame plays in public conceptualization of women's agency. Before concluding, in the final section of this chapter I discuss rape crisis feminism's ethos of survivorship and the recent SlutWalk movement as visible examples of feminist negotiation with the ethical problem posed by established forms of victim-blame. On my reading, the ethos of survivorship and the SlutWalk movement can be read as efforts to make women's agency, vulnerability and the problem of victim-blame visible all at once. The idioms 'rape survivor' and 'SlutWalk' strive to avoid making agency visible at the expense of vulnerability or in a way that is victim-blaming.

Survivorship and SlutWalk: resisting victim-blame

I noted earlier that the postmodern feminist critics take issue with anti-rape feminism's apparently singular focus on criminal law, leading them to offer an unduly narrow account of the scope of feminist anti-rape activism. In particular, these critiques discount rape crisis feminism's ethos of survivorship, according no attention to the distinctive language of victimization and agency articulated therein. Rape crisis feminism's ethos of survivorship has largely been developed by rape survivors and subverts the concept of expertise by situating rape survivors as 'theorists of their own experience' (Alcoff and Gray, 1993, p. 283). The ethos of survivorship steps back from the exercise of judging good and bad victim behaviours and advances instead a non-expert approach that confers authority upon women's own (examinable, multiple and changing) perspectives on their experience of rape, giving rise to unique and subversive conceptualizations. Survivor discourse makes agency and vulnerability visible amidst the critique of victim-blame. At first sight, rape crisis feminism appears to participate in anti-victimism because it critiques the term 'victim' and champions instead the alternative term 'survivor'. But rape crisis feminism in fact subverts the victim-blaming orientation of anti-victimism, problematizing 'victim identity' on very different grounds.

Critics of victim feminism tend to assume that 'victim' is an easy and readily available identity for women to take on, and that, in 'victim society', compassion for the victim is unreservedly supplied, tempting women to renounce personal responsibility and instead 'play the victim'. As Rene Denfeld (1995) put it in her critique of victim feminism, 'And let's face it. Seeing ourselves as victims is often far easier than taking responsibility for those aspects of our lives we can control' (p. 87). Taking his cue from the popular press critiques of victim feminism, American psychologist Robert Felson (2002) presents victim identity as desired by women and readily available, arguing that when young women make rape complaints, it is not likely to be because they have experienced rape, but because 'the victim label confers a special status that brings various social psychological rewards. It leads to sympathy and respect from others and offers a convenient explanation of any personal troubles one might be experiencing' (p. 136).[11] Felson assumes rape complaints automatically and unilaterally trigger 'sympathy and respect'. Rape crisis feminists, on the other hand, emphasize that rape complaints are difficult to make in part because they are met with victim-blame. Felson and Denfeld ignore a crucial factor that rape crisis feminists underline: far from embracing victim identity eagerly and with ease, women who have experienced rape often 'experience only self-directed anger' (Alcoff and Gray, 1993, p. 284), and are encouraged in this response by the wider context of victim-blame. Rape crisis feminists thus constitute the problem of 'victim identity' in a unique way – as a problem concerning the activity of self-blame and the way it reflects the wider context of victim-blame, rather than as a problem concerning women's apparent readiness to relinquish personal responsibility.[12]

According to Dawn McCaffrey's (1998) research, the terms 'victim' and 'survivor' carry two different sets of meaning in the context of rape crisis feminism's ethos of survivorship.[13] The first set of meanings is literal: 'victim' denotes the dead (women who were murdered by their assailant or subsequently committed suicide) while 'survivor' refers to those who literally survived. In the second set of meanings 'victim' and 'survivor' describe two distinct forms of self-identity and modes of response to sexual victimization. Rather than being defined in terms of agency and its lack, a different form of agency is associated with each term: the term 'victim' is associated with the agency of self-blame while the term 'survivor' is associated with a form of agency beyond self-blame. Women who have experienced rape are therefore always conceptualized as 'agentic', with rape crisis feminists complicating the term 'agency' and distinguishing between different forms of it. In this way, even though rape crisis feminism contrasts the terms 'victim' and 'survivor', it avoids the victim/agent dichotomy and the victim-bad/agent-good formulation. In this context, victim identity is not seen as leading to an individual's renunciation of agency and responsibility but, paradoxically, to an unwillingness to see oneself as a victim: a willingness to see oneself instead as responsible for or deserving of victimization. In accord with this understanding of victim identity, for rape crisis feminists, survivor identity is not about ceasing to regard oneself as a 'victim' or as having been 'victimized'. Instead 'survivor' is used because it incorporates acknowledgement that victimization took place: 'Survivor rhetorically establishes that one has been victimized, yet also implies that one should be recognized for overcoming the often debilitating effects of sexual victimization' (McCaffrey, 1998, p. 278). Hence the 'survivor' is not a non-victim but rather one who is subverting the experience of victimization, a subversion often marked by refusal to cooperate with the idea that they themselves and women in general are responsible for rape. In this respect the ethos of survivorship is noticeably at odds with the Christian heritage of 'the victima label' that Van Dijk (2009) describes, its political effort to subvert victim-blame breaking with the Christian ethic of enforced self-sacrifice and forgiveness.

Mardorossian (2002) clarifies that self-blame 'is a coping mechanism in reaction to the rape as well as to social responses to sexual violence' (p. 753). Self-blame is reinforced when the perpetrator directly blames the victim, is often co-mingled with conflicting emotions (Van Dijk, 2009) and can either alter or abide amidst the changing situation, experience and perspective of the victim over time and the life course (Kelly, Burton and Regan, 1996). In the context of rape crisis, feminism self-blame is thought about as a grasp on agency, in the sense that it can restore the sense of self-control that is lost or diminished in an experience of victimization. Second-guessing that one could have acted otherwise but elected not to can restore a sense of autonomy. Assuming the authority to judge one's own 'part' in victimization can confer strength. Rather than view self-blame as a purely natural or voluntary reaction, or interpret self-blame as a sign that victim-blame is legitimate,[14] rape crisis feminism emphasizes that self-blame reflects the wider cultural reflex towards victim-blame in cases of sexual harm, as evinced by the rape myths embedded in rape law and in social perceptions of rape.

Rape crisis feminists associate the identity 'victim' with self-blame, reflecting the idea that, from the perspective of rape culture, the self-blaming (thus non-complaining) victim is ideal. The objective here is not to take issue with rape survivors who are self-blaming. Instead, rape crisis feminism takes issue with the wider social context in which rape survivors, whether or not they are self-blaming, are effectively encouraged to be so. This means giving visibility to survivors' perspectives that are not dominantly or at all self-blaming – not in order to contradict survivors who are self-blaming, but in order to interrogate the non-accidental resonance between survivors' self-blame and the wider social context of established forms of victim-blame – to challenge not self-blaming but the adjacent and distinct social activity of victim-blaming.

In the wide variety of contexts in which the concept 'survivor' is invoked today, the unique meanings that rape crisis feminism ascribes to 'victim' and 'survivor' are rarely visible or visible only in depoliticizing ways. Along with the other 'best ideas' of second-wave feminism that Nancy Fraser (2009) argues have been 'resignified' in neoliberal times, the concept of survivorship has been mainstreamed and recuperated (see McLaughlin, 2012, Bumiller, 2008 and Alcoff and Gray, 1993). Even as the ethos of survivorship continues to powerfully inform the ongoing work of rape crisis feminism, in many contexts today, notions of survivorship and resilience operate on behalf of neoliberal victim theory. Where rape crisis feminists actively critique the social construction of victimhood and draw a distinction between self-blame (victim identity) and self-responsibility (survivorship), neo-liberal victim theory collapses this distinction, situating the ideal would-be victim as already self-blaming – individually responsible for preventing, resisting, surviving and recovering from all manner of threats to personal safety, psychic stability and economic security. The media reception of Charlene Smith's (2002) narrative of rape survival provides a good example of the way feminist meanings have been evacuated from the concept of survivorship and replaced with a credo of enforced resilience and personal responsibility. In one syndicated report Smith is described as a 'survivor' and it is noted that she 'hates the word victim' (Hosking, 2002, p. 5), but the concept of survivorship and rejection of victimhood are de-linked from feminism. Feminism is associated with 'victim identity' and an attitude of 'blam[ing] men' (p. 5), while 'survivor' is used to mark a move beyond this feminist negativity. The meanings rape crisis feminists ascribe to 'victim' and 'survivor' are then reversed. According to the columnist, Smith regards the word 'victim' as 'a term of abuse' (p. 5) not because it fails to convey the resilience of rape survivors, but because it invites victims to renounce personal responsibility.

Rape survivors who 'blame men' are making 'excuses' and indulging in 'self-pity' (p. 5). Accordingly, 'survivor' no longer refers to overcoming self-blame, but rather to overcoming the self-pitying deflection of responsibility presumed to constitute victim identity. In a full reversal of meaning, the 'victim' is defined as self-pitying rather than self-blaming, while the 'survivor' is praised for replacing other-blame with personal responsibility. Smith's book is a powerful indictment of rape culture in South Africa, yet this report frames the purportedly self-pitying and blame-laying tendencies of rape survivors as an equally spectacular problem.

Despite the evident mainstreaming and recuperation of the notion of survivorship, one would still expect that rape crisis feminism's ethos of survivorship would have some visibility within scholarly feminist investigations of feminism and victimhood, and not as an example of victim feminism, but rather as an example of an existing progressive feminist discourse of agency, progressive because it attempts to give women's agency visibility without eliding vulnerability and redrawing victim-blame. Perhaps in some way compensating for the mainstreaming of the notion of survivorship and its elision in scholarly feminist discussion, the recently emerged SlutWalk movement has vigorously renewed the effort to create a feminist discourse that makes victimization *and* agency visible while foregrounding the feminist critique of victim-blame. The SlutWalk movement was ignited by the now infamous statement of a Canadian police officer that 'I've been told I'm not supposed to say this – however, women should avoid dressing like sluts in order not to be victimized' (Michael Sanguinetti, 2011, cited in Ringrose and Renold, 2012, p. 333). Contesting the derogation of women as 'sluts',[15] and rejecting the logic that victim behaviour and attire explain rape, the movement has spread internationally and hosts vibrant public demonstrations against slut-shaming and victim-blaming. As Ringrose and Renold (2012) argue, SlutWalk launches a Butlerian politics of re-signification:

> Taking the word queer as the most common example of this dynamic, re-signification theorises how an injurious term is re-worked in the cultural domain from one of maligning to one of celebration. This dynamic is apparent in the use of slut as a point of celebration and a banner for political action, rather than shame. The SlutWalks as a collective movement are thus attempting to turn the blaming the victim of sexual violence for attack on its head! One of the goals is to push the gaze off the dress and behaviour of the victim of sexual violence back upon the perpetrator, questioning the normalization and legitimization of male sexual aggression.
>
> (p. 334)

SlutWalk has been contentious and subject to competing interpretations among feminists, including the rejection of SlutWalk as properly feminist. In my view, SlutWalk is strongly feminist in the sense that it is continuous with long-standing feminist critique of victim-blame and secondary victimization in the context of sexual harm. Moreover, SlutWalk can more specifically be interpreted as a feminist riposte to neoliberalism, in particular, the new lines the situational approach to crime prevention has drawn between ideal and deviant femininities, as Gotell (2008) describes. By contesting the label 'slut', the movement rejects the neoliberal construction of the risky woman.

It is highly significant that the phrase igniting the movement came from an officer of the law whose statement puts in a nutshell neoliberalism's address to the would-be victim of sexual harm: you are responsible for defending against your vulnerability to rape. Also significant is the preceding phrase, in which the police officer positions himself as speaking against an injunction to silence, as though his victim-blaming logic is the minor view: 'I've been told I'm not supposed to say this – however . . .' (Michael Sanguinetti, 2011, cited in Ringrose and Renold, 2012, p. 333). As I argued in Chapter 1, this claim on minoritized identity is a staple feature in contemporary rhetoric that constructs and opposes 'victim feminism' and 'political correctness'. SlutWalk demonstrations directly attack the logic of victim-blame with blunt, pithy placard slogans and counter-phrases, exposing and critiquing the status of victim-blame as a major view that carries significant practical consequences: 'Don't tell us how to dress – tell men not to rape', 'My clothes are not my consent', 'Clothes don't rape people – rapists do', 'Rape: a crime of opportunity, not appearance', 'It's a dress, not a yes', 'Society teaches "don't get raped", not "don't rape"', 'The only thing I'm asking for is a revolution', 'SlutWalk: because survivors deserve our support, not our scrutiny', 'SlutWalk: The radical notion that no one deserves to be raped' and 'SlutWalk: Because we've had enough'.[16] In view of the critical work this movement undertakes to counter the logic of victim-blame, I interpret SlutWalk as a powerful feminist riposte to the way the neoliberal rubric of personal responsibility has played out in legal and social perceptions of rape. The postmodern critiques discussed earlier suggest that victim feminism has successfully captured prosecutorial power, installing feminists and feminist concepts throughout contemporary justice systems. But the SlutWalk movement does not attest to this degree of institutional success, instead expressing profound impatience that after years of sustained feminist anti-rape activism, legal and social perceptions of rape continue to shame and blame the victim, indeed do so more intensely with the roll-out of the situational approach to crime prevention (O'Malley, 1992).

This reading of SlutWalk as feminist and as a powerful riposte to neoliberalism is at odds, of course, with the reading of SlutWalk suggested by postmodern feminist critiques of victim feminism. According to Ratna Kapur (2012), whose earlier postcolonial and postmodern critique of victim feminism I discuss in Chapter 3, SlutWalk is not continuous with existing feminist anti-rape politicizations and instead dramatically marks women's final rejection of these politicizations and their domination by victim feminism. Invoking Catharine MacKinnon, Kapur terms victim feminism 'dominance feminism' (p. 4), mobilizing this term as a total description of anti-rape feminism since MacKinnon's mid-1980s feminist theory work. Addressing the context of postcolonial India, Kapur situates the Pink Chaddi campaign and the SlutWalk movement in India and internationally as the successors of dominance feminism, which maintained 'overwhelming focus on a victimization politics in the context of sexual violence' (p. 4), led an 'anti-sex agenda' (p. 8) that denied sexual agency and pleasure, reduced all sex to rape and cast all women as 'always already victimised' (p. 11).

Focusing on SlutWalk as an international movement, Kapur argues SlutWalk is challenging feminism, not patriarchy: 'It is not seeking the overthrow of some elusive, universal, patriarchal order. Its function as a march is to unmask and un-do a feminist politics that asphyxiates and mummifies the sexual subject' (p. 17). For Kapur, SlutWalk is about breaking with dominance feminism and creating a new feminism that uniquely claims 'a space for respect of bodily integrity as well as assertions of sexual autonomy' while also 'gutting arguments about rape that have plagued law reform efforts for decades' (p. 12). Kapur reduces SlutWalk to its purported challenge to earlier feminism and then critiques SlutWalk as 'a politics of feminism "lite"' (p. 12): it is not genuinely radical. Where I read SlutWalk as challenging the politics of neoliberalism as they are brought to bear on sexual harm, Kapur considers that SlutWalk reflects the forms of sexual subjectivity and consumer agency circulating in 'the neo-liberal moment' (p. 18). Suggesting that SlutWalk is, in the end, all about clothing, Kapur argues that SlutWalk 'serves up an eclectic range of political possibilities in the form of SlutWalk couture and Pink Chaddis, re-fashioning the image of feminism' (p. 18). SlutWalk is valuable 'as a space clearing gesture' that opens up possibilities beyond dominance feminism, but is not by itself a 'transformative or revolutionary politics' (p. 1).

Kapur and I clearly differ in our interpretations of SlutWalk in relation to feminism and neoliberalism, demonstrating that the way one understands the recent history of feminist victim politics will profoundly influence one's reading of the political present. More specifically, much depends upon whether one reads recent feminist history solely through the victim feminism construct, or expands the analytic frame to also scrutinize derogating constructions of victimhood and feminism articulated from a variety of places with the political field. I concur with Kapur's interpretation that SlutWalk is 'gutting arguments about rape', and that the movement hosts intra-feminist critique. But rather than see SlutWalk as primarily a critique of feminism, I see its work of 'gutting arguments about rape' (p. 12) as continuing the feminist work of bearing witness to the differend. SlutWalk furthers long-standing feminist efforts to make women's agency visible without eliding vulnerability and redrawing victim-blame – efforts that do not neatly conform to, and are obscured by, Kapur's dominance feminism construct. In its defiance of victim-blaming and victim-shaming, SlutWalk noticeably echoes what I described above as rape crisis feminism's rejection of the self-sacrificial ethos of forgiveness attending 'the victima label'. With regard to neoliberalism, rather than merely blend into its consumer capitalist surroundings while clearing a space for the dawn of agency feminism, as I have argued, SlutWalk mounts a powerful challenge to the situational approach to governing crime and its revival of victim-blame in the context of sexual harm, offering a cogent feminist critique of the way the rubric of personal responsibility converts vulnerability to rape into responsibility for preventing rape. As such, SlutWalk appears not as 'feminism lite', but as an important feminist presence within the wider constellation of new and renewed protest movements that directly challenge the politics of neoliberalism, posing a radical threat to its almost 40-year ascendance. This radical and potentially transformative dimension of the SlutWalk movement, which I interpret as a feminist critique of neoliberal victim theory, is not visible from within the dominance feminism construct because this construct elides the negative operation of woman-as-agent constructions in victim-blame, instead treating agency as coterminous with liberation, as per the victim-bad/agent-good formulation.

In terms of the future of the constellation of protest initiatives making up the SlutWalk movement internationally, much depends on the position these initiatives take in relation to feminist intersectionality. The most important site of intra-feminist debate within the SlutWalk movement has not consisted in the rejection of 'dominance feminism', but more specifically in debate concerning feminism, intersectionality and the need to create a feminist movement that does not centre and universalize the interests of privileged white women, that instead exposes and critiques white privilege and politicizes the operations of racial hierarchy and inequality in the contemporary politics of rape. This debate arose most noticeably in response to a placard in the 2011 New York SlutWalk that featured a racist slur.[17] Responding not just to the appearance of this placard in the protest but also to the defences of it that subsequently appeared in online forums such as Facebook, Flavia Dzodan (2011) wrote a strong critique of the failure of the New York SlutWalk to counter racism and create a movement characterized by intersectional feminist politicization of rape. Dzodan's response is entitled, 'My feminism will be intersectional or it will be bullshit!' Though it marks Dzodan's disaffiliation from feminism, this phrase has also gone on to become a banner for those seeking to advance intersectional feminism within the movement, thus also marking the way forward for the movement. The radical and potentially transformative dimension of SlutWalk can only be realized in the context of intersectional feminist theory and politics.

Conclusion

I have argued in this chapter that Lyotard's theory of the differend provides a valuable alternative to the reductive logic of 'victim-bad/agent-good' for thinking about the encounter between feminist politics and rape law. The victim-bad/agent-good formulation blinds us to theorizations and politicizations of victimization that are not based in a presumption of the victim's passivity or haplessness, and to instances in which recognition as a victim is progressive; it also blinds us to instances in which recognition as an agent is problematic, deflecting critical attention away from the various ways in which agency is constituted. Rather than accept the negativity of vulnerability-victimhood and the positivity of agency-prevention, Lyotard's theory encourages investigation of rape law's effacement of rape: the various ways in which rape complainants are able to be divested of the means to prove that a wrong occurred. My investigation has shown that in rape law differends take shape through women-as-agent constructions that support enduring forms of victim-blame. This indicates the need to treat with caution the turn to agency called for in critiques of victim feminism as well as their political reading of the way 'male supremacist thinking' plays out in rape law, where femininity is typically linked with the responsibility to enact appropriate agency rather than with natural hapless vulnerability. Instead of reviving patriarchal scripts of feminine vulnerability, feminist efforts to reform rape law have sought to make various forms of vulnerability visible as such, challenging rape law's effacement of rape and its reduction of female agency to the ability to be blamed for suffering a wrong.

In making this analysis, I have also brought to light a dimension in the relationship between feminism and neoliberalism: the way agency-affirming feminism dovetails with the victim-blaming discourses of neoliberal crime control. I concur with Gruber and others that feminists need to critically examine the way their efforts to reform the criminal law of rape have fed into the neoliberal wars on crime. What is missing from this picture, however, is the other site of feminist intersection with neoliberalism: the agency-affirming rejection of victim politics that takes place across the spectrum of critiques of victim feminism, from popular to postmodern. Feminist derogation and abandonment of the language of victimization and the subsequent turn to agency directly reflect the other side of the neoliberal war on crime: the responsibilization of would-be crime victims that takes place in the privatization of social risk, which celebrates personal agency in order to institute victim-blame as policy, as per the victim-bad/agent-good formulation. 'Progressive' anti-victimist feminist messages about resilient rape-preventing agents are as strongly recruited in the neoliberal war on crime as are 'regressive' feminist efforts to signify sexual victimization in criminal law. In this way the feminist turn to agency is not a turn away from complicity with neoliberalism but rather a further site of intersection between feminism and neoliberal transformations in the government of crime.

Notes

1 In Australia, the 'victim feminism' debate was shaped primarily as an inter-generational critique, with second-wave feminists Beatrice Faust (1993) and Helen Garner (1995) criticizing an emergent generation of feminists as invested in the victim mantle, provoking a strong critical response from Virginia Trioli (1996) and Jemma Mead (1997). Beatrice Faust wrote the Foreword for the Australian edition of Rene Denfeld's (1995) critique of victim feminism *The New Victorians*. Speaking as a young feminist in agreement with the critique launched by Faust, Kathy Bail (1996) sought to steer fellow young feminists away from 'victim feminism' and towards an individualist feminist practice of self-reliance, dubbed 'do-it-yourself feminism'.

2 Reflecting the structure of *The Differend*, references to this text provide section numbers rather than page numbers.

3 For postmodern feminist work on rape that takes its bearings in Marcus' (1992) analysis see, for example, Haag (1996), Heberle (1996), Hall (2004), Halley (2006) and Gruber (2009).

4 In a speech subsequently published in *Our Blood* (1976), Dworkin wrote:

> As women, nonviolence must begin for us in the refusal to be violated, in the refusal to be victimized. We must find alternatives to submission, because our submission – to rape, to assault, to domestic servitude, to abuse and victimization of every sort perpetuates violence. The refusal to be a victim does not originate in any act of resistance as male-derived as killing. The refusal of which I speak is a revolutionary refusal to be a victim, any time, any place, for friend or foe. This refusal requires the conscientious unlearning of all the forms of masochistic submission which are taught to us as the very content of womanhood.
>
> (p. 72)

5 See especially Gruber (2009), Halley, Kotiswaran, Shamir and Thomas (2006) on 'governance feminism' and Bernstein (2010) on 'carceral feminism'.

6 Several commentators engaged critically with the critiques of victim feminism in the 1990s, including Abrams (1995), Smith (1997), Davis (1997), Eisenstein (1997), Walters (1998), McCaffrey (1998), McLeer (1998), Atmore (1999) and hooks (1999). Mardorossian does acknowledge Gavey (1999).

7 Drawing on Halley et al. (2006), Gruber (2009) explains that governance feminism 'refers generally to the "quite noticeable installation of feminists and feminist ideas in actual legal-institutional power," which often manifests as a substantive project that "emphasizes criminal enforcement" and "speaks the language of total prohibition"' (p. 604, citing Halley et al., 2006, pp. 340–341). See also the section 'governance feminism' in Halley's book, *Split Decisions* (2006, pp. 20–22) and the discussion of 'subordination feminism' and 'sexual subordination feminism' in Halley (2002). As Davinia Cooper (2010) describes, Halley argues for

> a break from subordination politics . . . because feminism (and, by implication, other analogous social justice politics) reinforces and capitalises upon women's passive victim status, generating a moralising desire for revenge. Feminism, in this sense, is performative. By constructing rape as sexual violence, by telling women they have been injured and hurt, feminism risks erasing women's agency, fixing and intensifying their distress.
>
> (p. 346)

Halley's critique of 'victim-focused' feminism draws on Sharon Marcus' critique of anti-rape feminism and invokes Nietzsche's concept of *ressentiment*, drawing on the theorizations of feminist *ressentiment* I examine in Chapter 3 (see Brown and Halley, 2002). In various ways Halley's depiction of feminism resembles those found in conservative anti-victimism and popular press critiques of 'victim feminism'. While I do not discuss Halley's work as an example, it fits into the archive of feminism's anti-victim texts that I am examining in this book.

8 The US prison population boom began in the 1980s (Greenfeld, 1997). Between 1980 and 1994 the average annual growth in the numbers of prisoners was 7.6 per cent. The number of prisoners who had been convicted of drug offences grew annually by 18.4 per cent. The second highest rate of annual growth was in prisoners who had been convicted of other sexual assault, which includes child sexual abuse (15.4 per cent). Behind assault (9.2 per cent) and murder (7.6 per cent), the number of prisoners who had been convicted of forcible rape rose annually by 6.9 per cent (Greenfeld, 1997).

9 Literally, in Halley's case. See Halley's reading of *Twyman v. Twyman* (Halley, 2006, pp. 348–363), particularly the depiction of Sheila Twyman.

10 In addition to the points I argue below, I would also add points that have arisen in discussion of Marcus' piece with undergraduate students. Having taught Marcus' piece in an undergraduate feminist theory class for over ten years, I have observed a

recurring pattern of response. On one hand, students enjoy the empowering element of Marcus' analysis – its focus on women's ability to 'take the ability to rape completely out of men's hands' (Marcus, 1992, p. 388). On the other hand, discussion of the piece invariably questions the way Marcus' analysis may lead to victim-blame, and problematizes the way Marcus' model of resistance presumes an able-bodied adult (and not, for example, a child, someone who is differently abled, or someone who is unconscious, drunk or drugged) and a scenario of stranger rape, when in reality rape predominantly occurs between people known or related to one another.

11 For a critical discussion of Felson's account of rape, see Peterson and Muehlenhard (2004). These authors argue Felson grossly exaggerates the tendency of women who experience date rape to cast their experience as rape, pointing out that studies in this area yield high numbers of women who have had experiences that would legally be classed as rape, yet who do not themselves cast these experiences as rape (see also Gavey, 1999).

12 For feminist analyses of self-blame in rape survival, see Breitenbecher (2006), Ullman (2006), Allison and Wrightsman (1993), Katz and Burt (1988), Kidd and Chayet (1984) and Sales, Baum and Shore (1984).

13 On conceptions of victimhood and survivorship in rape crisis feminism, see also Kelly (1988) and Kelly, Burton and Regan (1996).

14 As Mardorossian describes, Sharon Lamb takes the view that it is unjust to contradict the self-blaming victim, and that self-blame provides a justification for victim-blame. Lamb argues that:

> [W]e should 'honor their [the victims'] perspective,' but what [Lamb] means is that, since victims blame themselves, 'by informing them that they are sadly mistaken in their perception of choice and free will we do them an injustice.' Thus, out of respect for their point of view, we too should blame victims.
> (Mardorossian, 2002, p. 754, citing Lamb, 1996, p. 22; cf. Lamb, 1999)

Lamb's (1996) position elides the difference between self-blame and victim-blame (laying blame on oneself and laying blame on another are by no means identical), interpreting self-blame as a sign that victim-blame, within reason, must be legitimate. In contrast to Lamb's response, the rape crisis feminist response neither judges that the victim is simply 'mistaken' (unknowing, and in this respect non-credible) in their self-blaming view, nor considers that the self-blaming victim justifies victim-blame – the different gesture of laying blame on another.

15 SlutWalk has been criticized for 'reclaiming' the word 'slut' instead of critically rejecting it, but as Georgia Knowles (2013) points out in her SlutWalk speech, the objective of SlutWalk is to critique this term rather than simply embrace it:

> Our aim for this march is not to call ourselves sluts, as we do not believe that such a thing exists. It is useful here to note that 'reclaim' has multiple meanings. Reclaim has its origins in the Latin *reclamare*: 'to cry out' or 'appeal' in protest. Our SlutWalk movement is about 'crying out' against a word that is used to police women's sexualities according to sexist binaries. We want to highlight that 'slut' has no meaning beyond what patriarchy imbues it with. Our aim is to highlight the way slut is used against many women to police our sexuality and behaviour, to degrade and humiliate us. We want to draw attention to the way that slut is used to justify sexual violence, to wrongly blame survivors for sexual abuse and minimise the actions of perpetrators.

16 I have drawn this collection of placard slogans from images of SlutWalk marches found on the web and from the Dunedin SlutWalk marches in 2011, 2012 and 2013.

17 The placard adopted the title of a song written by John Lennon and Yoko Ono. See: www.youtube.com/watch?v=Uk_tcu1Xq3l (accessed 7 June 2012).

3

INJURY INCORPORATED?

Feminism and the politics of *ressentiment*

In the popular press critiques of victim feminism examined in Chapter 1, academic feminism is identified as steeped in victim feminism, indeed, as one of the primary sources of its political hold. As shown in Chapter 2, however, this depiction of academic feminism in the 1990s is profoundly misleading. It is instead the case that academic feminist theory operated concurrently as another site of critical interrogation of the theme of victimhood in feminism, with many feminist theorists making a departure from the 'language', 'politics' and 'paradigm' of victimhood in favour of new forms of agency-affirming feminism. As Gudrun Dahl suggests, this is typical rather than exceptional. In the 1990s, what Dahl calls the 'Agents Not Victims trope' (2009, p. 396) became firmly established in the discourses of the humanities, and academic feminist theory is no exception to this trend.

This chapter continues my exploration of the presence of anti-victimism in feminism and focuses primarily on an influential set of feminist political theory texts that critique 'victimhood' amidst a Nietzschean reading of feminism as a 'politics of *ressentiment*' – a political form characterized by moral righteousness and 'reiterative attachment' to, in feminism's case, a universalist conception of women as powerless victims. While the popular press critiques decried 'victim feminism' and called for 'power feminism', their companion texts in feminist political theory diagnosed the problem of 'feminist *ressentiment*', calling for Nietzschean feminism and 'feminism without *ressentiment*', also broadly conceiving of this shift as overcoming fixation on passive victimhood in favour of new feminist conceptions of power, subjectivity and agency. In this chapter, I first discuss feminist engagements with Nietzsche, before examining and comparing Joan Cocks' (1991) critique of *ressentiment* in the feminist movement against rape and sexual harassment, Anna Yeatman's (1993, 1997) critique of feminist *ressentiment* and the politics of democracy and difference and Wendy Brown's (1995) critique of *ressentiment* in modernist feminism and identity politics. All of these theorists also extend their diagnoses of *ressentiment* beyond feminism, characterizing adjacent progressive political projects such as anti-colonialism, anti-racism and revolutionary socialism as afflicted with *ressentiment*. In the final section of the chapter, I consider this stance in relation to anti-racist and postcolonial feminist articulations of the anti-victim critique, and explore the roll-out of neoliberal victim theory in the contexts of neoliberal globalization and the settler colonial state.

The theorizations of feminist *ressentiment* I examine in this chapter mirror the popular press critiques of victim feminism in a range of ways, while at the same time being conceptually more sophisticated, with their location in the different textual spaces of 1990s poststructuralist and postcolonial feminist political theory giving rise to different points of emphasis within the anti-victim critique. Overall, I argue that their engagement in Nietzschean critique works both for and against their analyses, setting the scene for a dual relationship with neoliberal victim theory. On one hand, the 'pathology-laden language' (Solomon, 1994, p. 99) of the Nietzschean critique of *ressentiment* provides striking discursive support for neoliberal constructions of victims, victimhood, victimization and agency. On the other hand, however, engaging with Nietzsche also enables the theorists of feminist *ressentiment* to mark important departures from neoliberal victim theory, suggesting ways of critiquing and subverting anti-victimism.

To introduce the theorizations of feminist *ressentiment*, I want to foreground three key differences between this body of work and the popular press critiques of victim feminism examined in Chapter 1. First, Cocks, Yeatman and Brown all conceive of *ressentiment* as the death of democratic politics in feminism and its replacement with an inflexible authoritarian morality. Thus, like the popular press critics of victim feminism, their questioning of victimhood is intimately linked with the question of what kind of political agency feminism should assume. Yet, as my comparative analysis will show, there is an intriguing lack of consensus among these theorists when it comes to locating *ressentiment* in feminist politics. While Cocks and Brown associate *ressentiment* with reformist political projects that seek social change through law and state power, Yeatman associates *ressentiment* with political projects that refuse to participate in this kind of reformism. Many have been ready to follow the call for 'feminism without *ressentiment*', but, as I show here, the direction in which this call would lead feminists is by no means clear. This and other conflicts in judgement serve to create a body of work that is heterogeneous in comparison with the chorus-like critiques of victim feminism, and more ambiguous in its relationship to neoliberalism.

Second, unlike their counterparts in the popular press, the theorizations of feminist *ressentiment* are not anchored in the empirical claim that masculine dominance is at an end, and do not ascribe to the argument that feminist political claims about gendered relations of oppression are simply fictional or exaggerated.[1] As Brown (1995) puts it, feminists need 'different tools of storytelling than the phenomena of hegemonic or ubiquitous formations of power', but this does not mean 'feminist claims about masculine dominance . . . thereby disintegrate' (p. 166). Cocks, Yeatman and Brown draw on Nietzsche's concept of *ressentiment* in order to advance critique of feminism as a politics of fixed identity, and feminist investment in a 'Manichean', pre-Foucauldian conception of power as domination. Cocks, Yeatman and Brown shape the problem of *ressentiment* as a problem concerning the way victim subjects can interpret their victimization as a sign of their virtue, and in this way enter into a resubordinative relation of reiterative attachment to victim identity, losing sight of what Gatens (1996) calls the '*sine qua non* of movements for social change': 'Becoming something other than that which we presently are' (p. 77). Rather than become something other than that which they presently are – a victim of oppression – the subject of *ressentiment* revalues what they are as good, recoding victimhood as virtue and powerlessness as the seat of moral superiority, politicizing victimization while remaining attached to it as an identity and source of ethical knowledge, a knowledge that is, however, limited by Manicheanism in the theorization of power. Deleuze (1983) precisely captures this version of the problem of *ressentiment*: '*Ressentiment* is the triumph of the weak *as* weak, the revolt of the slaves and their victory *as* slaves' (p. 117, original emphasis). In their focus on *ressentiment* as paralysed victim identity that equates suffering with virtue and results in totalizing accounts of women as powerless victims, the theorizations of feminist *ressentiment* are not entirely distinct from the popular press critiques of victim feminism, which also complain about 'victim' as a fixed identity that operates as a seat of moral superiority. Unlike the popular press critics, however, Cocks, Yeatman and Brown are seeking to theorize relations of oppression differently, rather than erase their existence.

The third difference I want to foreground is implied above. Where the popular press critics frame feminism's woman-as-victim theme as an *outmoded fiction* that no longer applies to women in the post-feminist West, theorists of feminist *ressentiment* tend to frame this theme instead as a *false universal* that problematically fixes identity and obscures power relations among women. Where the popular press critics of 'victim feminism' are very ready to identify non-Western women as still shackled by the yoke of patriarchal domination, Yeatman's and Brown's theorizations in particular emerged in dialogue with critiques of Western feminist universalism, responding to the need to rethink feminist conceptions of gender and power in view of differences among women, and mindful of challenges to Western feminist identification of non-Western women as fellow or more authentic victims of patriarchal domination (Spivak, 1988; Mohanty, 1986).[2] This brings us to the most compelling area of complaint about the theme of victimhood in feminism: the complaint that this theme carries an imperialist heritage and is strongly racialized, but unavowedly so, its racialist configurations requiring critical work to make them visible, at least to Western eyes. While the popular press critiques of victim feminism do not acknowledge this line of critique, Yeatman and Brown respond precisely to it. This is a significant difference, even though I argue here that Western feminists have tended to pick up and develop the critique of the notion of 'victim' in Western feminism, without taking on the same wariness of 'agency' that is evident in the anti-racist and postcolonial work they are responding to.

Although the theorizations of feminist *ressentiment* differ significantly from the popular press critiques of victim feminism, I argue in this chapter that they do nonetheless create another venue where feminist and neoliberal values visibly merge around the themes 'victim', 'agent', 'blame' and 'responsibility'. Their handling of these themes demonstrates the circumstance Harvey (2005) describes as 'vulnerability to incorporation within the neoliberal fold' (p. 42), or the making of an analysis that, unwittingly or otherwise, reflects tenets of neoliberal philosophy – a claim we are used to hearing in relation to feminisms other than poststructuralist feminism. Despite their greater conceptual sophistication and the different way in which they draw the problem of resentment – as a problem of fixed identity and of theories of subjectivity and power, rather than as a problem of mendacity – they nonetheless uphold rather than deconstruct the victim-bad/agent-good formulation that is essential to neoliberal victim theory. Indeed, the 'victim-bad' component of this formulation is dramatically strengthened through their diagnostic use of Nietzsche's concept of *ressentiment*, which at times serves to pathologize victim identity and victim politics with an intensity not seen in the popular press accounts of victim feminism. The Nietzschean turn in these texts sponsors a negative, judgemental focus on the character of victims and of those engaged in victim politics. As Robert C. Solomon (1994) observes, 'Whatever else it may be, Nietzsche's emphasis on nobility and resentment is an attempt to stress character and virtue (and with them, tradition and culture) above all else in ethics' (p. 101). In the contemporary context, the Nietzschean emphasis on the character and motivations of the moralist dovetails with neoliberal victim theory's similar recasting of victimhood as a question of individual character.

Nietzsche's account of the psychology of *ressentiment* is organized around repeated condemnation of the resentful slaves and the morality they elaborate in response to conditions of oppression. Theorists of feminist *ressentiment* continue in this Nietzschean vein of condemnation, rendering resentment as toxic psychology and re-circulating existing depictions of the bad victim as vengefully Manichean, prone to authoritarianism, dangerously irresponsible, and in various ways benighted by fixation on suffering, their attachment to victim identity leading them away from 'healthy' forms of agency. In terms of the 'agent-good' component of this formulation, the theorists of feminist *ressentiment* value agency over victimhood but they do so in different ways. Yeatman values agency in the forms of self-regulation and Nietzschean mastery, while Cocks and Brown value agency in the form of radical political agency as a practice of freedom – the ability to 'impose a new imprint on the world' (Cocks, 1991, p.152) – which they contrast with the bad political agency that springs from *ressentiment*. While their formulations differ from those of their counterparts in the popular press, they retain the basic structure of the victim-bad/agent-good formulation: victim identity is wholly negative, agency is progressive, and subjects who are advancing claims from victimhood need to be disciplined away from this approach to politics, through a process of responsibilization. To the extent that the theorizations of feminist *ressentiment* pursue a Nietzschean discourse of diagnosing the political pathology of *ressentiment* and derogating the figure of the complaining victim, they lend discursive support to the wider body of conservative anti-victim critiques produced in their time and since.

Rather than take the view that Nietzsche's theory of *ressentiment* is not relevant for thinking about feminist politics, I concur with theorists of feminist *ressentiment* that Nietzsche's theory offers contemporary feminists important lessons about politicizing gendered victimization. But I have a different view about what those lessons are, and I identify in this chapter that there are serious limitations to approaching Nietzsche's theory diagnostically, that is, in the vein of aligning feminism with *ressentiment* construed as a toxic psychological malaise. This approach recalls the disease model Susan Sontag (1978) discusses in *Illness as Metaphor*, where she contrasts the Greek conception of disease as punishment with the modern conception of disease as reflection of inner self, pointing out that this latter view is no less moralistic and punitive than its forebear: 'Psychological theories of illness are a powerful means of placing the blame on the ill' (p. 57). The diagnostic approach readily devolves into derogation of individual character, yielding little insight into wider political dynamics. While I problematize their diagnostic use of Nietzsche, my analysis also identifies the moments where they clearly depart from this approach, particularly the way Wendy Brown, amidst her diagnoses of feminists and identitarians as afflicted with *ressentiment*, makes the significant sociological claim that liberalism's individualist ethos of self-determining agency is profoundly generative of *ressentiment*. This strikes an important blow against the championing of self-determining agency in the wider body of anti-victim critiques and opens a window onto a different kind of anti-*ressentiment* critique, one that focuses not on the character of the resentful but on the conditions of possibility for their resentment. In Chapter 4, I amplify this sociological approach to *ressentiment* and develop an interpretation of Nietzsche's concept of *ressentiment* that exposes the potential of this concept to challenge, rather than participate in, neoliberal victim theory.

Nietzsche and feminism

The theorizations of feminist *ressentiment* I examine in this chapter form part of what I will call the Nietzschean turn in feminist theory, which began in the late 1980s and consolidated in the 1990s when feminist theory reached its high tide mark as a disciplinary presence in the academic humanities, enlivened by the new heuristics of postmodernist and poststructuralist thought. The Nietzschean turn reflects the status of Nietzsche's philosophy as an important touchstone in poststructuralism (Foucault, [1979] 1984; Derrida and McDonald, 1982; Derrida, 1979) and marks the emergence of a different style of feminist engagement with Nietzsche, namely, a shift away from the focus on anti-feminism and misogyny in Nietzsche's philosophy, and towards a practice of drawing on Nietzsche's philosophy to rethink feminist theory, a development Maudemarie Clark (1994) welcomed as the appearance of 'feminism beyond good and evil' (p. 12). The latter practice assumes an autonomous feminist relation with Nietzsche's philosophy, recognizing that this philosophy is protean and demands active reading, finding what is useful in Nietzsche's work for poststructuralist feminist theory, rethinking the labelling of Nietzsche as straightforwardly anti-feminist and misogynist, and pointing out where his philosophy departs from, and helps to critique, the gendered metaphorics of Western philosophy.[3]

Reflecting this engagement, Nietzschean concepts are strongly present in contemporary feminist theory. Nietzsche's perspectivism (see GOM: III, 12) informs Donna Haraway's (1991) conception of 'situated knowledges', while his account of the way the slave type produces 'being behind doing' is a central resource in Judith Butler's conception of gender as performative (Butler, 1990, p. 25). Rather than ignore anti-feminism and misogyny in Nietzsche's thought and its heritage of deployment by fascists, postmodern feminist uses of Nietzsche assume what William Connolly calls a relation of 'agonistic indebtedness' to Nietzsche, where one uses what is productive in Nietzsche's philosophy while remaining alert to its limits and prejudices, in this way 'using Nietzsche against himself' (Connolly, 1997, p. 194; see also Brown, 2000). As we will see, the theorists of feminist *ressentiment* follow this pattern of engagement, using Nietzsche's concept of *ressentiment* to critique feminist politics while also marking out disagreements with aspects of Nietzsche's political views.[4] If before the Nietzschean turn feminists predominantly asked feminist questions about Nietzsche, after the turn, they began to ask Nietzschean questions about feminism. This can be seen when we compare the different ways Linda Singer in 1983 and Avital Ronell in 1991 speak to the question of feminist *ressentiment*. Singer launches a feminist critique of Nietzsche's concept of *ressentiment*. Ronell, on the other hand, launches a Nietzschean critique of feminism as a politics of *ressentiment*, providing an early articulation of the anti-*ressentiment* critique that has continued to resound in feminist theory.

Singer ([1983] 1998) situates Nietzsche within 'a long tradition of thought which caricatures woman's anger in order to delegitimate it' (p. 178) and argues that the gendered theme of *ressentiment* in Nietzsche's philosophy operates as an apologetics of male dominance. Nietzsche treats resentment, hostility and vengefulness as 'entirely unoccasioned' (p. 176) quintessentially feminine instincts – character traits, rather than effects of domination – and deduces from this women's weakness, thus their suitability to a position of social inferiority. Nietzsche mistakes 'survival tactics' for 'instincts' (p. 177): resentment, hostility and vengefulness are responses to social inferiority, not signs of its naturalness. Singer argues:

> The refusal of women to accept this situation [patriarchal dominance] is
> a sign of their strength. So long as women are kept secondary and inferior
> they have no good reason not to resent their predicament. Nietzsche's
> demand that women abandon that attitude is an impossible and self-serving
> demand.
>
> (p. 179)

As Singer points out, feminism is first situated as a politics of *ressentiment* by Nietzsche himself. Rather than see feminism as a bid to move beyond the circumstances that breed resentment, Nietzsche sees feminism as an expression of feminine resentment that assumes the form of intra-female vengeance:

> [Nietzsche argues] that any effort by women to transcend their situation is in fact only a retrospective movement of resentment. Any effort toward emancipation by women is transformed by this analysis into a gesture of vengeance by 'abortive women' against their fertile and well-adjusted sisters.
>
> (p. 175)

Against Nietzsche, Singer argues that resentment is not quintessentially feminine but is instead occasioned by patriarchal social relations; and Singer situates resentment not simply as a burden of oppression but as a sign of strength and of the ability to challenge the configurations of power that occasion resentment.

In contrast to this, Avital Ronell's (1991) Nietzschean critique of feminism situates 'feminism today' as completely trapped within the 'reactive, mimetic, and regressive posturings' of '*ressentimental* politics' (p. 127). Asking how feminism can possibly free itself from 'the values of resentment and anger', Ronell observes that feminists are 'grim and humorless' rather than 'noble' in their response to masculine dominance (p. 128). Feminism is merely 'reactive' and 'subversive' (p. 128):

> [S]ubversion is a problem—it implies a *dependency* on the program that is being critiqued—therefore it's a *parasite* on that program . . . Is there a way to produce a force or intensity that isn't merely a reaction to *what is*? In other words, could feminism be a pointer towards a *future of justice* that isn't merely reproducing *what is*, with small reversals?
>
> (p. 128, original emphasis)

Where Singer ([1983] 1998) critiques the way Nietzsche figures 'women's existence as the negative face of the Nietzschean ideal' (p. 178), Ronell critiques feminism as the negative face of the Nietzschean ideal. Feminism is a 'very bad and allergic' (Ronell, 1991, p. 128) reaction to patriarchy rather than a noble departure from it; feminism merely reverses patriarchal values, instead of creating its own values; feminism thus corresponds with *ressentiment* and the slave-type, rather than the master-type Nietzsche lauds, who posits his own values.

Ressentiment and sexual politics

The Nietzschean turn described above is apparent in Joan Cocks' work on feminism and sexual politics. In *The Oppositional Imagination* (1989), Cocks defends radical feminism's 'political critique of sexuality in the name of an emancipatory moral ethos' against social and political theory's newfound 'fascination for Nietzsche, who saw morality *per se* as a mere cover for the resentments of the lowly' (p. 126). Where Nietzscheans have condemned radical feminists as sexually repressive moralists, Cocks defends radical feminism's 'egalitarian' and 'cooperative' ideals (p. 126). Then, in her subsequent 1991 article 'Augustine, Nietzsche and Contemporary Body Politics', Cocks shifts her position, using a combination of theoretical insights from Nietzsche and Augustine to critique radical feminists as sexually repressive moralists. Positioning herself as speaking against an injunction to silence, Cocks (1991) observes that to critique radical feminism is a 'hair-raising enterprise' (p. 158) that is bound to attract moral opprobrium. In anticipation of this, Cocks adopts a circuitous mode of critique, noting that radical feminism 'is best crept up on with delicacy and indirection' (p. 144). Accordingly, her article works through Augustine and then Nietzsche, before finally 'meeting head-on' (p. 155) with its object of critique. Cocks' object of critique is a 'malaise of oppositional politics' affecting anti-colonialism, socialism and radical feminism (p. 152).

Cocks proposes that these political forms have degenerated into 'victim politics', discarding the transcendent ambitions of revolutionary political change in favour of a therapeutic and litigious political sensibility oriented to gaining public recognition and compensation for past sufferings (p. 155). A transfiguration of the political relation takes place within this degeneration. Radical politics is no longer a noble politics of militant slave revolt against a master class; it is instead an ignoble politics of victim complaint directed to a group of victimizers:

> The slave relies for its understanding and articulation of enslavement less and less on the discordant triptych oppression-revolution-emancipation, more and more on an endless series of synonyms—violation, degradation, humiliation, abuse—for the passive recipience of evil . . . there is not a challenge to the master but a stepping up of demands to the victimiser: demands for a guilty conscience ('Look what you've done to us!') and for reparations ('Look what you owe us!') . . . the slave's noble hatred of the master's monopoly on freedom and pleasure decays into the victim's determination to outlaw for everyone any freedom and pleasure that any kind of victim is unable to enjoy.
>
> (p. 154)

In the case of radical feminism the degeneration Cocks describes manifests as a protectionist and authoritarian approach to sexual politics. Radical feminism's original 'Yes to the body', its 'expansive celebration of female Eros' gives way to a broad feminist repudiation of 'sexual desire per se' (p. 154). Rather than affirm female concupiscence, feminist victim politics offers only 'a No, a refusal of power and pleasure to the female body for the sake of protecting it from victimization' (p. 154). This degenerative sensibility commissions strict government of the body:

> We find in segments of the population hyper-alert to the sexual harassment and abuse of women and children (a real enough harassment and abuse,

to be sure), a suspicion of all socio-physical entanglements . . . There is an urge . . . to prohibit an increasing number of bodily gestures and movements that might be expressions of sexual power.

(p. 154)

In this context, the victim subject induces guilt in others in order to gain the upper hand and is thereby accorded unparalleled authority in the articulation of subjective suffering: 'In an age of victim politics the subjective feelings of victimization will always have the moral edge' (p. 155).

Cocks frames feminism's degeneration into victim politics as the death of politics and its replacement with psychotherapy. Victim politics trades 'the struggle for power' for the invention of 'psychotherapeutic techniques for treating and eradicating the will to power' (p. 155). At the same time, however, through her mode of critique Cocks herself makes a psychotherapeutic turn. Apart from observing that the degeneration she perceives reflects a 'general shift in the Zeitgeist of the West' (p. 152), the explanatory context Cocks sets up for this degeneration mobilizes insights from Augustine and Nietzsche in order to identify and diagnose the subterranean forms of psychological disturbance characteristic of those who participate in victim politics. Cocks argues that leading feminist figures such as Catharine MacKinnon, Andrea Dworkin and Mary Daly are driven by the degenerative forces of Augustinian asceticism and Nietzschean *ressentiment*. But she also observes that these forms of psychological disturbance have their 'most vital life outside of texts' and are present generally in the 'speech, common sense . . . and practices of counter-publics and individuals influenced by oppositional ideas', particularly those engaged in feminist movement against rape, sexual abuse and sexual harassment (p. 152).

Cocks converts the operative contradictions of Augustine's *Confessions* into tools of psychological diagnosis, in order to unveil the hidden psychology of feminist victim politics. The *Confessions* is at once an ascetic repudiation of bodily pleasure *and* a 'voluptuous' text that is 'preoccupied with bodily desires' (p. 146). This operative contradiction yields a lesson in reversals: 'a great hatred of bodily pleasure can veil a great love of it, from which we can infer that a great love of the body can veil a great hatred' (p. 145). Cocks identifies this latter configuration with radical feminist body politics. When feminists politicize rape, sexual harassment and sexual abuse, they appear to love the female body because they are asking that women's bodily integrity be respected and that women's bodies be protected from harm. This will to respect and protect the female body, however, is not what it seems: it expresses an 'urge to bring authoritative power to bear on bodily life' and in this way reveals an underlying ascetic rejection of 'bodily intensity and pleasure' (pp. 154–155). Hence, argues Cocks, the protectionist orientation of radical feminist body politics can be interpreted as a 'hatred of the body that masquerades as love' (p. 145).

Cocks similarly draws upon the textual disjuncture between style and substance evident in the *Confessions* – Augustine's substantial repudiation yet stylistic embrace of sensuality – to interpret the theme of power within feminist body politics. As we have seen, Cocks is arguing that radical feminism has left behind the politics of the militant slave and is now set around the degenerate figure of the complaining victim. Yet, she observes, proponents of radical feminist politics 'speak not in the peevish, hurt tones of the victim but in the proud, angry tones of the militant slave' (p. 153). Cocks interprets this outward appearance of militancy as a textual disjuncture. Just as Augustine denounced sensuality, so too do radical feminists 'deny the existence of power for women and denounce power as a political ideal' (p. 153). And just as Augustine embraced sensuality in his textual style, thus revealing his hidden love of sensuality, so too do radical feminists embrace the will to power in their mode of public address, revealing their underlying attachment to an authoritarian will to power. In sum, the actual affective economy of feminist victim politics has a repressed, subterranean quality: it can be glimpsed in the fervent style of its advocates and is revealed in the new tyrannies permitted by its ostensibly altruistic will to protect the female body. Feminist politicizations of sexual victimization outwardly appear to love the female body and to contest female victimization; inwardly, however, these politicizations hate the female body and are co-opting the agency of the law in order to sate their authoritarian will.

While Augustinian asceticism enables Cocks to probe the hidden psychology of feminist victim politics, Nietzsche's concept of *ressentiment* provides her with an overall diagnosis of feminist victim politics. In an interesting complement to her use of this concept in diagnostic mode, Cocks suggests that conscious knowledge of *ressentiment* acts as an 'antidote' (p. 145) to *ressentiment*. Knowledge of *ressentiment* is an antidote in the sense that the slaves, as Nietzsche draws them, are so repugnant that once we have engaged with Nietzsche's account, we are sure to want to avoid their psychology of *ressentiment*:

> However ugly it is as a politics on its own, Nietzsche's theory of *ressentiment* offers an antidote to the sanctimonious inclinations of any politics of the oppressed. Nietzsche shows us how a critique of dominative power can turn into a sanctification of powerlessness, a celebration of weakness, a championing of victim status, a witch hunt against strength, talent, charm, or any other positive distinction, and finally, with respect to the body as well as what used to be called the spirit, intellect, and will, a tyrannical suppression of all in life that is forceful and fierce.
>
> (p. 145)

Cocks' handling of Nietzsche's concept is both complex and equivocal, with Cocks situating Nietzsche as a politically conservative thinker who nonetheless offers radical important truths. In order to grapple with this aspect of her account, let us visit the basic architecture of Nietzsche's theory.

On Nietzsche's account, the economy of negative affect he calls *ressentiment* is an effect of human socialization felt most acutely among those who are politically subordinated. All humans are oppressed by the creation of social organization in the form of a state, but those occupying subordinated positions are more extremely subject to this oppression and are most lacking an 'outlet' to express their distress, a condition that will eventually lead to their rebellion. In Nietzsche's *On the Genealogy of Morals* ([1887] 1989), the concept of *ressentiment* unfolds as a drama involving three key figures: the master, the slave, and the ascetic priest. Pressing against the Hegelian conception of the master's power as dependent on recognition by the slave, Nietzsche casts the original masters as inherently powerful. Actively self-defining and self-affirming, the original masters value themselves and all that is powerful and vigorous as 'good'; subsequently they evaluate the slaves and all that is 'low' and 'common' as 'bad'. The distinctive morality of the masters, their conception of good and bad, is centred on self-affirmation, and does not require the slave. Cocks (1991) rejects the anti-Hegelianism at work in Nietzsche's concept of master morality, asserting that Nietzsche is 'starry-eyed . . . about the morality of the master' since 'the substance of the master is determined by the dialectic of the master/slave relation' rather than by the master's unique capacity for self-affirmation (p. 155).

According to Nietzsche, where master morality is centred on self-affirmation, the morality of the slave is centred on other-negation. This is the 'dependent', 'reactive' and 'parasitic' quality Ronell (1991, p. 128) ascribes to *ressentiment* above. In the moment of political rebellion, the slave, driven by *ressentiment*, reverses master morality. The slave meets the master's 'I am good, he is bad' with a reversing syllogism: 'He is evil, therefore I am good.' That which the master has valued as 'good' (mastery, power, strength, vigour) is revalued as 'evil'; and that which the master has valued as 'bad' (servility, lowliness, weakness, suffering) is revalued as 'good'. In this way the slave enters a relation of reiterative attachment to their identity as a slave. Even as the slave contests their condition, they revalue that condition as the seat of moral virtue. In an interesting intervention on Nietzsche's theory, Cocks argues that slave revolt does not necessarily fall into this trap. Cocks (1991) affirms slave morality while maintaining that *ressentiment* is bad, insisting that these are separable elements of Nietzsche's theory: 'slave morality is not, as Nietzsche supposed, a morality of *ressentiment* by definition', even as slave morality 'is always in danger of succumbing to *ressentiment*' (p. 155). In other words, it is possible for a slave revolt to take place, and for those who revolt to generate their own set of moral values, in a way that exceeds the immanent negations and reversals that Nietzsche associates with *ressentiment*.

Cocks identifies this 'healthy' form of slave revolt with modern radical politics in its original incarnation. Prior to their degeneration into victim politics, anti-colonialism, socialism and feminism were vigorous and passionate projects to 'seize freedom, power, and pleasure from the monopoly of the master and to impose a new imprint on the world' (p. 152). Led by 'a noble hatred for the master' they sought the 'dissolution of mastery and servitude via the slave's political action' (pp. 152–153). Now, however, they have 'succumbed to *ressentiment*' and are 'more aptly called resistance politics' (p. 152). According to this reading, radical political projects exceed the politics of *ressentiment* where they pursue emancipation through revolutionary action. Contrawise, they succumb to *ressentiment* where they merely bargain for reforms that accord recognition and compensation for suffering, creating venues not for transcendent political action, but for 'recitation of the slave's suffering' (p. 152).

As Nietzsche tells it, the role of the ascetic priest in the drama of slave revolt is to contain the *ressentiment* of the slaves, by turning their *ressentiment* back on themselves. In order to quell slave rebellion and conserve the social order, the priest induces the slave to blame themselves, rather than the masters, for their suffering. As Cocks elucidates:

> Religious asceticism . . . provides a solution for the strong to the *ressentiment* against them of the weak. By representing the natural characteristics of the weak as spiritual virtues, religious asceticism flatters the weak without allowing their will to power an outward outlet, forcing them instead to stamp out any tendencies to pride, strength, and aggression in themselves; teaching them to blame themselves for the ills they suffer as punishments for their sins.
>
> (p. 151)

Bringing together the Augustinian and Nietzschean strands of her theorizing, Cocks observes that Augustine's *Confessions* is a perfect example of priestly asceticism operating in the way Nietzsche describes. The *Confessions* calls for 'unquestioning obedience of all servants to all masters' and renders such obedience as the slave's passage to spiritual virtue (p. 151). Augustine lends moral value to the slave – they will stand in for all that is 'virtuous' and 'good' – while simultaneously withdrawing any possibility of factual power from the slave since their value is contingent upon their maintaining slavish obedience. In this context the slave becomes self-blaming: their suffering is no longer interpreted as the questionable deed of the master, but as punishment for sin. As we have seen, Cocks aligns feminist victim politics with the figure of the *ressentimental* slave. Problematically, however, she also argues that the 'great orators and writers of victim politics' play the role of the ascetic priest, so described (p. 155; see also Conway, 1993).

In what sense can feminist politicizations of sexual harm be said to participate in the incitement to self-blame Nietzsche associates with priestly asceticism? Cocks' (1991) answer is that the final destination of feminism's hatred of the body is to cast 'embodiment itself' as 'the fundamental crime': 'having a body makes one a potential victim of physical and sexual abuse and/or a potential abuser' (p. 155). Her argument, then, is that feminist victim politics ultimately blames the problems of rape, sexual abuse and sexual harassment on the body, on the having of a body, and in this way produces the self-blaming consciousness Nietzsche associates with the ascetic priest. This disregards, however, a cardinal feature of feminist victim politics that Cocks has previously recognized and maligned: the fact that feminist victim politics precisely does not direct blame in this way. Cocks argues elsewhere that the problem with feminist victim politics is that it is a politics of complaint: it directs blame externally, creating contexts in which sexual suffering is visible as wrong and demanding recognition and compensation from a specific group of victimizers. Cocks' argument, then, is that feminist victim politics is problematic because it encourages victims/survivors to blame victimizers *and* because it cancels out this possibility, by enveloping the victim/survivor in an ethos of ascetic self-blame. As I observed in Chapter 2, feminist efforts to position perpetrators rather than victims/survivors as responsible for sexual harm take place in response to victim-blame and self-blame prevailing in contexts of masculine dominance. To the extent that feminist victim politics does direct blame externally, it undoes the ascetic priest's solution to the problem posed by the *ressentimental* slave. As one ready to complain, the victim/survivor subject of this feminist politics refuses to be self-blaming, refuses to take on the ascetic conscience. In her case, the efforts of the priest have failed. While its directions of blame are perplexing, Cocks' theorization rightly emphasizes the theme of asceticism in Nietzsche's theory. When in Chapter 4 I return to and discuss Nietzsche's theory of *ressentiment* in greater depth, we will see that there is scope for conceptualizing neoliberal victim theory, rather than feminist politics, as a contemporary form of 'asceticism' in Nietzsche's sense.

In sum, for Cocks, what is lost in the 'age of victim politics' (p. 155) is the possibility of true radicalism – revolutionary transcendence of the status quo. She frames the politics of *ressentiment* as radicalism's degeneration into an essentially reformist posture in which the agency of the state and the law are co-opted in the name of a political programme that seeks recognition and compensation for suffering, and which denounces power at the same time as it harnesses the power to govern bodily life in authoritarian mode. Accordingly, Cocks sets up the solution to the problem of *ressentiment* as a return to true radicalism. She suggests feminists return to an Augustinian 'depiction of the world as made of relations between mastery and servitude', while jettisoning, of course, Augustine's recommendation that slaves be obedient (p. 156). Such a depiction of the world will inspire a properly radical rebelliousness in the slave, restoring the capacity for militant action that victim politics, in its campaigns against violence, has threatened to extinguish. Hence Cocks' account of feminism as a politics of *ressentiment* is set around two contrasting types: the feminist of *ressentiment*, a faux radical bent on immanent complaint rather than transcendent action; and the feminist of slave morality, a true radical who, in style *and* substance, directs their will to power towards imposing 'a new imprint on the world' (p. 152), thus remaining immune to the malaise of *ressentiment*. As we will see, Anna Yeatman's account of feminist *ressentiment* reverses this typology.

Ressentiment and the politics of difference

Anna Yeatman's theorization of feminist *ressentiment* explores the ethics and politics of representing women as victims in the 'contemporary era of multiply contested oppressions' (Yeatman, 1993, p. 228; see also Yeatman, 1995). Yeatman argues that the era of multiply contested oppressions has thrown into relief the partial character of feminist politics, forcing feminists to rethink their insistence on the primacy of gender oppression, a circumstance Yeatman describes as a loss of innocence. Innocence is lost in the realization that feminist universalism has been tailored to the particular interests of white bourgeois women, creating a politics that is 'incommensurable with the emphases of emancipatory movements oriented to different axes of oppression' (Yeatman, 1993, p. 228). Yeatman's view is that much can be gained in the way of knowledge of the political in view of this realization. She sets out to rethink feminism's work as a politics of difference in view of its 'internal' politics of difference, arguing that the manner in which feminists approach the 'custodians of the established order' (p. 229) must shift in view of the position of white bourgeois women as the custodians of feminism's established order. Emancipatory movements typically view the custodians of the order they are challenging as 'interested' rather than 'ethical'. Yet this typical view, Yeatman argues, cannot be sustained by those 'positioned as custodians of the established order within an emancipatory politics' (p. 229). Given that the emergence of a politics of difference within feminism has revealed the extent to which the universals of feminism have been particularized around the interests of white bourgeois women, and given that these same women are answerable to the demand that this particularization be recast, their position complexly combines 'interest' and 'ethics', where the latter denotes an 'ethical orientation' to such recasting (p. 231). According to Yeatman, the politics of difference within feminism thus leads to the realization that this same combination of interest and ethics characterizes the position of the custodians of the patriarchal gender order that feminism is challenging. On this basis Yeatman sets up a contrast between two political strategies or postures that feminism, and emancipatory movements more broadly, can adopt: a pseudo-political radical posture in which it is assumed that the custodians inevitably are interested rather than ethical, which she identifies with *ressentiment*; and a properly political reformist posture that is open to democratic interlocution and participatory reconstruction of the liberal polity, thus overcoming *ressentiment*.

In setting up this contrast, Yeatman is working with a particular theory of democratic politics, one that emphasizes its relational and dynamic character.[5] She observes that the ethical universals that express the values of a democratic polity (participation, freedom, equality) 'must be particularized in order to exist' (p. 231), where particularism necessarily undercuts universalism. Thus the proper achievement of an ethical universal such as equality is 'perpetually deferred' (p. 229). But with particularism comes the possibility of 'politics'. In establishing a bounded community that centres some while marginalizing others, particularism calls into being or 'interpellates' (p. 234) contestation from the margins. That is, particularism always wrongs the universal it particularizes, and this wrongdoing positions the custodians of the bounded community as answerable to the wronged who, in being wronged, are positioned to show how this community's political discourse 'fails to live up to its own professions of universalism' (p. 231). Articulation of the wrong on the part of the emancipatory subjects, and answerability to the wrong on the part of the custodians, comprise the interlocutory relation that is 'politics': 'Politics requires and depends on the interlocutory and performative dynamics of what is a contestatory *relationship*, demanding an ethical response from both those who are positioned as privileged by policy and those who are positioned as wronged by policy' (p. 230, original emphasis). Thus, 'politics' is brought into being by and will intervene upon the wrongs particularism must commit. By extension, democracy is here understood as constitutively unstable: between the promise and failure of universalism lies what must be a site of restless contestation.

In locating politics in this way, Yeatman seeks to establish that professions of universalism on the part of custodians of an established order do not proceed solely in the name of interest. Rather, all such professions have an 'ethical component' insofar as they are 'continually accountable to politics', so described (p. 234). Yet this is not to say that this ethical component, nor the demand that it be brought to account, necessarily will engage politics. Yeatman is concerned with the ways in which politics can be foreclosed by both parties to the political relation. On the part of the custodians, politics is foreclosed through 'the simple reassertion of established policy and a correlative refusal to listen to the contestatory voices of emancipation; or a more subtle version, the appropriation of the contestatory and emancipatory voice' (p. 235). Such refusals to engage in the 'act of listening' stymie the emancipatory subject's articulation of the wrong, conserving rather than renegotiating 'the established procedures of who gets to participate within the process of governance' (p. 236).

Yeatman's primary concern, however, is with the emancipatory subject's mode of foreclosure. On the part of the emancipatory subject, politics is foreclosed when it is assumed that the custodians inevitably will 'subordinate claims on equality to their interest in conserving their privileges' (p. 237). Yeatman reads this mode of foreclosure through Nietzsche's concept of *ressentiment*, characterizing the politics of *ressentiment* as a reign of 'moral terror':

> The result of this type of foreclosure is that the subject is forced to define itself in terms of the status of exclusion, namely as lying outside positive, political capacity. A politics of *ressentiment* follows whereby the emancipatory subject turned victim alternately practices moral appeal to and blackmail of what is now hypostatised as the dominant subject custodian of the established order. This is a pseudo-politics oriented to the exercise of force, moral terror in this case.
>
> (p. 230)

Yeatman characterizes the politics of *ressentiment* as a form of radical sedition that is non-transformative, undemocratic and vested in a Manichean reading of power relations. Yeatman then develops this reading in her later essay 'Feminism and

Power', arguing that *ressentiment* produces a mistaken view of power (Yeatman, 1997).

In 'Feminism and Power', Yeatman argues that the emancipatory subject-turned-victim remains fixed on a reductive view of the custodians as engaged in undemocratic coercion. The power of the powerful is seen as limited to 'all the coercive and non-benign senses of "power over"' (p. 145). This view is mistaken because it fails to perceive the positive, democratic form that state domination can assume, namely a 'non-extractive' or productive form that serves to build or enhance, rather than suppress or curtail, the capacities and freedoms of citizens. The victim subject's mistaken view of power produces a Manichean reading of power relations, with the political field carved up into two mutually antagonistic groups, one dominant, the other perfectly deprived of power. Yeatman identifies this form of Manicheanism with feminism, revolutionary socialism and anti-colonialism:

> the emancipatory movement sees itself as representing those who are dominated by some kind of ruling class: the bourgeoisie, the colonialists, men, etc. The focus for change thereby becomes this movement's efforts to throw off this relationship of domination and exploitation by a mix of various means: ideological contestation of this relationship, mobilisation of mass resistance, revolutionary struggle. Since power is equated with force, counter-power has to be a counter-force. This being the case, the emancipatory movements including feminism tend to pursue an undemocratic and often non-political practice of counter-force . . . This is a politics which cannot discern within modern statist systems of domination the difference between the democratic and undemocratic features of such systems.
>
> (pp. 145–146)

Yeatman views the politics of *ressentiment* as non-transformative in two senses. First, it forecloses politics in favour of oppositionality: 'if those who are positioned differently, in terms of privilege and its lack . . . are simply articulating given and opposed interests, there can be no change' (Yeatman, 1993, p. 237). Second, the politics of *ressentiment* is non-transformative because it converts the 'politics of emancipation' into the 'politics of identity' (p. 237). Rather than challenge and destabilize the identities conferred upon those who are excluded and marginalized, emancipatory efforts confirm and stabilize these identities when they claim outsider-status and victim-status as a first and last political posture: 'When these movements "stand outside looking in" they act to confirm [their] interpellated identities, not to challenge them' (p. 233). In feminism's case, identity is further hypostatized around sexual difference ('a feminism oriented by rancor and *ressentiment* casts women as good, men as evil' (Yeatman, 1997, p. 148)), with this lack of subjective transformation similarly linked to an incapacity to effect political transformation: 'All that is permitted a feminism oriented by rancor is a separatist retreat from the world' (p. 148).

It is significant that, in the context of a theory of politics that emphasizes its dynamic and relational character, Yeatman discusses the modes of foreclosure of the custodians and the emancipatory subjects without considering what the emancipatory subjects are to do when the custodians enact their modes of foreclosure. What is to be done in response to custodians who neglect the act of listening or appropriate the contestatory voice? Is it these foreclosures that incite the 'moral terror' Yeatman associates with *ressentiment*? Further questions are raised by Yeatman's characterization of *ressentiment* as 'undemocratic'. What does it mean to interpret something which consistently emerges within a political regime as not of that regime? Insofar as liberal democracy's necessary acts of particularism posit as constitutive its failure to fulfil the promises of universalism, its mode of perpetual deferral would seem to provide a potent condition of possibility for *ressentiment*. This suggests *ressentiment* is not 'undemocratic', but is rather germane to liberal democracies. *Ressentiment* is bound to appear when particularism, necessarily and repeatedly on Yeatman's account, wrongs universalism. Yeatman frames *ressentiment* as a form of toxic psychology that develops in response to domination: 'A politics of *ressentiment* is a politics which makes sense to a subject who is systematically brutalized and exploited by more powerful forces' (p. 147). Yet her account also suggests the politics of *ressentiment* makes sense as a response to unresponsive custodians – a response to a political regime that is perpetually engaged in successive forms of marginalization and exclusion.

Yeatman associates the politics of *ressentiment* with the same breadth of radical political forms as does Cocks: socialism, anti-colonialism, feminism. But Yeatman and Cocks offer conflicting judgements in terms of their readings of these as politics of *ressentiment*. The very political strategies and postures Yeatman identifies with *ressentiment* – mass resistance, revolutionary struggle, seditious determination to work outside and against the established order – are seen by Cocks as the healthy forebears and remedies of political *ressentiment*. Where Cocks recommends radicals overcome *ressentiment* by returning to an Augustinian conception of the world as comprised of relations of mastery and servitude, Yeatman considers that precisely such a conception of power relations is germane to the 'moral-political passion and worldview of *ressentiment*' (p. 147). For Cocks, *ressentiment*'s reiterative attachment to victim identity inheres in political reformism; for Yeatman, it inheres in the radical politics of the revolutionary outsider, beginning with their trenchant refusal to engage in reformism. Cocks (1991) wishes to revive radicalism's 'noble hatred of the master' (p. 154), yet for Yeatman this is the hatred of hypostatized identity – the inability to see the powerful as ethical as well as interested. In this way, Cocks' and Yeatman's accounts of the politics of *ressentiment* pull in completely different directions. What one theorist sets up as the problem, the other sets up as the solution, and vice versa.

In Yeatman's later essay on feminist *ressentiment*, there appears at first to be some ground of agreement between her and Cocks, with Yeatman including a particular mode of reformist politics within the category of political *ressentiment*: feminist protectionism. Drawing on Sharon Marcus' (1992) critique of anti-rape feminism, Yeatman argues that feminist efforts to co-opt the agency of the state and the law in order to protect women from male violence serve to re-victimize women. Such efforts reinscribe paternalism and constitute women as 'innocent victims' who require rescue:

> [T]hese subjects interpret their powerlessness as moral virtue, and in casting their oppressors as evil, seek in some way to be rescued from this evil by someone more powerful than they . . . Liberalism interprets state intervention on behalf of women's rights as the legitimate extension of state protection to a vulnerable group. This being the case, women's rights-bearing status may be a qualified one, namely one that exists only to the extent that it is reconcilable with the idea of state-sponsored patriarchal protection of women.
>
> (Yeatman, 1997, pp. 147–149)

Like Yeatman, Cocks reads feminist protectionism as a politics of *ressentiment* that reiterates feminine vulnerability. Yet for Cocks the alternative to protectionism is the revolutionary politics of the militant slave, while for Yeatman the alternative is a superior strategy of liberal reformism – a strategy that conceives power as capacity rather than as coercion or protection, and that asks the liberal state to constitute women not as victims who require protection, but as self-regulating autonomous agents. In this regard, Yeatman beckons a 'feminist counter-discourse of women as subjects of power, capable of exercising the full range of agentic capacities' (p. 154). The victim-bad/agent-good formulation clearly emerges here, and leads eventually to Yeatman's measured endorsement of neoliberal welfare reform as post-patriarchal.

Yeatman identifies this woman-as-agent counter-discourse with Nietzschean master morality. Where Cocks rejects the anti-Hegelianism at work in Nietzsche's concept of master morality, Yeatman embraces master morality as an instructive alternative to the slave morality in which feminists have engaged. Arguing that *ressentiment* has stymied feminist appreciation of the 'historical achievements in regard to self government' (p. 146) that the powerful have made, Yeatman invokes the traits of Nietzsche's master: autarky, freedom of action, self-affirmation, self-legislation. She argues this form of personhood is enabled when the liberal state employs legitimate domination to constitute citizens as self-regulating agents: 'such a state constitutes women as agents in their own right' (p. 154). In crossing from theoretical explication to practical illustration, Yeatman situates neoliberal welfare reform, in particular the use of workfare schemes, as a positive example of this state–citizen relation. Here Yeatman's account links strongly with the terrain of Nancy Fraser's (2009) argument about neoliberal resignifications of feminism, in particular the resignification of feminism's critique of the patriarchal welfare state as a critique of the 'nanny state'. Rather than seeing in neoliberal welfare reform a *resignification* of feminism, Yeatman perceives a *reflection* of feminism and an opportunity to advance feminist political goals in critical alliance with neo-liberalism.

Yeatman (1997) argues that neoliberal welfare reform represents an 'equal opportunity approach to income support' (p. 155). Unlike the Keynesian welfare state, which was originally a male breadwinner's welfare state that provided assistance to certain categories of women if they lacked a male provider (Pateman, 1988, 1989), the neoliberal welfare state disregards the gender of welfare beneficiaries, expecting all beneficiaries on income support to display market readiness. Yeatman (1997) characterizes the neoliberal welfare state as post-patriarchal because it 'withdraws paternalistic protection from women, and thereby challenges the patriarchal division between a master and his dependents' (p. 155). Breaking with the historical constitution of women as economic dependants, neoliberal welfare reform constitutes women as self-determining agents, requiring that 'women on welfare participate in labour market programs whether they are mothers of small children or not' (p. 155). Yeatman acknowledges that neoliberalism is narrowly focused on a 'market-oriented version of self-regulation' (p. 155). Yet, since this version of self-regulation is consonant with the feminist demand that women be seen as equally entitled to economic autonomy, 'feminism cannot argue for a reinstatement of women as economic dependents of either individual patriarchs or the state as a corporate patriarch' (p. 155). Rather, feminists must work 'with rather than against the self-regulatory features of this situation' (p. 155).

Here we see Yeatman narrow the scope for critical feminist response to neoliberal welfare reform, in the name of overcoming *ressentiment*. This aspect of her account is reminiscent of the popular critiques of victim feminism, where a certain resignation to the status quo is set up as the answer to the ills of victim politics. Workfare schemes are problematic for a range of reasons. They fail to acknowledge that women beneficiaries with dependent children are already working, and they further the undervaluing of women's unpaid work in the home, unfairly situating solo mothers as individually responsible for overcoming their systematic marginalization in the economy. And these schemes *do not* disregard gender. As Handler and Hasenfeld (2007) have clearly shown, workfare schemes are legitimated through the 'explosive combination of race and gender discrimination' embodied in the 'welfare queen' stereotype (p. 9). But in the schema Yeatman sets up, to argue against workfare schemes in these ways is to step back into a *ressentimental* constitution of women as dependent victims. This indicates that Yeatman's account is structured around a particular dynamic concerning agency. The scope for women's agency rhetorically broadens in the same measure as the scope for feminist political agency narrows. Measures by which women are constituted as 'agents' rather than 'victims' are championed, while feminist political agency is reined to a relatively conciliatory posture within the established order, with neoliberalism cast as a political force feminists need to work with rather than antagonistically reject.

Yeatman's treatment of neoliberal welfare policy seems to perform that discernment of democratic from undemocratic features of the liberal state she argues is lacking in the politics of *ressentiment*. Yeatman (1997) suggests that neoliberal values of self-regulation are democratic, while its market-oriented version of self-regulation is undemocratic because employment contracts are still governed by employer prerogative, thus are not 'adequately contractual' (p. 155). In other words, women welfare beneficiaries who have dependent children are expected to be self-regulating job seekers in a context where employers have no obligation to recognize and meet their particular needs. Here Yeatman acknowledges the key problem with neoliberal workfare schemes: they expect a particular form of self-regulation without creating its conditions of possibility. Significantly, Brown (1995) theorizes that precisely this circumstance – one in which the citizen is hailed as a self-regulating individual yet is unavowedly regulated by wider forces that lie beyond their individual control – is profoundly generative of *ressentiment* (p. 67). For Brown, liberal citizens 'quite literally seethe with *ressentiment*' (p. 69) because their self-regulating capacities are at once assumed (by liberalism) and sabotaged (by capitalism and disciplinarity). Hence, for Brown, the ethos of self-regulation at work in neoliberal welfare policy would not take us beyond *ressentiment* since this ethos is itself productive of *ressentiment*. What in Yeatman's account is set up as a solution to the problem of *ressentiment* – a strategy of desisting in themes of female victimization, dependence and vulnerability by working with neo-liberalism's agency-oriented ethos of self-regulation – appears in Brown's account as a context that leads back into the problem of *ressentiment*. As we will see, the accounts of Yeatman and Brown also differ significantly in terms of their respective readings of *ressentiment*, identity politics and liberalism's universalist political culture.

In sum, for Yeatman, what is lost in the politics of *ressentiment* is the prospect of properly political and genuinely democratic engagement in the affairs of the polity. Rather than assume a reformist posture that permits the participatory undertaking of reconstructive work, political forms that are led by *ressentiment* remain dogmatically attached to an identity as a victimized outsider and to a purist political strategy of revolutionary transcendence of domination. In this way, Yeatman reverses the typology set up in Cocks' account. Both theorists render *ressentiment* as a form of psychological disturbance that arises from relations of domination. But where Cocks associates this disturbance with a descent into a litigious and reformist politics, Yeatman identifies it with stubborn refusal to engage in the genuinely transformative politics of reformism. There is little difference between the stubbornly antagonistic outsider whom Yeatman maligns and the rebelliously militant slave Cocks champions, except that they are assigned contrasting roles in these theorists' respective theorizations of feminist *ressentiment*.

Ressentiment and the politics of identity

As Cocks (1997) suggests in her review of Brown's book *States of Injury* (1995), there is an affinity between their respective accounts of *ressentiment* and radical politics. Just as Cocks argues that radicalism's degeneration into the politics of *ressentiment* entails a loss of transcendent political orientation, so too does Brown (1995) contrast the 'uncritical statism' of political *ressentiment* with 'a vital politics of freedom' (p. 79). Yet there is greater caution in Brown's account when it comes to imagining a politics beyond *ressentiment*. Brown sets up the transcendent orientation of revolutionary Marxism as an instructive point of contrast with the unemancipatory *geist* of identity politics, and suggests that in feminism's case the answer lies with postfoundationalist feminism. But we also find Brown criticizing revolutionary Marxism as a 'science of revolution' (p. 49) and airing serious doubts about the political efficacy of postfoundationalist feminism (p. 79). Thus unlike both Cocks and Yeatman, Brown offers a set of theoretical-political provocations concerning feminism and *ressentiment* and urges movement beyond *ressentiment*, but without delivering a fully fledged counter-image or 'antidote' to the problem of *ressentiment*. As Brown puts it, as a political theorist, her task is not to provide 'blueprints for political action', but to critically diagnose political tendencies so they do not 'metamorphose unchecked into political expression' (p. xiii).

Brown's more equivocal account also differs from those of Cocks and Yeatman in terms of how she mobilizes the concept of *ressentiment*. Across two chapters of *States of Injury* Brown uses the concept of *ressentiment* to critique modernist feminism and identity politics. In both cases Brown uses this concept in diagnostic mode – to uncover veiled psychological structures and proclivities – while also mobilizing this concept sociologically. As the examples of Cocks and Yeatman show, diagnostic use of the concept of *ressentiment* performs what Lisa Duggan (2003) calls political othering: entire groups of political actors are rendered as sufferers of psychological disturbance and emotional imbalance. As Vikki Bell (1999) observes, feminist readers of theorizations of feminist *ressentiment* are asked to 'accept an image of ourselves as fuelled by *ressentiment*, attached to our wounded identities' (p. 50). In Brown's account, we certainly find a pathologizing portrait of *ressentimental* political actors as plagued by toxic psychology: her political genealogies are designed to expose the way 'paralysing recriminations and toxic resentments [are] parading as radical critique' (Brown, 1995, p. xi). As Carine Mardorossian (2002) describes, Brown's account pathologizes and individualizes 'an oppositional political movement that is made to sound like it is more in need of therapy than of a renewed political emphasis' (p. 760) and, as we will see, in its reception, Brown's critique of *ressentiment* has been interpreted as a clinical description of a politico-psychological illness called 'victimhood'. Despite these factors, however, in Brown's account, we also glimpse a very different approach to the idea of *ressentiment*, as Brown makes significant sociological claims about the historically specific conditions that serve to generate *ressentiment* in the contemporary era. The sociological approach to the concept of *ressentiment* is at odds with the diagnostic approach, producing tensions in Brown's account. Unlike the diagnostic approach, the sociological approach does not isolate *ressentiment* from its conditions of possibility. It shifts the analytical focus away from *ressentiment* as toxic psychology and towards questions about how the social world generates and might become less generative of *ressentiment*. The sociological approach to *ressentiment* appears in nascent form in Brown's account and forms part of my rethinking of the concept of *ressentiment* in Chapter 4.

In a similar vein to Cocks and Yeatman, Brown also considers that *ressentiment* leads feminists to be something other than properly 'political'. Cocks and Yeatman respectively describe *ressentiment* as a descent into psychotherapy and pseudo-politics. For Brown (1995; see also Brown, 2001), *ressentiment* is a descent into moralism, which she casts as fully anti-political and anti-democratic. In the first of her two chapters addressing *ressentiment*, Brown focuses on feminism in the context of postmodernity, placing feminism and left politics within a spectrum of political forms that participate in what she calls reactionary foundationalism, defined as a 'coping strategy for our "lost" condition of postmodernity', a response to the dislocations of the postmodern condition by which political subjects cling to and fetishize 'some indisputable good, for example, Western civilization, the American way of life, feminism, or left politics' (Brown, 1995, pp. 35–36). Brown reads 'feminist panic' (p. 39) in the face of postmodernist theory as symptomatic of reactionary foundationalism. Rather than understand the postmodern turn in feminist theory as 'an attempt to articulate and engage the characteristic powers of our age', feminists arrayed against postmodern theorizing instead 'kill the messenger' (p. 33), adopting a defensive posture in relation to postmodernist deconstruction of the subject and the category 'women'. Feminist antipathy to postmodernist theory provides the context for Brown's argument that 'much North Atlantic feminism partakes deeply of both the epistemological spirit and political structure of *ressentiment*' (p. 46).

Brown situates feminist standpoint theory and second-wave feminist knowledge practices such as consciousness-raising and speak-outs as a form of epistemological positivism, a 'science of woman' that follows in the footsteps of Nietzsche's *ressentimental* slave. Feminist efforts to value women's voices and perspectives as valid knowledge that gives a 'view from below' are seen to be centred on a homogenizing conception of the oppressed subject as possessed of privileged access to truth: unlike the powerful, the oppressed subject's reading of worldly power relations is undistorted by interest in perpetuating those power relations, and is therefore more credible. This epistemology thus appears to romanticize power-lessness, granting the oppressed subject the same exalted position the slave is granted in slave morality: women's knowledge, points of view and accounts of their worldly experiences are positioned as the good and the true and are beyond criticism, even as feminist standpoint theorists regard women as 'socially con-structed to the core' (p. 42). As Brown describes, in the epistemology of *ressentiment* '[p]owerlessness is implicitly invested in the Truth while power inherently distorts. Truth is always on the side of the damned or the excluded: hence, Truth is always clean of power, but therefore also always positioned to reproach power' (p. 46).

Brown renders this feminist epistemology as a moralism rather than a politics, a rancorous 'moral apparatus' that evades genuine political engagement in favour of 'complaint against strength', encouraging feminists to cling to 'the subjectivity of the subject' (p. 44) in response to postmodernism. Brown's question then becomes whether feminism can prevail without this moral apparatus and develop instead a 'politics without *ressentiment*' (p. 48). Reminiscent of Cocks' call for a revitalized radicalism that will 'impose a new imprint on the world' (Cocks, 1991, p. 152), Brown (1995) urges feminists to desist from moralistic complaint and proceed instead on 'the strength of an alternative vision of collective life' (p. 47). In terms of the place of women's voices and perspectives in postfoundationalist feminist epistemology, Brown argues for a shift away from identity-based speech focused on the private self ('who I am') and towards 'postidentity' public speech turned to world and common ('what I want for us'); and a shift away from the purportedly confessional locution of consciousness-raising, towards the impersonal, contestable, and accountable locutory mode she calls 'political argument' (p. 51):

> [D]ispensing with the unified subject does not mean ceasing to be able to speak about our experiences as women, only that our words cannot be legitimately deployed or construed as larger or longer than the moments of the lives they speak from; they cannot be anointed as 'authentic' or 'true' since the experience they announce is linguistically contained, socially constructed, discursively mediated, and never just individually 'had'.
>
> (pp. 40–41)

Importantly, Mardorossian (2002) disputes Brown's critique, arguing that feminist epistemology has not operated predominantly as a site where 'experience was unproblematically taken up as the basis of feminist epistemology' (p. 765). Rather than centre on confessional locution revealing incontestable truth, practices such as consciousness-raising and speak-outs create sites of 'collective enunciation' in which women 'examine the very terms they use to describe their experience' and 'come to understand that an experience they might previously have perceived as interpersonal in nature is in fact rooted in historical and social relations' (p. 764) As such, these forums do not 'preclude so much as foster the analysis of processes of subject construction', often entailing 'precisely the kind of denaturalizing postmodernists advocate' (p. 764). Lisa Duggan (2003) has similarly argued that Brown's critique of identity politics as *ressentimental* is strongly didactic and flattens out this political form, ignoring its most compelling instantiations and proponents: '[t]he impulse to caricature identity or cultural politics as political "other" underwrites the critic's authority more than it usefully describes the political landscape' (p. 80). Mardorossian's and Duggan's criticisms are important because they reflect one of the profound limitations of using the concept of *ressentiment* diagnostically. The diagnostic approach fends ambiguity, tensions and contrary signs, imparting a totalizing account of the object of diagnosis, in this case entire groups of political actors, as 'all bad'. That said, neither Mardorossian nor Duggan identifies the sociological aspect of Brown's account of *ressentiment*, which is considerably more compelling.

Like Cocks and Yeatman, Brown (1995) also extends the anti-*ressentiment* critique beyond feminism, moving on to critique identity politics in general as a politics of *ressentiment*: '[The] effort which strives to establish racism, sexism, homophobia as morally heinous in the law, and to prosecute its individual perpetrators there, has many of the attributes of what Nietzsche named the politics of *ressentiment*' (p. 27). In her chapter 'Wounded Attachments', Brown documents what she regards as the failings of identity politics: its self-subversive investment in reified identity categories, its depoliticizing entanglement in liberalism's games of inclusion, recognition, protection and right, its legitimation of law and the liberal state in the effort to outlaw social injury, which trades genuine emancipation for 'the satisfactions of revenge' won through law reform and litigation (p. 70).

> [T]he effort to 'outlaw' social injury powerfully legitimizes law and the state as appropriate protectors against injury and casts injured individuals as needing such protection by such protectors . . . in its economy of perpetrator and victim, this project seeks not power or emancipation for the injured or the subordinated, but the revenge of punishment, making the perpetrator hurt as the sufferer does.
>
> (p. 27)

Brown's Foucauldian critique works from the insight that 'political "resistance" is figured by and within rather than externally to the regimes of power it contests' (p. 3). Brown asks that we recognize identity politics' 'disciplinary, liberal and capitalist parentage' and the extent to which identity politics annexes and legitimates its tripartite parentage, curtailing its transformative potential by reiterating rather than contesting 'the "political shape" of domination in our time' (p. 28). Brown's focus on the forces conditioning the production of identity politics recalls Yeatman's insistence on the interpellated character of politicized identity, and both of these theorists problematize identity politics because it reifies the identities it politicizes, ensuring that disenfranchised identities will continue to be marked as such, as in the *ressentimental* scenario Deleuze draws as 'victory of the slave *as* slave'. But where Yeatman considers that politics is foreclosed when the disenfranchised refuse to work with the custodians towards inclusion recognition and subjective transformation, Brown considers that precisely such work leads to a depoliticizing foreclosure of political freedom. In stark contrast to Yeatman, Brown considers that asking liberalism to live up to universalism is the problem with identity politics rather than the solution to its ills.

Brown frames late modernity as a context in which, on one hand, state universality wears thin in view of liberalism's increasingly naked investment in 'particular economic interests, political ends, and social formations' (p. 56) while, on the other hand, the production of particular identities proliferates as disciplinary powers perform increasingly intricate classificatory labours. Identity politics has emerged in a context where identities become 'available for politicisation because they are deployed for purposes of political regulation' (p. 56). As Brown elaborates:

> In this story, the always imminent but increasingly manifest failure of liberal universalism to be universal—the transparent fiction of state universality—combines with the increasing individuation of social subjects through capitalist disinterments and disciplinary productions. Together, they breed the emergence of politicized identity rooted in disciplinary productions but oriented by liberal discourse toward protest against exclusion from a discursive formation of universal justice.
>
> (p. 56)

As Brown has it, identity politics is problematic because it inhabits rather than interrogates the articulation of identity categories on the part of capitalism and disciplinary power, then pursues what is actually a *de*politicizing route of politicizing along the lines set out by liberalism: generic claims of particularism baited by failed universalism, excluded orders of interest seeking inclusive recognition. Liberalism's pre-emption of the 'articulation of difference as political—as effects of power' (p. 56) is effectively obeyed as politicized identity claims emerge as eminently digestible complaint, rather than as deep challenges to the forces conditioning their production. In this way liberalism's economy of inclusion and exclusion, as distinct from its exclusiveness, is protected from critique, and capitalism is re-naturalized and class politics muted as the white, bourgeois, masculine ideal operates as the yardstick by which exclusion is measured and inclusion imagined.[6] Just as Avital Ronell (1995) situates feminism as trapped in a position of parasitic dependence, Brown (1991) considers that identity politics is ensnared in a political strategy that is ultimately self-subversive: 'Politicized identities generated out of liberal, disciplinary societies, insofar as they are premised on exclusion from a universal ideal, require that ideal, as well as their exclusion from it, for their own continuing existence as identities' (p. 65).

In the course of Brown's account, the object of her anti-*ressentiment* critique shifts from feminism and identity politics to liberalism's discourse of social being. Cocks and Yeatman suggest without specification that where there is domination, there is *ressentiment*, whereas Brown makes the very specific sociological claim that liberalism's discourse of social being – its constitution of citizens as self-governing individuals – is a *ressentiment*-producing machine. In the context of late modernity the liberal subject is 'starkly accountable yet dramatically impotent' and, therefore, 'quite literally seething with *ressentiment*' (p. 69). As Brown elaborates:

> It is . . . the prior presumption of the self-reliant and self-made capacities of liberal subjects, conjoined with their unavowed dependence on and construction by a variety of social relations and forces, that makes *all*

111

liberal subjects, and not only markedly disenfranchised ones, vulnerable to *ressentiment*: it is their situatedness within power, their production by power, and liberal discourse's denial of this situatedness and production that cast the liberal subject into failure, the failure to make itself in the context of a discourse in which its self-making is assumed, indeed, is its assumed nature. This failure, which Nietzsche calls suffering, must either find a reason within itself (which redoubles the failure) or a site of external blame upon which to avenge its hurt and redistribute its pain.

(p. 67, original emphasis)

In Brown's account, we thus glimpse a critical sociological claim about liberalism's 'generalized incitement' (p. 66) of its subjects to *ressentiment*, demonstrating that Brown's is a critique of liberalism and its companion powers rather than solely a critique of toxic psychology among feminists and identitarians. It is also a critique of *neoliberalism* given the intensification of the rubric of individual responsibility for individual socio-economic fate that is central to that political formation and, according to Brown, to the production of *ressentiment*. Cocks and Yeatman suggest the problem of *ressentiment* resides in the errant proclivities of those engaged in victim politics, whereas for Brown this problem resides in liberal-capitalist societies, where *ressentiment* emerges as 'both product and reaction' (p. 69) to liberalism's discourse of social being. Rather than set up 'agency' as the solution to the problem of *ressentimental* victim politics, Brown locates the material situation of constrained agency – the demand that one be autonomously self-making and the impossibility of that demand – as profoundly generative of *ressentiment*. The tension between the diagnostic and sociological approaches to *ressentiment* is clear when we consider the different questions they give rise to. While the diagnostic approach leads to the question of how feminists and identitarians need to change in order to free themselves of *ressentiment*, the sociological approach opens wider and more difficult questions about how the social world generates and may become less generative of *ressentiment*. Unlike the diagnostic approach, which sees *ressentiment* as bereft of value, the sociological approach also opens onto the idea that *ressentiment* is a generative source of ethical insight and a force for social change.

To conclude my discussion of Brown, however, I want show how the different way the problem of *ressentiment* is drawn in her account is not generally visible in its reception. In its reception, the diagnostic aspect of Brown's account has proven more resonant and a certain marriage of this account with neoliberal victim theory has taken place. Whereas Brown situates liberalism's responsibilization of the individual as a cardinal source of *ressentiment* in liberal societies, a cardinal theme in Brown's reception has been that feminists and identitarians need to be disciplined away from *ressentiment*, through a process of responsibilization. This is expressed when Brown herself calls upon feminists to 'assume responsibility for our situations' as an answer to the problem of *ressentiment* (p. 51). Echoing this call, Moira Gatens (1996) invokes Brown's and Yeatman's critiques of feminist *ressentiment*, arguing that together they indicate the need for feminists to 'take responsibility for what we are' (p. 88). If they are to develop a politics without *ressentiment*, feminists must examine 'notions of complicity, responsibility and accountability' (p. 88) in order to better understand the ways in which the subordinated and excluded are implicated in their own subordination and exclusion. Laid bare here is what Fredric Jameson (1981) calls the 'autoreferential' (p. 202) or recursive structure of the theory of *ressentiment*. Those identified as afflicted with *ressentiment* become objects of the critic's resentment. As Jameson observes, 'What is most striking about the theory of *ressentiment* is its unavoidably autoreferential structure . . . the theory of *ressentiment*, wherever it appears, will always itself be the expression and the production of *ressentiment*' (p. 202).

In terms of Nietzschean critique, an intriguing turn takes place within the recursive structure of the *ressentiment* critique and its effort to responsibilize the resentful. The diagnostician of *ressentiment* assumes the role of Nietzsche's ascetic priest, encouraging the resentful towards introspective self-blame. The solution to the problem of *ressentiment* is identified with improved conduct of political agency on the part of feminists and identitarians – not analysis and politicization of the socio-economic forces conditioning the production of *ressentiment* in the social world. In this interpretive scenario, Brown's critical sociology of *ressentiment* disappears and is replaced with something more akin to Max Scheler's ([1915] 1961) sociology of *ressentiment*.

Drawing on Nietzsche, Scheler developed a sociology of *ressentiment*, arguing that there are 'typically recurrent situations' in social life which are '*charged* with the danger of *ressentiment*' (p. 38, original emphasis). In a similar vein to Brown, Scheler argues that *ressentiment* 'would be slight in a democracy which is not only political, but also social and tends towards equality of property', and is 'strongest' in a society where 'approximately equal rights (political and otherwise) . . . go hand in hand with wide factual differences in power, property and education' (p. 50). In other words, in a formulation similar to Brown's, Scheler considers that formal equality amidst factual inequality produces *ressentiment*. Yet when it comes to addressing what is to be done about *ressentiment*, Scheler takes a conservative turn. Scheler observed that *ressentiment* is 'chiefly confined to those who *serve* and are *dominated*' who 'fruitlessly resent the sting of authority' (p. 31, original emphasis). Their resentment is fruitless because, according to Scheler, inequality is given by nature:

> [I]t is false to interpret legal inequality as the imperfect expression of an underlying ideal of equal rights, which is perverted by factual power relations. Quite on the contrary, every factual legal equality conceals a basis of inequality of rightful claims which is founded on the unchangeable natural difference between 'slaves' and 'free men'.
>
> (p. 102)

For Scheler, those who serve and are dominated become vulnerable to the 'inner venom of *ressentiment*' when they harbour thoughts of resistance (p. 31). To prevent being engulfed by *ressentiment* – which, Scheler insists, is 'incurable' (p. 6) – the dominated must vent their spleen, but they must do so privately, without disturbing the natural order of things. In the case of the 'ill-treated servant', for example, rather than openly complain to the master, the servant should 'vent his spleen in the antechamber' (p. 31), privately bringing their inimical feelings under control, in this way 'assuming responsibility for themselves' in the sense of acting as the respondent to one's own suffering. Brown and Gatens clearly would not share Scheler's belief in natural inequality, but their focus on disciplining feminists and identitarians away from *ressentiment* is strongly reminiscent of Scheler's conservative turn. The diagnostic approach to *ressentiment* very easily slides into a depoliticizing argument for treating the 'condition' of resentment, instead of challenging the wider social structures that constitute its conditions of possibility.

A visible merging of Brown's theorization of feminist *ressentiment* with neoliberal victim theory takes place in John Hoffman and Paul Graham's (2006) political theory primer, *Introduction to Political Theory*. This text interprets Brown's discussion of Nietzsche as clinical evidence for the claim that 'victimhood is a pathology' (Hoffman and Graham, 2006, p. 512): 'Brown identifies Nietzsche's critique of "slave morality" with what we have called the pathology of victimhood' (p. 518). Hoffman and Graham frame 'victimhood' as a 'new problem' (p. 510) for students of political theory to examine, but they do so in a way that raises concerns about the kind of pedagogy their discussion of 'victimhood' provides. They furnish students with a narrow account of the 'problem of victimhood', one that strongly reflects neoliberal victim theory. As though following the example of the first victimologists (Van Dijk, 2009), Hoffman and Graham depict victims and 'victimhood' in ways that should themselves be the object of critical scrutiny. Their discussion of victimhood and *ressentiment* reflects rather than analyses the wider context of anti-victim critique within which it appears. As such, it fails to recognize the importance, to students of political theory, of examining anti-victimism – of factoring the contemporary prevalence of anti-victim discourses into the analytical frame when theorizing contemporary victim politics. Below I outline three respects in which Hoffman and Graham's depiction of 'victimhood' reflects neoliberal victim theory, before positing that Jean Améry's (1980) perspective on victimhood provides a potent counter-depiction of a kind also worthy of consideration by political theorists.

Reflecting neoliberal victim theory, Hoffman and Graham (2006) first of all present contemporary society as pervasively overrun by claims to victim status: 'We live in a society in which it has become increasingly common for people to identify as victims', as evinced in the rise of 'victim feminism' (p. 510). Here Hoffman and Graham are ignoring political theorists who suggest that the opposite is true – that in contemporary society people are actively *discouraged* from identifying as victims and are urged instead to align with an ideal subject who resists victimhood in favour of a key virtue of market individualism: personal responsibility. In contrast to Hoffman and Graham's image of a multitude of citizens clamouring for recognition as victims, political theorist Engin Isin (2002), for example, sees a multitude of citizens constituted as individually responsible risk-averse non-victims by and through neoliberal technologies of responsibilization: '[j]ust as avoiding risk becomes the responsibility of individuals as authors of their own destiny, ill-fate and misfortune also become the responsibility of individuals: the unemployed, the homeless, and the poor are constituted as responsible for their own condition' (p. 248). Where Hoffman and Graham claim victims now enjoy unparalleled visibility and political sway, Isin observes the *erasure* of victimization in neoliberal times. For example, tracing the rise of the category 'homelessness' across the 1980s and 1990s, Isin observes the term 'homeless' veils a process of victimization: rather than being 'constituted as "the evicted," signifying a victimised status', the homeless are constituted as active subjects whose individual entrepreneurial skill determines the having or lacking of a home (p. 271).

Second, Hoffman and Graham uncritically affirm the values of the victim-bad/agent-good formulation. Victim identity is wholly negative while agent identity is wholly positive, and victimhood is ostensibly agency's opposite and demise: 'Victimhood . . . involves the belief that being a victim renders a person or group powerless, a mere object, lacking in agency and thus the capacity to exert independent action . . . Hence victimhood paralyses agency' (Hoffman and Graham, 2006, pp. 512–513). Paradoxically, of course, though they identify victimhood with paralysed agency, they associate victimhood with various forms of bad agency. Victims afflicted with victimhood gain power and influence through an identity of powerless victimhood, are purveyors of a dangerously mistaken Manichean view of power relations as 'polarised and dualistic' (p. 514) and are led by thirst for vengeance: 'What makes victimhood pathological is that "victims" easily slip into the position of perpetrators . . . If the state cannot inflict the violence on their behalf, they do it themselves!' (p. 525). In contrast to this, stands good agency, which carries the usual meanings: action, self-determination and responsibility.

The third respect in which Hoffman and Graham's text reflects neoliberal victim theory is that the problem of victimhood is strongly identified with feminism, with women victimized through rape and violence called up as examples of the bad victim. Drawing on Brown, Hoffman and Graham align feminism with authoritarianism, reverse sexism, misogyny and protectionism: 'Radical feminists "blame" men and assume that women are impotent or . . . must rely on the state and the law as their "protector"' (p. 516). Accordingly, the solution to the problem of victimhood is envisaged as the disciplining of 'victim feminism' and 'victims of victimhood' away from the position of *ressentiment* and towards a healthier orientation to agency:

> Feminism must find a way that sees women as victims, but avoids victimhood through developing strategies that give women the power and confidence to make inroads into male domination, to act in a way that increases agency and self-determination.
>
> (p. 516)

Here again we see the diagnostic approach to *ressentiment* arrive finally at priestly asceticism – a programme of improving victim behaviour by encouraging intro-spective responsibilization, in order to cultivate the self-determining agency and capacity for action victims are presumed to lack.

In Hoffman and Graham's text, 'victimhood/*ressentiment*' is bequeathed to political theory as a narrow problem concerning the psychology and motivations of victim subjects, rather than a complex problem concerning the conditions, forms and effects of victimization in a given social world. In their interpretation of Brown's anti-*ressentiment* critique as a clinical description of the pathology of victimhood, Hoffman and Graham not only ignore the sociological dimension of Brown's account, they fully convert Brown's account into a critique of victim-hood from the anti-sociological perspective of neoliberal victim theory. Assuming authority as diagnosticians of *ressentiment*, they withdraw authority from those who would speak as victims, powerfully delegitimating this speaking position as bereft of value and insight, blinded by Manichean passions of revenge, and inimical to responsibility. While Brown cautions feminists to pull back from the roman-ticization of powerlessness as a source of truth, Hoffman and Graham delegitimate the epistemology of powerlessness altogether and suggest the perspective of 'victimhood' is inevitably corrupt and misleading. Hoffman and Graham depict the 'victims of victimhood' as benighted and incapable of truth: they are 'unable to understand the real causes of [their] woes and ascribe an imaginary causality to the suffering concerned' (p. 527). They also invoke the motif of the 'vengeful victim' to undermine the notion of a legitimate victim's perspective on ethics, trafficking in the very kinds of representations of the victim one would expect them to critically examine.

Vengeance is an essential trait of the disease of 'victimhood/*ressentiment*' as Hoffman and Graham draw it. Hoffman and Graham suggest that, on the victim's part, an experience of victimization inevitably leads to struggle with the urge for revenge, a struggle that diseased victims resolve by becoming violent avengers and 'easily slipping into' the position of perpetrators (p. 525). As Van Dijk (2009) advises, the motif of the vengeful victim needs to be approached with caution, not only because 'the presumption of the victim's intrinsic punitiveness is largely a myth' (p. 20), but also in view of the semantic heritage of this motif within Christianity, which idealizes the conciliatory, forgiving victim over the angry, vengeful victim and in this way sets the scene for reactive victim scapegoating – the dramatic withdrawal of compassion from victims who are seen to defy the conventions of ideal victimhood, who speak from a place of anger and resentment, who refuse to be conciliatory and forgiving, who want to assume authority in the narration and understanding of their experience of victimization. Victims who 'defy the expected victim role' are positioned as threats to the Christian ethic of forgiveness, which succeeded and outlawed the ancient right (and in some contexts the obligation) to enact revenge with impunity (p. 5). The Christian ethic of forgiveness calls upon the victim to sacrifice the right to revenge and instead practise forgiveness, thus becoming Christ-like, 'seen as a person in the image of Jesus

Christ' (p. 5). The vengeful victim is the foil of the forgiving, Christ-like victim, positioned as a negative icon, an anti-Christ. Rather than excavate and examine the meanings already attached to the figure of the vengeful victim, Hoffman and Graham trade in these meanings, resonating with the Christian ethic of forgiveness as they give vengefulness – the victim's purported will to 'inflict violence' (Hoffman and Graham, 2006, p. 525) – a special place as essential to the pathology of victimhood/*ressentiment*.

Just as we are able, indeed, obliged, to excavate the meanings already attached to the idea of revenge, we are also able to consider the meanings victims ascribe to revenge. The Christian ethic of forgiveness promotes the assumption that the vengeful victim wants to inflict counter-violence, reclaiming the law of *lex talionis*. In his book, *At the Mind's Limits*, Jean Améry discusses his experiences of being subject to this discourse and perceived by others as a vengeful, uncooperative victim in the wake of the Second World War and his experience of capture and torture by the Gestapo. Améry (1980) writes, 'I speak as a victim and examine my resentments' (p. 63). Keenly aware of Nietzsche's influence in discussions of resentment and of the way these discussions readily devolve into judgements of the victim's character, Améry observes that the feeling of resentment 'has been condemned by moralists and psychologists alike. The former regard it as a taint, the latter as a kind of sickness' (p. 64). Pressing against these depictions of resentment, Améry's discussion situates resentment as a profound source of ethical insight. Améry directly critiques the Christian ethic of forgiveness: 'Over two decades of contemplating what happened to me, I believe to have recognised that a forgiving and forgetting induced by social pressure is immoral' (p. 72). His discussion subverts the Christian motif of the vengeful victim in a unique way, providing a different kind of response to the question of what the victim wants.

Améry's response is *not* that the victim wants to inflict violence in return, making the victimizer suffer in the same way they were made to suffer. In fact, for Améry, the idea that one might torture to avenge torture is abhorrent: such revenge would bring torture – for Améry, the horror – back into the world, placing him again in its presence (even as torture has not truly departed his world, for it is unforgettable). With this insight, Améry responds to the way others interpreted his experience of victimization as vulnerability to the will to torture in return, showing how egregiously false this construction of the victim can be: 'Nowhere else could the *jus talionis* [an eye for an eye] make less historic and moral sense than in this instance' (p. 77). Améry's vision of practical settlement between victim and victimizer is somewhat less politically dramatic than a grand scheme of counter-violence: 'The problem could be settled by permitting resentment to remain alive in the one camp and, aroused by it, self-mistrust in the other' (p. 77).

Améry's resentment began *after* his experience of torture, in response to how others attempted to govern his response to this experience. This is the scenario I described in Chapter 2 as 'vulnerability after wounding': Améry's resentment constitutes a form of second-order victimization, a harm added to the original harm. He documents the pressure placed on him to 'let go of hard feelings' as the German nation state recomposed itself in the wake of the Nuremberg trials. Rather than bow to conciliatory survivorship and its erasure of his suffering, Améry 'held against Germany its twelve years under Hitler' (p. 67) – not in the name of violent revenge, but in order to actualize an ethical moment in which 'two groups of people, the overpowered and those who overpowered them, would be joined in the desire that time be turned back and, with it, that history become moral' (p. 78). Améry holds firm to German 'collective guilt', asking for a post-Holocaust Germany that 'would no longer repress or hush up the twelve years that for us others really were a thousand, but claim them as its own negative possession' (p. 78). His resentment wants to affect the future of German consciousness, not through a practice of counter-violence, but by making the bearers of collective guilt share the after-effects of victimization, also experiencing the victim's disrupted time-sense and their situation as 'the captive of the *moral truth* of the conflict' (p. 70, original emphasis). 'My resentments are there in order that the crime become a moral reality for the criminal, in order that he be swept into the truth of his atrocity' (p. 70).

This discussion has sought to demonstrate that on the topic of victimhood students of political theory need to do more than learn how to diagnose the 'pathology of victimhood'. Instead of schooling students in received neoliberal and Christian constructions of the bad victim, Hoffman and Graham's primer ought to prompt critical analysis of these very constructions, as well as engagement with victims' perspectives on primary and secondary victimization, and awareness of the Christian heritage that implicitly informs our purportedly secular forms of victim talk and ways of reacting to victims. Van Dijk (2009) beckons a critical victimology that examines constructions of the victim and values the victim's perspective. In view of the way Hoffman and Graham draw the 'problem of victimhood', the same case can be made for developing critical perspectives on victimhood in the context of political theory.

Beyond *ressentiment*?

The theorizations of feminist *ressentiment* examined in the previous sections complicate Michèle Le Dœuff's (1987) dictum, 'For feminism does not create its object for itself. Sexism comes first' (p. 41). While feminism does not create its object for itself, it does, according to these theorizations, host knowledges, practices, identities and postures that 'recreate' the scenarios of sexist oppression: the politico-legal constitution of women as vulnerable subjects who require protection, the conception of patriarchal power as total and unflinching, and reiterative attachment to victim identity. Despite this apparent unanimity, however, my analysis has shown that theorists of feminist *ressentiment* make conflicting judgements concerning where and how the resubordinative dynamics of *ressentiment* play out in the heterogeneous domain of feminist politics. Cocks and Brown ask that we imagine feminism's politics of *ressentiment* as a vengeful moralism that is uncritically statist and insufficiently radical, while Yeatman identifies feminist *ressentiment* with the radical's refusal to engage in statist reformism. Yeatman suggests we imagine feminism beyond *ressentiment* as a politics that works critically within, rather than antagonistically against, liberalism's universalist political culture and neoliberalism systems of self-regulation and personal responsibility. Yet Brown situates liberal universalism as a path to depoliticization and to the forfeiting of political freedom, while also identifying the role of (neo)liberal discourses of self-regulation in the very production of *ressentiment*. Many have been ready to echo the call for feminism to move 'beyond' the politics of *ressentiment*, yet the theoretical accounts issuing this call offer mixed messages about where feminism can be said to engage in or exceed the politics of *ressentiment* in the first instance.

In terms of their entanglement in the politics of neoliberalism, the discussions of feminist victim politics by Cocks, Yeatman and Brown are more subtle and generative compared with those of their popular press counterparts, and they are not centrally concerned to render feminist accounts of masculine dominance as irrational fictions. Yet, like their popular counterparts, they overlap with neoliberal victim theory in various ways, from Yeatman's measured endorsement of neoliberal welfare reform through to their participation in the pathologization of *ressentiment*, by which victimization is framed as a problem concerning the inner psychology of victim subjects rather than as a problem concerning systemic injustice and inequality in the wider social world. Brown's sociological approach to *ressentiment* is promising because it strikes against this trend, opening a window onto a different kind of engagement with feminism, *ressentiment* and the politics of victimization – one that focuses on *ressentiment*'s conditions of possibility rather than its 'symptoms', deepening the question of what it means to move 'beyond *ressentiment*' by suggesting that such a move requires reckoning with the conditions of possibility for *ressentiment*, not self-improvement on the part of the resentful. I will explore this different approach among other dimensions of *ressentiment* in Chapter 4, where I analyse the intriguingly protean form of victim theory Nietzsche proposes in his account of an unfolding history of slave revolt.

Having explored the Nietzschean theme of the theorizations of feminist *ressentiment* and their diagnoses of feminism, in the final section of the chapter I want to return to and consider the way these theorizations extend the diagnosis of political *ressentiment* beyond feminism and apply it to anti-racist and anti-colonial political struggles. As my discussion above makes clear, the theorizations of feminist *ressentiment*, especially those of Yeatman and Brown, are responding to anti-racist and postcolonial feminist critiques of Western feminist universalism, furthering warranted scrutiny of the themes of victimhood and agency in Western feminist depictions of gendered suffering. Yet where Cocks, Yeatman and Brown identify the problem of *ressentiment* with anti-racist and anti-colonial political struggles, they seem to double the anti-*ressentiment* critique back on the political forms that have given rise to the very critique of Western feminist universalism that they are responding to. To consider this predicament I explore a last set of anti-victim texts: anti-racist and postcolonial feminist articulations of the anti-victim critique.

Western feminism and the victim/agent dichotomy

As Gudrun Dahl (2009) observes, in the academic humanities the 'Agents Not Victims' trope represents a shift in the ethics of 'respectful writing' (p. 392), particularly in the context of Western scholars engaging in cross-cultural or transnational research, away from writing that addresses 'the other' as valuable depending on their perceived degree of rationality, towards writing that is seen to assume a relation of 'respectful co-humanness' with 'research informants' (p. 392). Situating research informants as 'Agents Not Victims' avoids the discursive foreclosure of the informants' agency that is seen to take place when informants are represented as '"damned victims, rather than capable people"' (p. 392). In particular, addressing the other as an agent rather than a victim is thought to mark a break with the Western colonial history of representationally effacing the humanity and contemporariness of colonized peoples. Dahl's examples of the Agents Not Victims trope, drawn from academic discussion and media, demonstrate that non-Western women are seen as being especially subject to stereotypical representation in the West as agency-less victims, thus standing in greatest need of the ethical shift to agent identity. As Kaplana Wilson (2011) has observed, the shift to agent identity in the representation of Third World peoples, in particular, women, is in part a response to landmark postcolonial feminist critiques of the theme of victimhood in Western feminism by theorists such as Chandra Mohanty (1986) and Gayatri Chakraborty Spivak (1988).

In this section I explore the anti-victim critiques that take shape in the work of bell hooks (1984), Ratna Kapur (2002) and Rey Chow (2002), before engaging with Wilson's recent critique of the category 'agent' in the politics of Third World development. Collectively this work reveals a complex web of gendered and racialized constructions of victimhood and agency, productively interrogating cultural essentialism and the permeable borders between feminist, imperialist and settler colonial tropes in the representation of gendered suffering. In this work we find familiar complaint about the concept of 'victim', but also a discernible wariness of 'agency' as a suitable thematic replacement to 'victim' in the representation of subaltern subjects. Though they are said to have inspired the Agents Not Victims trope, neither Mohanty nor Spivak advocated a move to 'agency' as a solution to the victim problem. In the work I survey here, it is only Kapur (2002), following Brown (1995), who positively advocates a shift to 'agency', though Kapur sees agency as situated and constrained and briefly but explicitly distinguishes her conception of agency from the liberal discourse of agency as autonomous self-making. Similarly, hooks problematizes victimhood without advocating a shift to agency, instead invoking a language of survivorship. This greater wariness of the concept of agency and the overall critique of the victim/agent dichotomy as racialized distinguish this work from other versions of the anti-victim critique, marking a break with the logic of neoliberal victim theory though by no means an active critique of it. Only in more recent work such as Wilson's, which I discuss at the conclusion of this section, does an active critique of neoliberalism in relation to the racialized categories of 'victim' and 'agent' fully take shape.

We saw in Chapter 2 that bell hooks' (1984) critique of victim identity in feminism sought to expose the gendered dynamics of race-ethnicity and class set around feminism's woman-as-victim theme. Challenging second-wave feminism's global call for women to bond on the basis of a shared identity as victims of male domination, hooks deftly shows how this gesture reproduces white privilege within and beyond feminist politics. When white bourgeois feminists discursively constitute 'other women' as fellow victims of patriarchy within a politics that pits 'woman' against 'man', they erase differences among women, the power structures that produce inequality among women and their own situatedness within those structures. Rather than claim that 'other women' are *not* victimized in a context of hierarchy, segregation and inequality, hooks invokes the language of survivorship, an alternative conception of resilience-amidst-victimization that bears witness to the daily actions women take to sustain themselves amidst poverty, disenfranchisement and marginalization.

Following Mohanty (1986) and Spivak (1988), in the 1990s and 2000s, postcolonial critics developed this argument in a different direction, focusing on the way the Western feminist conception of non-Western women as fellow victims tends to devolve into a conception of non-Western women as more extremely abject victims of 'barbaric cultural tradition'. In the representational scenario Mohanty critiqued in her landmark essay 'Under Western Eyes', the Third World woman, portrayed as 'ignorant, poor, uneducated, tradition-bound, domestic, family-oriented, victimized', provides a ground of contrast for the '(implicit) self-representation of western women as educated, modern, as having control over their own bodies and sexualities, and the freedom to make their own decisions' (Mohanty, 1986, p. 337). Mohanty's argument thus reveals the status of 'agency' as an articulation of empowered feminine whiteness. Reminiscent of Etienne Balibar's (1991) argument that neo-racism has replaced biology with culture as the marker of essentialized racial difference, critics such as Uma Narayan (1997) and Ratna Kapur (2002) have traced the workings of cultural essentialism in Western feminism's address to non-Western women, arguing that cultural essentialism shows itself in Western feminist portrayal of non-Western women as extreme authentic victims.

In a powerful critique of international feminist human rights campaigns targeting violence against women, Ratna Kapur (2002) argues that these campaigns centre on 'the victim subject', a discursive trope that can reinforce exoticizing constructions of gendered violence in non-Western contexts as timeworn cultural practices, reviving the imperialist view of the 'native subject as different and civilizationally backward' (p. 12). Drawing on Uma Narayan's (1997) critique of cultural essentialism in media representations of dowry murders in India, Kapur (2002) observes that dowry murders are rendered in Western national contexts as a cultural phenomenon, a form of 'death by culture' (Narayan, 1997, p. 42), while analogous forms of violence in Western contexts, such as domestic violence murders, are not. Culturally essentialist feminist depictions of gendered violence in non-Western contexts representationally cleanse the West of patriarchalism, rendering non-Western women in ways reminiscent of 'the colonial construction of the Eastern woman' (Kapur, 2002, p. 18). Positioned as 'not yet a "whole or developed" person' (p. 19, citing Kempadoo, 1998, p. 11), the non-Western woman is representationally 'emaciated', while the Western woman is representationally 'emancipated':

> The image that is produced is that of a truncated Third World woman who is sexually constrained, tradition-bound, incarcerated in the home, illiterate, and poor . . . In striking contrast to this emaciated image stands the image of the emancipated Western woman; she has 'control over her income, her body and her sexuality'.
>
> (Kapur, 2002, pp. 18–19, citing Kempadoo, 1998, p. 11)

The emaciated/emancipated binary 'reproduces the colonialist rationale for intervening in the lives of the native subject' (Kapur, 2002, p. 19), renewing the discursive figuration of the West as 'white saviour'.

Kapur's analysis situates 'victim' and 'agent' as political signs with gendered and racialized colonial histories, the tropes of which can be reproduced or interrupted in the context of international feminist politics. Kapur urges feminists away from shaping international feminist movement around the victim subject, beckoning alternative representations of non-Western women as 'peripheral' and 'resistive' subjects and encouraging a 'deeper and more rigorous kind of contextual analysis' (p. 17). Kapur conceives this as a representational shift from 'victim' to 'agent', but at the very end of her essay she briefly specifies her conception of agency, distinguishing it from the liberal conception of autonomous self-making: 'It is an agency that is neither situated exclusively in the individual nor denied because of some overarching oppression. It is situated in the structures of social relationships, the location of the subject, and the shape-shifting of culture' (p. 37). Kapur counsels movement away from the victim subject but persists in using the term 'victim'. She argues that part of the problem with international feminism's focus on violence against women is that this focus marginalizes other significant respects in which non-Western women are 'victims of rights violations' (p. 17).

Developing the view that white bourgeois feminism *imposes* a shared or more extreme victim identity upon the 'other woman', Rey Chow (2002) discerns that Western feminism can also move in the other direction, *monopolizing* victim identity on behalf of white bourgeois women, disregarding the victimization of the 'other woman'. Chow discusses victim identity in the context of colonial captivity narrative, observing that dominant tropes of white femininity have been conceptualized historically around the culture-crossing figure of the white woman captive, wrought in the widely read epistolary texts of seventeenth-century captivity narrative and its offspring in fiction in the centuries since. Chow draws on Nancy Armstrong's argument that at the apex of its power the British Empire paradoxically imagined Englishness through the altero-referential racist trope of the abducted white woman: 'a kind of epistolary heroine, whose ability to read and write distinguished her, more than anything else, from her Indian captors' (Armstrong, 1998, p. 204).[7] In this narrative trope the white woman captive's unfolding experience of suffering and endangerment is centred and humanized, becoming a symbol of settler colonial identity that performs the ideological work of marking the Indigenous other as malicious and profane, obscuring the actual geopolitical situation of colonial capture and occupation of Indigenous lands. In a representational reversal, the trope of the white woman captive conceals the power of Empire, rendering colonized peoples as threateningly dominant. Developing on Armstrong's argument that in English fiction captivity narrative becomes protofeminist in the sense of giving rise to a critique of white bourgeois masculinity, Chow (2002) argues that the trope of the white woman captive carries over into feminist politics, with Western feminism characterized by a 'racialist reluctance to give up the hold on victimhood', a 'tendency to monopolise and capitalise on victimhood' and a reluctance to 'dislodge white women from their preferred status as the representatives of alterity throughout Western history' (p. 179).

In relation to Chow's argument that white feminism monopolizes victimhood, it is worth noting the ambivalence of the figure of the white woman captive. As conveyed in the deliberate double-meaning of the title of Christopher Castaglia's book about this figure, *Bound and Determined* (1996), in captivity narrative the white woman captive is not figured as an agency-less victim: she is figured as a victim and an agent, 'bound up' and 'bound for', 'determined by' and 'determining'. Supporting my argument in Chapter 2 that where figurations of femininity, victimhood and agency are concerned, there is rarely a simple victim/agent dichotomy in play but instead a complex maths of victim-agent combinations and distinctions, the white woman captive most commonly is figured as a resilient victim – an active but endangered subject whose return from capture and subsequent narration of her experience reiterate the legitimacy of the colonizing mission, visibly affirming her natal values and ways of life while visibly exoticizing Indigenous values and ways of life. In light of the captive's ambivalent figuration as an agentic victim, the monopolization of victimhood by white feminism identified by Chow is consistent with the racialized emancipated/emaciated binary identified by other scholars, by which Western women are said to monopolize agency. Colonial captivity narratives bequeath an agentic, resilient, literate and eventually emancipated victim, rather than a helpless, passive and silent victim.

Collectively the critical work I have surveyed here suggests that feminist efforts to signify female suffering can be bound up in processes of racialization in ways that serve to humanize white Western women as actively signifying and authoritative, relegating non-Western women either to invisibility, or to an objectifying representation as being both 'unseen' and 'unseeing' sufferers (Moreton-Robinson, 2003, p. 67). Either the non-Western woman is excluded from victim recognition while the struggles of white women are centred and humanized; or the non-Western woman is included by way of a dehumanizing representation as a more complete victim – totally or more abjectly dominated by male despotism, robbed of the ability to actively signify her own experience, standing in need of rescue by Western feminists, who appear in contrast as personally and politically more knowing and agentic. As such, the critical work I have surveyed raises the concluding points of my analysis, concerning the politics of difference in feminist anti-victim and anti-*ressentiment* critique.

The critical work I have surveyed helps to show the thematic context in which the theorizations of feminist *ressentiment* emerged, speaking to a significant difference between these theorizations and the popular press critiques of 'victim feminism'. While Yeatman and Brown are clearly responding to anti-racist and postcolonial critiques of the racialist tropes of western feminist universalism, in contrast, their counterparts in the popular press *reiterate* these racialist tropes, boldly replicating the emancipated/emaciated binary in their shared assertion that Western women are no longer victims while non-Western women still are. As discerned in Chapter 1, from the perspective of the popular press critiques of victim feminism, calling Western women victims is insulting, infantilizing, destructive and misleading, for these women now have autonomous agency, living as they do in the postfeminist West. On the other hand, from the perspective of these critiques, calling non-Western women victims is appropriate and ethical. Mired in the kinds of really existing conditions of patriarchal oppression that belong to the Western past, these women lack autonomous agency, their cultural settings standing in need of the modernizing interventions of Western feminism.

That the popular press critiques of victim feminism are racialized in this way explains why Hoff Sommer's critique in the 1990s segued neatly into her support for the wars on terror in the 2000s, wars that sought legitimacy in part through discursive self-presentation as movements for Islamic women's liberation (see Riley, Mohanty and Pratt, 2008). In replicating this binary of Western women as 'emancipated agents' and non-Western women as 'emaciated victims' and 'agents-in-waiting', the popular press critiques of victim feminism demonstrate how temporal constructions of the contemporary West as 'postfeminist' can participate in what Helliwell and Hindess (2005, 2013) call the temporalizing of difference, or the perception of non-Western people as existing in conditions of life previously overcome in the West. As Helliwell and Hindess (2013) argue, far from being politically benign, the temporalization of difference carries the consequence of differential valuing of life: 'in contemporary Western social thought, those who are seen as belonging to the present assume a greater moral and political significance than those who are seen as belonging to the past' (p. 73). More specifically, 'perceived temporal backwardness' is associated with 'a perceived lack of real individuality', thus is 'accorded a lower value' (p. 79).

Unlike their counterparts in the popular press, the theorizations of feminist *ressentiment* avoid participating in cultural essentialism and the emancipated/emaciated binary. Yet there are problems with how they respond to anti-racist and postcolonial feminist versions of the anti-victim critique, and here I want to return to the point that in the anti-racist and postcolonial feminist critiques 'agency' is nowhere posited as an unproblematic alternative to 'victim'. The critical work by Mohanty, Spivak, hooks, Kapur and Chow is anti-victim critique in the sense that their different analyses all press against Western feminism's woman-as-victim theme; yet it cannot be said that this body of work advances anti-victim critique through the Agents Not Victims trope, or the related phenomenon I am calling the victim-bad/agent-good formulation. In this body of work the criticisms of 'victim' do reflect 'victim-bad': hooks and Kapur frame 'victim' as an inevitably reductive identity carrying necessary connotations of passivity and helplessness, while Chow's analysis foregrounds the theme of the suspect victim as a bad agent whose claim on victim identity is a bid for power. Yet the real object of critique in this work is not 'victim' but, more broadly, the victim/agent dichotomy, with 'agency' actively critiqued as a racialized concept and nowhere posited as an unproblematic alternative to 'victim'. Despite this, however, anti-racist and postcolonial feminist articulations of the anti-victim critique have been interpreted as establishing the need to see non-Western women as 'Agents Not Victims', rather than the need to critically reappraise the victim/agent dichotomy and recognize its racialist configurations.

This interpretation is evident in the theorizations of feminist *ressentiment* by Cocks, Yeatman and Brown, which pick up and develop the critique of the notion of 'victim' in Western feminism, but without carrying over the same wariness of 'agency' that is evident in the anti-racist and postcolonial feminist work they are responding to, instead articulating a Nietzschean version of the victim-bad/agent-good formulation, cast in the Nietzschean distinctions between reactive and active forces, states of sickness and health, and the slavish and noble human types. As Kaplana Wilson (2011) observes, 'Critiques of the essentialisation of people in the South—and of women in particular—as passively suffering victims have been widely interpreted as an imperative to represent these women as universally enterprising, productive and happy' (p. 328). Reflecting my scepticism in Chapter 2 about the emancipatory potential of 'woman-as-agent' constructions in the politicization of rape, Wilson provides an important critique of the visual production of women-as-agent constructions in the context of neoliberal capitalism and the globalization of citizenship. I will briefly outline her critique, before reaching my final point, concerning the way, on the margins of their texts, theorists of feminist *ressentiment* bundle anti-racist and anti-colonial political struggles in with the spectrum of political forms they diagnose as afflicted with *ressentiment*.

Wilson and Gudrun Dahl warn that, while the shift to agent identity in the representation of Third World peoples appears to remedy the victim label's egregious foreclosure of agency, this shift is a neoliberal turn that requires scrutiny. The Agents Not Victims trope works on behalf of neoliberalism in the context of supra-national programmes of structural adjustment in the 'developing' world, normalizing the privileging of autonomous entrepreneurial agency and the derogation of victimhood as self-made (Dahl, 2009, pp. 404–405). The Agents Not Victims trope has become generalized with the globalization of citizenship, which enacts a partial shift in the Western perception of non-Western peoples in relation to citizenship and the capacity for autonomy and self-government. As Hindess (2002) has observed, in non-Western contexts, neoliberal programmes of structural adjustment promote democratization, 'good governance' and citizenship concurrently with market regulation and integration within the international market system. The promotion of democratization and 'good governance' globalizes citizenship, while the concurrent promotion of market regulation and integration hollows out the social and political rights that go with citizenship. Social rights are noticeably more restricted in parts of the world designated as 'developing', which unlike the neoliberal states of the West are 'subject also to the further rigours of the international development regime' (Hindess, 2002, p. 140). The promotion of citizenship in parts of the world identified as 'developing' in many cases reverses an historical exclusion of colonized peoples from citizenship, displacing imperialist perception of colonized peoples as lacking the capacity for civil self-government and thus fitness for citizenship, with a post-imperialist perception of colonized peoples as 'autonomous agents' within the global market system (p. 139). In this ostensibly decolonizing representational shift from 'victim' to 'agent' the capacity for self-government is recognized, but at the expense of recognizing new constraints on individual agency imposed by the market system in the context of neoliberal economic reform (p. 139).

Complementing this reading of 'victim' and 'agent' in the context of globalized neoliberal citizenship, Wilson (2011) observes that 'the notion of women's "agency" has become ubiquitous within approaches to gender and development, and has been incorporated into neoliberal development discourses', creating 'new,' 'positive' representations of women in the global South as 'hyper-industrious entrepreneurial agents' (p. 315). Wilson's analysis traces 'the shift to "positive images" of women in the global South by international NGOs, donor governments, the World Bank and other development institutions' (p. 315) which began in the late 1980s and accelerated through the 1990s and into the 2000s. Growing investment in the notion of women's agency in the arena of international politics is reflected in the way the General Assembly of European NGOs updated its *Code of Conduct on Images and Messages Relating to the Third World* in 1989. The updated code vows to bear witness to Third World peoples' 'ability to take responsibility for themselves' (cited in Wilson, 2011, p. 322) and to move beyond portrayals of Third World women as 'poor and powerless . . . dependent victims' through 'positive change in the images projected of Southern women' (cited in Wilson, 2011, p. 321) in NGO education materials disseminated in symbiotic relationship with media.[8] Rather than demonstrating ethically improved transnational address, as the Agents Not Victims move is presumed to do, Wilson's analysis shows that the shift to positive images serves to legitimate one of the most contentious aspects in the gendered politics of neoliberal programs of structural adjustment: their 'instrumentalisation of poor women' (Wilson, 2011, p. 319), or the use of women's intensified labour in low-income households 'as a buffer against the ravages of economic reforms' (p. 318). The shift to positive images also helps to make political resistance to imposed reform invisible (or, I would add, visible only in pathologizing and depoliticizing ways). Wilson's analysis shows that the shift to positive imagery does not create new postcolonial imagery, instead recalling and updating the visual tropes of colonialist representations of indentured workers. I quote Wilson at length as she elaborates the relationship between the feminization of survival, the silencing of dissent, and the perpetuation of colonial discourses in the turn to 'agency' and 'resilience':

> [C]ontemporary 'positive' visual representations of women in the South produced by development institutions are rooted in a notion of 'agency' consistent with—and necessary for—neoliberal capitalism. These 'new' constructions contribute to, rather than subvert, racialised regimes of representation . . . These 'positive' images are consistent with the current neoliberal development consensus which . . . portrays an intensification of labour applied by women in the South as the 'solution' to poverty as well as gender inequality. They operate in the same way as the images of 'contented and productive' women workers in colonial enterprises used in British advertising in the late 19th and early 20th centuries: to reassure the viewer of the legitimacy and justice of existing relationships and structures . . . Like their colonial predecessors, today's images work to silence or obscure multiple forms of resistance to contemporary imperialism.
>
> (pp. 328–329)

Importantly, Wilson's critique of the shift to positive images is not an argument for returning to the theme of the Third World woman as 'ultimate victim'. Instead, her critique shows how the theme of agency performs particular ideological work on behalf of neoliberalism, demonstrating the continued presence and practical consequences of liberal political reason in the lives of non-Western people.

While the shift to positive images Wilson describes involves development NGOs and media disciplining their own representations of non-Western peoples, the anti-victim critique is also directed against colonized peoples who, despite the globalization of citizenship and the decolonizing gestures of contemporary liberalism, persist in self-presentation as victims of colonization. Just as there have been critiques of 'victim feminism' within and against feminism, so too have there been critiques of victim identity within and against Indigenous politics. As Glen Coulthard (2012) describes, in the contemporary Canadian context the state's address to First Nations peoples is structured around the 'neo-colonial framework of forgiveness, recognition and reconciliation' (p. 1), promoted by government as 'morally superior', with government statements of apology for historical wrongs attended by the expectation that apology will be met with forgiveness, marking closure.[9] Reflecting the Christian ethic of forgiveness, in the morality of the reconciliation framework Indigenous forgiveness is valorized while Indigenous anger and dissent are pathologized as 'resentment' and 'victim mentality'. The anti-colonial political movement contesting the premises and processes of the reconciliation framework and giving visibility to the ongoing legacies and relations of colonization – to the status of Indigenous people as 'still subject to the ongoing structural and symbolic violence of dispossession and settler-state governance' –

127

is seen as arising from the vengeful emotion of resentment, portrayed as a disabling psychic attachment to anger over historical victimization (p. 1; see also Coulthard, 2007). In the Australian context, the critical stance against Indigenous resentment that Coulthard describes takes shape in the critique of 'black armband history' (Macintyre and Clark, 2003), articulated amidst a shift in Indigenous policy towards a neoliberal framework of 'practical reconciliation', which posits victim mentality and resentment as disruptive to, and ameliorated by, personal responsibility and market readiness (see Moreton-Robinson, 2009, 2011). Where Dahl's original analysis of the Agents Not Victims trope observes its role in altering Western representations of non-Western peoples, Coulthard's discussion indicates that the Agents Not Victims trope is also operative in the disciplining of Indigenous *self-presentation*, its construction of the good Indigenous citizen as a forgiving, responsible, market-ready individual masking the continued legacies of colonialism, framing colonialism as an 'event' rather than a 'structure' (Coulthard, 2012, p. 1; Wolfe, 2006).

Coulthard's analysis cautions that political theory's anti-*ressentiment* critiques easily become a discursive support for the values of the neocolonial reconciliation framework. In the theorizations of feminist *ressentiment* examined in this chapter the primary focus is feminist *ressentiment*, but Cocks and Yeatman both situate anti-colonialism within the broad downward trend towards *ressentiment* in radical political struggles, while Brown (1995) focuses on feminist *ressentiment* and then extends the analysis to identity politics more broadly, identifying *ressentiment* with the spectrum of 'politicized identities' centred on 'race, gender and sexuality' (p. 60). Their diagnoses of broad radical political malaise suggest that *all* those engaged in radical political struggles are at risk of or afflicted by *ressentiment* – including the domains of anti-racist and anti-colonial struggle, from which the challenge to Western feminist universalism emerged. Their development of the anti-racist and postcolonial anti-victim critique into the postmodern feminist anti-*ressentiment* critique is oriented to furthering warranted scrutiny of Western feminism. As Coulthard's analysis cautions, however, the anti-*ressentiment* critique is conceptually in step with neocolonialism, taking on conservative political uses in the context of settler colonial governance by reaffirming the official valorization of healthy responsible forgiveness over sick complaining resentment. Ultimately, then, the relationship between feminist political theory's anti-*ressentiment* critiques and the colonizing gestures of Western feminism needs to be weighed against the discursive support these critiques provide for the practical disciplining of Indigenous political subjects away from the attitude of resentment and towards the more compliant position of forgiveness idealized in settler colonialism's recon-ciliation phase.

Notes

1   The notable exception to this is Marion Tapper's (1993) theorization of feminist *ressentiment* in her chapter '*Ressentiment* and Power', which I do not analyse here because it closely approximates the popular press critiques of 'victim feminism',

presenting terrain already examined in Chapter 1. Tapper advances the same claims found in the 'victim feminism' critiques: that feminists regard women as passive victims, eliding women's agency and current position of equal opportunity amidst patriarchal decline. Addressing the sphere of Australian universities, Tapper (1993) argues that in this sphere 'women have roughly achieved equal power', but feminists are denying this because they are led by *ressentiment*, characterized by 'a need to see women as helpless victims' when factually they are not (p. 134). In hindsight we can see that Tapper's claims about the achievement of gender equality in universities were seriously overblown. As research in this area has continued to attest, Australian universities are sites of pronounced inequality. In a labour market pattern typical of professional workforces, as David Robinson (2006) observes, 'Women academics remain seriously under-represented and under-paid compared to their male colleagues. The gender gap is most pronounced within the most senior academic ranks' (p. 1; see also Dever, 2008).

2   Yeatman's discussion of feminist *ressentiment* arose in the context of the Huggins-Bell debate in Australia, concerning white feminist practices of marginalizing and appropriating the voices and perspectives of Indigenous women. On the Huggins-Bell debate, see Bell and Nelson (1989), Larbalestier (1990), Huggins et al. (1991), Yeatman (1993), Moreton-Robinson (2003), Due and Riggs (2012) and Stringer (2012).

3   Fully exploring feminist engagement with Nietzsche is beyond the scope of this chapter, but I do want to acknowledge and chart some of the discussions and engagements that have taken place in this area of Nietzsche scholarship. Many significant contributions to Anglophone feminist discussions of Nietzsche are collected in volumes edited by Clark and Lange (1979), Burgard (1994), Bar On (1994) and Oliver and Pearsall (1998). A number of feminist philosophers have provided important and influential discussions of Nietzsche, including Deutscher (1993), Diprose (1989, 1994), Irigaray (1991), Schutte (1984, 1994), Oliver (1995), Bergoffen (1989, 1994) and Picart (1999). A variety of perspectives on Nietzsche's philosophy in relation to feminism, gender and sexual difference can be found among Schrift (1994), Abbey (1996), Del Caro (1990), Wininger (1998), Appel (1997), Kennedy (1987), Behler (1993), Burney-Davis and King (1989), Bertram (1984) and Hatab (1981). A number of Nietzsche's feminist commentators have provided important accounts of the role of maternity in Nietzsche's metaphorics, including Oliver (1995), Kofman (1994), Picart (1999), Ainley (1988) and Graybeal (1998). Accounts of the feminisms contemporary to Nietzsche and influenced by him can be found in Diethe (1989), Aschheim (1992), Thomas (1983), Schmidt (1993), Evans (1976), Thonnessen (1973) and Bridenthal, Grossman and Kaplan (1984).

4   Cocks critiques Nietzsche's concept of master morality (Cocks, 1991, p. 155), while Brown (1995) argues Nietzschean values are 'excessively individualized' (p. 48). See also Brown (2000).

5   Yeatman's political theory draws on the work of Jacques Rancière (1992) and shares ground with the radical democracy project formulated by Ernesto Laclau and Chantal Mouffe (1985), initially in their book, *Hegemony and Socialist Strategy: Towards a Radical Democratic Politics*. Laclau and Mouffe's poststructuralist radical democratic project theorizes a form of democracy capable of conducting a pluralist mode of coexistence without, on the one hand, suppressing antagonisms arising from difference in the interests of achieving final harmony and, on the other hand, treating differences as given identities which simply require valorization (as in interest group pluralism and identity politics). As Mouffe (1996) outlines:

To acknowledge the existence of relations of power and the need to transform them, while renouncing the illusion that we could free ourselves completely from power: this is what is specific to the project that we have called 'radical and plural democracy' . . . In a democratic polity, conflicts and confrontations, far from being a sign of imperfection, indicate that democracy is alive and inhabited by pluralism.

(pp. 248–255)

Wendy Brown critiques this conception of radical democracy (Brown, 1995, pp. 11–13, 57 n.7).

6   Brown (1995) argues that identity politics centred on gender, sexuality and race-ethnicity may be interpreted as a 'peculiarly disguised form of class resentment' (p. 60) by which the injurious effects of capitalism are displaced from the category of class onto the explicitly politicized non-class category.

7   On the politics of captivity narrative, see also Tennenhouse (1996), Armstrong and Tennenhouse (1992), Spivak (1985), Castaglia (1996), Schaffer and Randall (2001), Logan (1993), Lougheed (2002) and Sharpe (1993).

8   Wilson acknowledges that with the rise of positive woman-as-agent imagery, the circulation of images of lone children did not abate (Wilson, 2011, p. 322, discussing Manzo, 2008).

9   These quotes are drawn from the abstract for Coulthard's (2012) public lecture at Dalhousie University, Halifax, Canada, 'Seeing Red: Recognition, Reconciliation and Resentment in Indigenous Politics'. The abstract can be found at: http://halifax.mediacoop.ca/events/9499 (accessed 10 November 2013).

4

RETHINKING *RESSENTIMENT*

Nietzsche and the victim subject
in neoliberal times

Where the previous chapters have focused on examining the presence of anti-victimism in feminism, this final chapter gives prominence to the second task I have been undertaking amidst these analyses, that of identifying progressive conceptions of the victim that provide alternatives to neoliberal victim theory and, as such, might aid in challenging its dominance in contemporary victim talk. In this light I have discussed, Lyotard's theory of the differend, the SlutWalk movement's campaign against victim-blaming, and anti-racist and postcolonial feminist critiques of the victim/agent dichotomy in Western feminism, among other examples. In this chapter I propose that Nietzsche's theory of *ressentiment* belongs to this archive of alternative conceptions of the victim, despite its affinity and current interconnection with neoliberal victim theory. As we saw in Chapter 3, Nietzsche's theory of *ressentiment* is presently a key resource for anti-victimism. Nietzsche's emphasis on character and psychology in the question of morality dovetails with the individualizing, psychologizing and pathologizing discourses that have redefined and reframed 'victimhood', 'resentment' and 'feminism' in the neoliberal era. This is reinforced in the diagnostic approach to Nietzsche's theory adopted in the theorizations of feminist *ressentiment*, which follow what Henry Staten (1990) calls Nietzsche's 'official attitude of condemnation' (p. 59) of *ressentiment*. Avoiding the diagnostic approach, in this chapter I interpret Nietzsche's theory through the alternative approach of critical exegesis, which proves fruitful for finding in Nietzsche's theory significant resources for unsettling, critiquing and countering neoliberal victim theory, rather than supporting its precepts. Van Dijk (2009, p. 5) has already observed that Nietzsche's critique of Christian morality – of the Christian valuing of 'what is unegoistic' and hostility to 'what is egoistic' (EH: Dawn, 2)[1] – is relevant to challenging contemporary versions of the Christian ethic of forgiveness that value 'unegoistic', forgiving victims and demonize 'egoistic', complaining victims. Concentrating on Nietzsche's account of the master–slave relation and the origins of the state rather than his critique of Christianity, my analysis finds further sites of productive intersection with the Nietzschean critique. In particular, I show where Nietzsche conceives of victim identity as a source of identificatory transformation rather than fixity; I argue that Nietzsche's discussion of asceticism provides a strikingly apt analogy for interpreting the contemporary relationship between feminism and neoliberalism; and I conclude with a critical interpretation of neoliberal victim theory as 'asceticism' in Nietzsche's sense.

Glen Coulthard (2012) has observed that contemporary anti-*ressentiment* critiques strip the concept of *ressentiment* of Nietzsche's elitism. They give insufficient visibility to the connection between Nietzsche's condemnation of *ressentiment* and his idea that, in order for human greatness to thrive among the 'healthiest' human types, human societies need to institute an 'order of rank' (BGE: 257) that segregates the higher and lower types. As we saw in Chapter 3, theorists of feminist *ressentiment* engage critically and autonomously with Nietzsche's philosophy and its 'ugly politics' (Cocks, 1991, p. 145). Yet the diagnostic approach to *ressentiment* they adopt continues to give voice to Nietzsche's elitism because it constitutes *ressentiment* as always already 'bad', assuming the classically elitist authority to mark the presence of lesser, decadent beings. As Robert C. Solomon (1994) observes in his discussion of Nietzsche's *On the Genealogy of Morals*, 'the unavoidable message of the diagnosis of resentment and the pathology-laden language that surrounds it is that slave morality is *bad*' (p. 99, original emphasis). Beyond the questionable ethics of the diagnostic gesture, a further problem with the diagnostic approach to Nietzsche's theory of *ressentiment* is that this approach operates as a kind of lightning rod that ushers attention away not only from Nietzsche's elitism, but also from the wider story Nietzsche tells about the unfolding of *ressentiment* within a dynamic master–slave relation. This wider story permits focus on the structural sources of *ressentiment*, as opposed to focusing on the ignoble traits of the resentful.[2] My discussion in this chapter brings out this wider story.

Anti-*ressentiment* critiques typically use the term *ressentiment* as though it were stable in meaning – a solid referent for an existing disease – but when we take in Nietzsche's wider story we see that '*ressentiment*' unfolds in phases within an inherently unstable power relationship and has at least three meanings. First, there is 'brute' (Deleuze, 1983, p. 126) or 'non-creative' (Ridley, 1998, p. 23) *ressentiment*. Second, there is creative *ressentiment*, referring to the moment in which a slave class creates a counter-morality that delegitimates their oppression. Third, and crucially, I argue here, there is explosive/contained *ressentiment*. This refers to the moment in which the *ressentiment* of the slaves poses a threat to the social order that has brought it into being (explosive) and is brought to terms (contained) through processes of resignification, responsibilization and recuperation. As I observed in Chapter 3, I concur with theorists of feminist *ressentiment* that Nietzsche's theory offers important political lessons about feminism and the dynamics of victim politics. But I argue here that our conception of what these lessons are shifts considerably when we take in the full sweep of the theory and reckon more openly with its elitism, which is embedded in the theory rather than being incidental to it.

Concentrating primarily on the theory of *ressentiment* as it unfolds in Nietzsche's *On the Genealogy of Morals*, in this chapter I follow *ressentiment* through its different phases and emerge with a reading that unsettles the dominant representation of *ressentiment* as delivering only the 'victory of the slave *as* slave' (Deleuze, 1983, p. 117, original emphasis), or a resubordinative equation of suffering with virtue that gives rise to fixed victim identity and naïve Manicheanism. I argue that in the moment of slave revolt the slaves do not become attached to a self-identity as virtuous victims; instead slave revolt leads to an identificatory upheaval that opens social being to contingency, making it possible for the slaves to take up political agency and contest the conditions of their existence. I use Nietzsche's theory to reflect on the distinction between two meanings of the word 'victim': victim in the sense of *victima*, or the sacrificed one, and 'victim' in the sense of the wronged victim. In their condition of enslavement the slaves are positioned as *victima* – the ones whose sacrifice is posited as necessary to the socio-political order. In the moment of slave revolt the slaves disidentify from *victima*, creating an emancipatory interpretation of their enslavement as a wrong. Nietzsche downplays this *de*subordinative element of slave revolt, making it visible only in its effects, because his objective in the *Genealogy* is to de-heroicize the slaves (and re-heroicize the masters). The first lesson I draw from Nietzsche's theory, then, is that the *ressentimental* category 'victim' can operate in this emancipatory manner, giving rise to political agency and identificatory upheaval, rather than necessarily devolving into depoliticization and fixed identities. Like the theorists of feminist *ressentiment* I also interpret feminism as a politics of *ressentiment*, but not in the sense of marking out a zone of political pathology and naivety. My interpretation of Nietzsche's theory situates *ressentiment* as an effect of domination that becomes a source of collective strength, creativity and, as such, a potent weapon against domination. Rather than being characteristically positivist, the epistemology of *ressentiment* can be sociological – concerned with the social constitution of subjects in relations of power and alert to the changing and transformable nature of those relations.

Second, my analysis suggests Nietzsche's account of what happens *after* slave revolt is perhaps most important for reflecting on feminist politics in neoliberal times. From the perspective of the powerful slave revolt, it will need to be brought to terms, the creative *ressentiment* of the slaves will need to be recuperated, redirected and thereby contained. I discuss the strategies Nietzsche says the powerful use to diffuse the threat posed by *ressentimental* social groups, focusing on priestly asceticism, or the use of religion to transform the 'other-blaming slave' into a 'self-blaming sinner'. Connecting this back to my analyses in previous chapters highlighting the role of discourses of victim-blame in neoliberal victim theory, I develop an analogy between neoliberalism and priestly asceticism, arguing that neoliberal victim theory and its supporting anti-victim and anti-*ressentiment* critiques perform discursive asceticism in Nietzsche's sense. The derogation of victim identity and victim politics that takes place in these texts corresponds more or less precisely with the task of asceticism, according to Nietzsche: the task of turning resentment 'back on itself', inducing those who advance claims from a position of victimhood to become self-disciplining, self-surveilling and self-blaming. Through the ministrations of priestly asceticism, radical complaint against victimization comes to appear as a forfeiting of responsibility and as a wrong in itself. The second lesson I derive from Nietzsche's theory of *ressentiment*, then, is that the emergence of neoliberal victim theory is a predictable, ascetic phase in the process of politicizing victimization in the form of structural oppression.

Throughout my analysis I adopt the monikers Nietzsche uses in addressing relations of power and domination – master, slave and priest – though this should not be taken as a signal of retreat into a Manichean conception of power relations as unflinching top-down domination. On the contrary, Nietzsche's account puts the master–slave relation as inherently dynamic and unstable – *ressentiment* is the source of political instability – and charts a path from political domination in the sense of rule by masters, through to political domination in the sense of government, or the conduct of conduct, represented by the priest, and in this sense the theory enables us to reflect on power in several evolving forms.

Nietzsche's reverse victimology

In my reading of Nietzsche's theory of *ressentiment* in this chapter I step back from Nietzsche's condemnation of *ressentiment*, but this is of course difficult to do because enjoining this condemnation is precisely what Nietzsche asks his reader to do in *On the Genealogy of Morals*.[3] At several points in the *Genealogy* Nietzsche speaks directly to and as his imagined reader, an honest democrat whose firmly democratic values and sympathies buckle and shift the further they venture into his genealogy of morality (GOM: I, 9). As with much of Nietzsche's work, the *Genealogy* is a performative critique designed to dramatically disconcert the reader and set them upon new tracks. In this case the honest democrat will be disabused of moral certainty, and the idea that modern democracy is the aristocracy's decisive historical opponent. Read through Nietzsche's *Genealogy*, modern democracy's apparent redistribution of power to the people is merely the latest in a long line of reverberative consequences of an original slave revolt which began two thousand years earlier, a 'protracted' revolt which 'we no longer see because it—has been victorious' (GOM: I, 7). Ignited by the slaves' resentment of the master, the original slave revolt altered the course of human history, interrupting the unfolding of human greatness among the dominant class. Thus began the era of the dominion of slave morality, the era to which we moderns are heir. Although the slave revolt has been victorious, this is not a victory in which the slaves themselves become great masters. Theirs has been a protracted victory at the level of moral values, with slave morality steadily defeating master morality and expelling the possibility of true mastery from the world. Slave morality has come to stand in for morality as such, its value and its values taken 'as given, as factual, as beyond question' (GOM: P, 6). The victory of the slaves consists in the continued dominion of their definitions of good and evil, which they have defined from a position of victimhood, demonizing the strong as evil and rendering suffering, not strength, as virtue.

To shake we honest democrats of modernity out of our unquestioned commitment to the values of the lowly, Nietzsche returns us to the 'twofold prehistory of good and evil' (BGE: 260), a prehistorical co-existence of master and slave moralities. Here we glimpse the original nobles in their unique glory and find that master morality is the original morality; here we see that the origins of our values, which we take to be universal, actually lie with the 'rancorous' resentment of ignoble victims of slavery – 'those in whom poisonous and inimical feelings are festering' (GOM: I, 10). The values of slave morality are degenerative, they are born of distress and impoverishment, and their dominion proceeds at great cost to the future of humanity. For Nietzsche, at stake in the question of morality is nothing less than the future of humanity (EH: Dawn, 2). Modernity's 'good man' may live 'more comfortably, less dangerously' (GOM: P, 6) than did the original nobles, but his slavish mediocrity is bound to pre-empt 'the type man' from attaining the 'highest power and splendour' (GOM: I, 11) possible for him. Nietzsche perceives within our conception of good and evil 'a symptom of regression . . . likewise a danger, a seduction, a poison, a narcotic' through which the present lives '*at the expense of the future*' (GOM: P, 6).

As Judith Shklar (1984) has observed, Nietzsche's account of the master–slave relation in the *Genealogy* turns the world upside down. Nietzsche reverses the customary democratic telling of political domination as a relation in which the weak are dominated by the strong. In Nietzsche's telling, as Shklar describes, 'The weak are the powerful, thanks to their guile and numbers, while the genuinely strong individuals are really the victims' (p. 41). As Rosalyn Diprose (1989) has remarked, Nietzsche's account of slave revolt singles out a 'sole aristocratic victim' (p. 31) and, as Lynne Tirrell (1994) points out, by presenting the oppressed as the oppressors, Nietzsche 'blames the victim' (p. 161). Nietzsche's rendering of the resentful slave as victor and the resented master as victim reflects the structure of reverse victimology identified in Chapter 1, and this helps to explain why Nietzsche's philosophy holds such resonance for contemporary anti-victim and anti-*ressentiment* critiques. One can see how useful Nietzsche's image of a triumphant slave morality is to those who regard late modernity as overrun with political correctness and victim mentality. Contemporary critiques of victim politics echo Nietzsche's complaint that humanity is in the worst of hands, 'governed by the underprivileged, the craftily vengeful' (EH: Dawn, 2). Indeed, these critiques update the *Genealogy*, continuing Nietzsche's story of an unfolding slave revolt into late modernity's struggles over the representation and recognition of social suffering. Unlike the reverse victimologies I have previously discussed, however, Nietzsche's reverse victimology is complex, equivocal and of formidable theoretical breadth. Readers of the *Genealogy* can take the place of the honest democrat and follow Nietzsche into steadily greater suspicion of slave morality, as critics of feminist victim politics in neoliberal times have tended to do. Alternatively they can, as I suggest, grapple with Nietzsche's reverse victimology by tracing the tensions and struggles within his portraits of the master and slave and their unfolding rela-tion. In the *Genealogy* Nietzsche asks that we suspend negative judgement of the nobles, the powerful, the dominating as 'evil', so that we can develop ways of thinking, being and valuing outside of slave morality. To grapple with his reverse victimology, however, we need to also suspend Nietzsche's negative judgement of the slaves and their morality as 'bad'.

Fragile strength: reading the master

Much of the intellectual work of the *Genealogy* hinges on Nietzsche's distinctive portrait of the master or original noble. With this figure Nietzsche rivals Hegel's master–slave dialectic and aims to confound moral universalism (Nietzsche argues 'good' has a double origin, noble and slavish, with contrasting, disunited definitions), moral utilitarianism (the idea that goodness consists in actions that benefit others, in 'unegoism' rather than 'egoism') and social contractarianism (a form of 'sentimentalism' [GOM: II, 17] that disavows the unquestionably violent origins of the state). Through the master Nietzsche is also positing a key concept of his philosophy, the concept *will to power*. These themes are woven through Nietzsche's portrait of the original nobles as uniquely autarchic creators of values. Understanding how and why Nietzsche characterizes the original nobles in this way is necessary for an understanding of Nietzsche's overall theory of *ressentiment* and slave morality. I will analyse Nietzsche's alternative account of the master–slave relation and consider whether his anti-Hegelian move succeeds.

Nietzsche first establishes this portrait of the nobles as uniquely autarchic creators of values in the book preceding the *Genealogy*, *Beyond Good and Evil*. In *Beyond*, he presents his thesis on master and slave morality and isolates ancient nobility as a vital and unique type of humanity: 'The noble type of man experiences itself as determining values; it does not need approval . . . it knows itself to be that which first accords honour to things; it is *value-creating*' (BGE: 260). In the *Genealogy* Nietzsche builds on his portrait of the nobles as value-creating with etymologies of the words good, bad and evil. His genealogy of ancient meaning in the language of morality shows that the first origins of the word 'good' are noble self-definitions:

> The judgment 'good' did not originate with those to whom 'goodness' was shown! Rather it was 'the good' themselves, that is to say, the noble, the powerful, high-stationed, and high-minded, who felt and established themselves and their actions as good, that is, of the first rank, in contra-distinction to all the low, low-minded, common and plebian.
>
> (GOM: I, 2)

The original nobles posited the first morality, the first conception of good and bad. Their morality is not a normative code of conduct. It is a spontaneous language of self-affirmation, indeed self-glorification, expressing the nobles' experience of power and nobility as ecstatically pleasurable. The noble mode of valuation:

> acts and grows spontaneously, it seeks its opposite only so as to affirm itself more gratefully and triumphantly—its negative concept 'low,' 'common,' 'bad' is only a subsequently-invented pale, contrasting image

in relation to its positive basic concept—filled with life and passion through and through—'we noble ones, we good, beautiful, happy ones!'

(GOM: I, 10)

Nietzsche never discusses the distinctive virtues of the original nobles without also describing their demise at the hands of slaves who contest their condition of slavery. We see the original nobles in their self-affirming and value-creating glory, always also witnessing their murder by a resentful and clever collective of slaves. These ways of representing the nobles – as uniquely self-affirming and as historical victims – soften the trait of the original nobles that Nietzsche also emphasizes: their unbridled cruelty. The original nobles embody will to power in its healthiest, strongest and least fettered guise. They are 'beasts of prey' who act as life itself acts: 'Life is *essentially* appropriation, injury, overpowering of what is alien and weaker; suppression, hardness, imposition of one's own forms, incorporation and at least, at its mildest, exploitation . . . life simply *is* will to power' (BGE: 259). Nietzsche characterizes the naturally occurring violence of the original nobles as an 'involuntary, unconscious' artistry that leads to the creation of the state, 'a ruling structure that *lives*' (GOM: II, 17). With this image of animal artistry Nietzsche is countering the idea that humanity has emerged from the state of nature through a peacefully brokered social contract.

> [T]he welding of a hitherto unchecked and shapeless populace into a firmer form was not only instituted by an act of violence but also carried to its conclusion by nothing but acts of violence . . . the oldest 'state' thus appeared as a fearful tyranny, an oppressive and remorseless machine . . . He who can command, he who is by nature 'master', he who is violent in act and bearing—what has he to do with contracts!
>
> (GOM: II, 17)

The original nobles enact their state-building animal artistry *in good conscience* (BGE: 258). They delight in violence and cruelty and dominate a slave class. Yet they do so, Nietzsche suggests, as pre-reflective Barbarians, as yet unconstrained by guilt and moral conscience, 'still in possession of unbroken strength of will and lust for power' (BGE: 257). The original nobles can 'emerge from a disgusting procession of murder, arson, rape, and torture, exhilarated and undisturbed of soul' (GOM: I, 11). Although cruel and imposing, the original nobles are essentially *innocent*. Theirs is an 'innocent conscience' (GOM: I, 10). They cannot be blamed for the violence they enact, the suffering they inflict. It cannot be expected that a lion not feast, just as it cannot be expected that a man 'who is by nature "master"' not dominate others: 'They do not know what guilt, responsibility, or consideration are, these born organisers' (GOM: I, 17).

It is the slaves who invent the concepts of guilt, responsibility, blame and ethical consideration of the victimized other. These concepts (slave morality) act like poison on the healthy body of the noble, signalling a degenerative turn in the course of human history. Slave morality introduces the grammar of causation, instituting a new way of knowing human action: as deliberate, calculable and accountable; as either praiseworthy or blameworthy, from the perspective of the other. The nobles' untrammelled will to power is crippled by slave morality's transformation of how human action is conceived. In the context of slave morality the beast of prey can no longer be what he is. His good conscience and animal innocence are destroyed by feelings of shame and guilt as he succumbs to the 'ugly growth' (GOM: I, 17) of bad conscience. Slave morality succeeds by '*poisoning the consciences* of the fortunate with their own misery, with all misery', making the 'happy, well-constituted, powerful in soul and body . . . doubt their *right to happiness*' (GOM: III, 14). Slave morality robs the nobles of the spontaneity of action necessary to their uniquely autarchic selves, making it steadily less possible for noble virtues, freedoms and pleasures to be sustained. Slave morality creates the metaphysics of substance, transforming spontaneous human action into rationalized human conduct.

In this story of slave revolt, Nietzsche theorizes that when the victims of violence, cruelty and domination speak, when the victimizer is made to contemplate the sufferings of the other, that which makes the victimizer a victimizer – in this case their capacity for untrammelled, unconscious, enjoyed violence – is destroyed. Slave morality's grammar of causation and accountability separates the doer from the deed, transforming the beast of prey into a subject of free will, overlaying the master's expression of power with a moral drama in which the master is cast as a subject who chooses to behave in the way they do, a subject who is, therefore, free to behave otherwise. The slaves invent the concepts of blame and free will, by which they are able to suggest that the beast of prey is responsible for the other's suffering and is free to choose not to enact violence on the other:

> For just as the popular mind separates the lightning from its flash and takes the latter for an *action*, for the operation of a subject called lightning, so popular morality also separates strength from expressions of strength, as if there were a neutral substratum behind the strong man, which was *free* to express strength or not to do so. But there is no such substratum; there is no 'being' behind doing, effecting, becoming; 'the doer' is merely a fiction added to the deed—the deed is everything.
>
> (GOM: I, 13)

By generalizing the concept of free will – the poisonous belief that '*the strong man is free* to be weak' – the slaves 'gain the right to make the bird of prey *accountable* for being a bird of prey' (GOM: I, 13). The slaves assume the right to hold the nobles accountable for their cruelty, which in turn deprives the original nobles of the 'right to exist' (GOM: III, 14). When their will to power is thus poisoned by the concept of free will, the original nobles' unique capacity for autarchic self-affirmation and value-creation is lost. Nietzsche characterizes slave morality as poisonous, degenerative and *fictional*. With slave morality begins the pretence that there is being behind doing, a strength that is free to not enact violence on the other, a human who can and should be 'good', according to the slave's definition of good, that is, 'undangerous' (BGE: 260). In a point to which I will return in the following section, we can see here that the concept of 'victim', in the specific sense of one who suffers a wrong, is given by the concept of free will.

As Deleuze (1983) has observed, 'Anti-Hegelianism runs through Nietzsche's philosophy as its cutting edge' (p. 8). Nietzsche's account of the noble mode of valuation is designed to rival Hegel's master/slave dialectic in the philosophy of power. Accordingly, Nietzsche's master is everything Hegel's master is not: inherently powerful, vitally creative and self-affirming. In Hegel's dialectic the master's power is not inherent but relational: his power depends on the slave's obedient recognition of him as powerful, among other contingent factors. In Hegel mastery is not a pleasurable condition of superabundant creativity. It is a circuit of desire met with satisfaction, a condition of creative stagnation, by which scope for creative deeds (work) and self-reflection is given over to the slave, whose condition of oppression demands both work and self-reflection. Against Hegel's image of mastery as a condition of stagnation and dependence on the slave, Nietzsche posits his born organizers: autarchic creators of values conducting instinctive drive and will. Nietzsche here describes an anti-Hegelian ethics of the self. The slave is not necessary to the original noble, the noble mode of valuation is aneconomic as it need not trade on a debt to the other. The other (the slave) is not 'needed' but rather is 'sought' as a further source of self-affirmation; the other provides a 'contrasting shade' rather than a contrast as such (GOM: I, 11). As Deleuze contends, Nietzsche not only rejects Hegel's vision of the master–slave relation as dialectical. Nietzsche's philosophy of power further suggests Hegelianism is 'the ideology of *ressentiment*' (Deleuze, 1983, p. 10). As Deleuze elaborates, 'The relation of master and slave is not, in itself, dialectical. Who is the dialectician, who dialectizes the relationship? It is the slave, the slave's perspective, the way of thinking belonging to the slave's perspective' (p. 10). Hegel's treatment of power as a question of relational recognition and representation is symptomatic of slave morality: 'The slave only conceives of power as the object of a recognition, the content of a representation . . . Behind Hegel's master we always find the slave' (p. 10).

Does Nietzsche's anti-Hegelian account of power relations succeed? It does in the sense that Nietzsche's account of the noble mode of valuation genuinely unveils a different morality and way of being, showing that the Hegelian framework is limited in its conception of power and value judgement. Nietzsche's etymologies and reflections on 'the entire hieroglyphic of the moral past of mankind' (GOM: P, 7) clearly show that moral values are neither universal nor absolute. Nietzsche convincingly frames the question of morality as a question of power and politics, of differences and conflicts in perspective among social groups (or, as Nietzsche posits, among different human 'types', types that differ physiologically, that are healthy or sick, active or reactive, noble or slavish, lordly or plebeian). Although Nietzsche succeeds in describing a form of power that exists in its own right (an inherent will to power, embodied by the original nobles), there are respects in which his anti-Hegelian move does not succeed. Rather than describe a master–slave relation that is non-dialectical, I contend that Nietzsche uses an innocent beast/guilty slave binary to disguise the dialectical movement in his own account of the master–slave relation. As Aaron Ridley (1998) observes, in the *Genealogy*, Nietzsche strives to distinguish the nobles from the slaves 'as sharply as possible' (p. 20). Nietzsche achieves the contrast with the innocent beast/guilty slave binary: emphasizing the innocent conscience of the beast of prey, he blames and condemns the slaves for the nobles' untimely demise. This innocent beast/guilty slave binary effectively downplays the original nobles' role in creating the dialectic that would lead to their demise. Like the texts he studied exhaustively as a philologist, Nietzsche's texts are many-layered and require active reading. Behind the *Genealogy*'s innocent beast/guilty slave binary we find of course a more subtle account of slave revolt.

Nietzsche's story of slave revolt puts the master as *differently dependent* on the slave, rather than independent of them. In *Beyond*, Nietzsche describes the nobles as a class that 'needs slavery' (BGE: 257) if they are to enact their nobility and develop higher forms of humanity. An 'order of rank' must exist in order for the nobles to further their 'development of ever higher, rarer, more remote, further-stretching, more comprehensive states', their 'enhancement of the type "man"' (BGE: 257). Albeit differently to Hegel's master, Nietzsche's master does depend on the slave. The master's capacity to enact mastery is indebted to the existence, the oppression and the obedience – but not the recognition – of the slave. The master's 'will to cruelty' depends on the availability of victims. Nietzsche's overall narrative of slave revolt suggests the untrammelled will to power Nietzsche prizes, to the extent that it needs and creates slavery, is inherently self-destructive. It has the character Jacob Burckhardt ([1860] 1995) ascribed to Renaissance despotism: 'As despotisms rise, grow, and are consolidated, so grows in their midst the hidden element which must produce their dissolutions and ruin' (p. 7). Nietzsche's will to power needs and creates slavery; in this way it sets the scene for the slave revolt that will destroy it. As Ridley (1998) has put this point, 'The original noble was doomed from the moment he oppressed the first slave' (p. 133).

As in the Hegelian philosophy of power, the master–slave relation in Nietzsche is unstable, the power of the dominant class being contingent rather than inherent. The power of Nietzsche's master originally is inherent, and with the creation of the state it becomes contingent upon particular conditions characterizing the nobility's early rule, conditions that permit them a more flexible relationship with socialization compared with the slave. As Nietzsche has it, once the state is created, both master and slave undergo 'man's most fundamental change': 'that change which occurred when he found himself finally enclosed within the walls of society and of peace' (GOM: II, 16). Nietzsche calls this change the 'internalization of man' (GOM: II, 16), a repression of animal instinct and the formation of an interiorized subjectivity or 'soul'. Nietzsche conceives of socialization as a form of suffering that proceeds as frustrated yet generative self-torture. After the 'forcible sundering of man from his animal past' the human becomes an 'animal soul turned against itself' (GOM: II, 16), with instincts present yet inhibited by social straitjacketing, and action increasingly mediated through consciousness. With the creation of the state, master and slave jointly suffer the 'homesickness' that attends the civilizing process (GOM: II, 16). Both are deprived of a seamless relation with instinct's '*more natural* vent' (GOM: II, 22). Yet master and slave are not equally subject to these first distresses of socialization.

In the time before slave revolt, Nietzsche's nobles can free themselves of the state, they can 'go outside' and 'go back to the innocent conscience of the beast of prey', savouring 'freedom from all social constraints' (GOM: I, 11). As Nietzsche puts it in *Beyond*, the nobles have recourse to 'drainage ditches' (BGE: 260) for their affects: means of venting the frustration and distress that attend socialization. In this way they the original nobles assume a flexible and agentic relationship with the process of socialization, making it a rich experience of self-creation. In the state the master is minimally repressed. The slave, on the other hand, is maximally repressed. As Ridley (1998) has observed, the slave suffers a comparatively 'high degree of internalization' (p. 27). The slave's condition of oppression means that they are 'denied the true reaction, that of deeds' (GOM: I, 10). Rather than act their reaction to socialization, their frustration and distress 'fester' (GOM: I, 10), lacking any outlet, held in check by the expectation of obedience and the threat of punishment. This experience of rancorous frustration is *ressentiment* in its 'brute state' (Deleuze, 1983, p. 126). The nobility's active relationship to socialization ensures that they are immune to *ressentiment*,[4] while the slaves' condition of oppression ensures that they are consumed by *ressentiment*. Despite Nietzsche's view of the slaves as inherently inferior beings, his theory of *ressentiment* thus lends itself to sociological interpretation. *Ressentiment* appears with the very establishment of society through a process of socialization – the 'sundering of man from his animal past' (GOM: II, 16). Social structure creates different degrees of vulnerability to *ressentiment*. Social change is brought about by creative *ressentiment*: the moment in which the brute *ressentiment* of the slaves 'becomes creative and gives birth to values' (GOM: I, 10).

In view of this reading of the figure of the master, *ressentiment* and slave revolt can be read as a *co-production* of master and slave, and as an effect of the original noble's will to power. In a thoroughly dialectical scenario, the will to power Nietzsche prizes sets the scene for the slave revolt he condemns. The innocent beast/guilty slave binary enables Nietzsche to understate the respects in which the master does depend on the slave, and to disguise the self-destructive character of will to power in its 'healthiest' form. Nietzsche avers precisely this when he states that slave revolt and the invention of the bad conscience 'would not have developed *without*' the masters (GOM: I, 17). He does nonetheless blame the slaves alone: 'One can see who has the invention of the "bad conscience" on his conscience—the man of *ressentiment*!' (GOM: I, 11). In blaming the slaves, Nietzsche is literally correct – their condition of maximal oppression leads them to invent slave morality. But this condition of maximal oppression, and with it slave morality, would not exist without the will to power Nietzsche prizes.

Nietzsche's 'official attitude of condemnation' (Staten, 1990, p. 59) of the slaves thus wears thin.

Nietzsche blames and condemns the slaves for altering the course of human history, but why should we expect the slaves to have behaved otherwise than to contest their condition of enslavement? One answer is that, for Nietzsche, in the creative moment of slave revolt the slaves are seeking to escape a condition that they should not be escaping, for they are the weak ones – they are fated to be slaves. While the nobles are 'born organizers', the slaves are 'born failures' (GOM: III, 14). The slaves are socially constituted as weak – they are 'deprived', 'oppressed', 'lowly' and 'failures from the start' (GOM: II, 13; III, 14) – but they are so, for Nietzsche, because of their essential weakness: the slaves are 'ill-constituted', 'dwarfed', 'atrophied', 'sick', 'impotent' and 'physiologically unfortunate' (GOM: I, 10, 7; III, 14). As Staten (1990) describes, 'Nietzsche continually reiterates his belief that there are higher human beings who are *more valuable* than the mass and *for whose sake* the mass exists and may be sacrificed' (p. 123, original emphasis). As Nietzsche writes, 'A good and healthy aristocracy . . . accepts with a good conscience the sacrifice of untold human beings who, *for its sake*, must be reduced and lowered to incomplete human beings, to slaves, to instruments' (BGE: 258).[5] As the connotation of sacrifice suggests, in this moment Nietzsche sees the slaves as victims, but not in the sense that they are victims of *wrongdoing*. Instead the slaves are victims in the sense of *victima*: the ones who exist to be sacrificed for a higher purpose.

Readers of the *Genealogy* can surely join Nietzsche in suspending judgement of the original nobles as 'evil', in order to appreciate Nietzsche's insights into the contested realm of moral values. Indeed, Nietzsche notes that we may be 'quite justified . . . in being on [our] guard against' (GOM: I, 12) the tyrannical noble, while urging us nonetheless to reconsider our investment in the forces that served to expel the noble's particular form of autarchy from the world – forces that are more readily discerned when the noble's role in their own demise is consistently understated. Yet there is also good reason to suspend Nietzsche's prejudice against the slave. Nietzsche laments the grammar that slave morality imposes on human action through the concepts of guilt, blame and free will. But, as I will argue in the following section, his story of slave revolt also lays bare the emancipatory potential of *ressentiment* and slave morality. In the moment of slave revolt the slaves reject their constitution as *victima* (the sacrificed ones) constituting themselves instead as victims of wrongdoing. This identificatory transition from *victima* to the wronged victim does the very opposite of fixing the slaves to victim identity. By recasting enslavement as a preventable wrong rather than a necessary sacrifice, slave revolt opens social being to contingency, enabling the slave to imagine becoming something other than a slave. In this way slave revolt poses a formidable threat to which the powerful will require a solution. If the powerful are to preserve their power, they will need to find ways of pressing the slaves back into *victima*.

Becoming political: reading the slave

As the theorizations of feminist *ressentiment* examined in the previous chapter make clear, the dominant understanding of slave morality is that it does not liberate anyone. Rather, it attacks the maximally free, making all unfree. All are forced to see things through the slave's perspective, which claims to be the only perspective; all are subject to the ways of thinking and being of slave morality, which repress strength, spontaneity and originality, valuing as 'good' only that which prevents and eases suffering; and when they revolt, the slaves fail ultimately to substantively alter their situation, in the sense that they merely recast their enslavement as a source of virtue while they vengefully poison the happy consciousness of the nobility. But is this dire scenario of generalized unfreedom really the only result slave revolt can have? Or is this a limited characterization of slave revolt, reflecting Nietzsche's prejudice against the slave? In the previous chapter we saw that Joan Cocks suggests the latter. Cocks (1991) intervenes on Nietzsche's theory, arguing that Nietzsche would have regarded 1960s and 1970s radical politics as a noble politics 'were he able to see nobility in any kind of slave revolt' (p. 152). Cocks separates *ressentiment* from slave morality, arguing that while *ressentiment* is irredeemably bad, slave morality can be good: it is possible for the slaves to rival the master's ability to generate and posit values, avoiding the resubordinative trap of merely reversing the master's values, thus making their own kind of claim on noble creativity. While I disagree that *ressentiment* and slave morality can be separated in this way – Nietzsche is very clear that slave morality arises from *ressentiment* – I concur with Cocks that slave morality can operate in this more positive and protean manner, and that we are able see this if we do not ascribe to Nietzsche's slanted telling of what happens when the slaves revolt and moralize. Unlike Cocks, however, I do not consider that when slave morality operates more positively it does so because it has avoided 'victim politics'. To the contrary, on my reading, the positive operation of slave morality consists precisely in the elaboration of victimization in the sense of wrongdoing, against victimization in the sense of *victima*. I will address Nietzsche's account of what happens when *ressentiment* 'becomes creative and gives birth to values', interpreting this process as an example of what Engin Isin (2002) calls 'becoming political', or a moment in which political actors 'constitute themselves differently from the dominant images given to them' (p. 275).

When he first presents his thesis on the moralities of master and slave in *Beyond*, Nietzsche performs one of the signature moves of his account of morality, that of switching between two perspectives on one social order. After describing the 'morality of the ruling group' (BGE: 260), Nietzsche takes us into the perspective of the ruled, 'the minds of those who suffered' (GOM: I, 11) from the master's cruelty, those whom the nobles deem 'bad':

> Suppose the violated, oppressed, suffering, unfree, who are uncertain of themselves and weary, moralise: what will their moral valuations have in

common? Probably, a pessimistic suspicion about the whole condition of man will find expression, perhaps a condemnation of man along with his condition. The slave's eye is not favourable to the virtues of the powerful: he is sceptical and suspicious, *subtly* suspicious, of all the 'good' that is honoured there—he would like to persuade himself that their happiness is not genuine. Conversely, those qualities are brought out and flooded with light which serve to ease the existence of those who suffer . . . Slave morality is essentially a morality of utility.

(BGE: 260)

In the *Genealogy*, Nietzsche introduces the concept of *ressentiment* into his account, referring to slave morality as the 'morality of *ressentiment*' (GOM: I, 11). From this point Nietzsche emphasizes that the slaves do not posit values, rather they invert the values of the master, furnishing master morality with competitive opposition from below. Slave morality produces an evaluative distinction in which the 'good' of master morality is recast as 'evil', while the 'bad' of master morality is recast as 'good'. Slave morality's revaluations provide self-preserving, utilitarian expediency and a path to self-affirmation, but only by way of a starkly reactive constitution of self.

The task of the slave is to conjure self-definition and self-affirmation from a starting position in which he '*was* only what he was *considered*: not at all used to positing values himself, he also attached no other value to himself than his masters attached to him' (BGE: 261). Being only what one is considered, and being thereby separated from what one can become, is the definition of oppression Nietzsche gives in his genealogy of morality. The possibility of self-making is outlawed for the slave. This notion of a self separated from the capacity to act and be self-creating is a compelling conception of oppression, though there is strong conjecture here: Nietzsche assumes that in the condition of enslavement the slaves are perfectly unable to develop a sense of self outside of their social constitution as slaves. The value the master attaches to the slave renders the slave 'bad', hence the slave's starting position is one of self-loathing: 'I am bad'. The slaves are nothing other than what they are considered, but the more internalized they become and the more their *ressentiment* mounts, the more their intelligence grows: Nietzsche notes that slaves are 'bound to become eventually *cleverer* than any noble race' (GOM: I, 10). It is through cleverness that the slaves are able to make their *ressentiment* over into a source of creativity. As Ridley (1998) puts it, 'cleverness, born of enforced prudence, is the ace up the slave's sleeve' (p. 26).

Slave morality's creative revaluation of the noble's values will remedy the slave's situation to the extent that they will be able to break with self-loathing. However, unlike the master, the slave's starting situation does not offer the possibility of autarchic self-definition and self-affirmation. In the *Genealogy*, Nietzsche is especially concerned to convey that negation must constitute the first evaluative step the slaves take when they moralize:

144

While every noble morality develops from a triumphant affirmation of itself, slave morality from the outset says No to what is 'outside,' what is 'different,' what is 'not itself'; and *this* No is its creative deed . . . in order to exist, slave morality always first needs a hostile external world; it needs, physiologically speaking, external stimuli in order to act at all—its action is fundamentally reaction . . . picture 'the enemy' as the man of *ressentiment* conceives him—and here precisely is his deed, his creation: he has conceived 'the evil enemy,' '*the Evil One*,' and this in fact is his basic concept, from which he then evolves, as an afterthought and pendant, a 'good one'—himself!

(GOM: I, 10, 11)

So both master morality and slave morality begin by evaluating the master. In the case of master morality, this valuation is one of positive self-affirmation; in the case of slave morality, it is one of negative other-negation. Only on the basis of this initial negation of the master can the slave achieve an affirmative sense of self: 'He is evil therefore I am good.' This places the slave's affirmation of self as an immanent perversion of – rather than a transcendent alternative to – master morality, a reversal of its terms, which, as a reversal, remains dependent on those terms. The slave achieves self-affirmation and breaks with self-loathing, but only by shifting the terms of their dependence on the master, not by eliminating this dependence. In short, the slave achieves an immanent form of emancipation rather than emancipation as such.

This suggests that lack of authenticity is continuous for the slave: while they are enslaved they are only what they are considered, and when they revolt they revalue what they are considered as good. As Nietzsche writes, in the 'dark workshop' of slave morality, the slave's condition of weakness 'is lied into something *meritorious*' (GOM: I, 14). This puts creative *ressentiment* as a reconciliation to slavery, rather than a rejection of it: when they lie their circumstance into something meritorious, the slaves forfeit the possibility of genuine political change, contenting themselves with moral superiority. This lack of authenticity in creative *ressentiment* and its position of reconciliation is the primary focus in the theorizations of feminist *ressentiment* examined in the previous chapter: it is the *ressentiment* that exists as a 'parasitic', 'secondary territoriality' (Ronell, 1991, p. 128), that fails to 'impose a new imprint on the world' (Cocks, 1991, p. 152) and to create 'an alternative vision of collective life' (Brown, 1995, p. 47), that is trapped within the equation of suffering with virtue and the romanticization of powerlessness, that is fixated on complaint and revenge. But focusing on this reactive quality of *ressentiment* discounts the way creative *ressentiment* turns reactivity into a source of action, by shifting the meaning of victim from *victima*, or the sacrificed one, to victim in the sense of one who suffers a wrong. If through creative *ressentiment* the slaves merely reconciled themselves to their condition of slavery, Nietzsche would not later describe creative *ressentiment* as an explosive threat that will need to be brought to terms (GOM: III, 15). The role of the category 'victim' in the morality the slaves elaborate is central to the threat *ressentiment* poses to the socio-political order within which it appears. Representationally dampening this threat – that is, portraying slave revolt as reconciliation to slavery, not rejection of slavery – *is* the 'slant' in Nietzsche's slanted telling of slave revolt.

As I observed in the previous section, the concept of free will leads to the notion of 'victim' in the sense of one who has suffered a wrong. This notion of victim enables the slave to recast the master's cruelty and domination as preventable wrongdoing, raising against cruelty and domination the ethic of the undangerous human. The notion of victim in the sense of one who has suffered a wrong critiques and replaces the notion of victim as *victima*, enabling the slaves to reject the idea that their enslavement is a natural and inevitable sacrifice that serves a higher purpose. Here we see that *ressentiment* gives rise to slave morality, which in turn targets the source of *ressentiment*, in this case, victimization as a wrong in the form of enslavement. In the moment of creative *ressentiment* the slaves conjure the ability to move from perceiving themselves as natural slaves – 'incomplete human beings' who are only what they are considered – to perceiving themselves as victims of slavery – a condition that is neither natural nor inevitable, but rather can be changed. The notion of the wronged victim reinterprets something that was naturalized as arbitrary. The position of the slaves is reactive – they are, as Avital Ronell (1991) puts it, reacting to 'what already exists as powerful and dominating' (p. 127). But this reactive position becomes a source of action. The notion of the wronged victim is denaturalizing and entails active disidentifcation from *victima*. It carries the sense that self and world could be otherwise, in this way opening up the very possibility of identificatory resignification, the very possibility of becoming something other than what one is considered. When in this way the category 'victim' opens social being to contingency it is not at odds with 'agency', instead giving rise to the very possibility of the slaves assuming political agency and claiming power in the world. Thus victim identity can be a vehicle of agency – not in the sense of the 'bad agency' of morality superiority, but agency in the sense of disputing the way oneself or the group has been constituted in the social order and moving to constitute oneself or the group differently. Rather than serve to stabilize their identity as victims, in creative *ressentiment*, the slaves' reconstitution of themselves as victims of a wrong is an identificatory upheaval for all concerned. When the slaves disidentify from *victima*, nothing can be the same for either 'master' or 'slave'.

This dimension of slave morality corresponds with what Engin Isin (2002), in his book on citizenship, calls 'becoming political'. Isin describes becoming political as a response to the condition of being political:

> Being political means being implicated in strategies and technologies of citizenship as otherness. When social groups succeed in inculcating their own virtues as dominant, citizenship is constituted as an expression and embodiment of those virtues against others who lack them . . . Becoming political is that moment when the naturalness of the dominant virtues is

called into question and their arbitrariness revealed . . . the moment in which strangers and outsiders . . . constitute themselves differently from the dominant images given to them.

(p. 275)

The moment Isin describes is reminiscent of an observation Sartre makes in *Being and Nothingness*: 'There are indeed many precautions to imprison a man in what he is, as if we lived in perpetual fear that he might escape from it, that he might break away and suddenly elude his condition' (Sartre, 1969, p. 59). On my reading of Nietzsche's theory of *ressentiment*, when the slaves disidentify from *victima* – when they reject their role as the sacrificed ones – they raise exactly this fear. The 'becoming political' dimension is *ressentiment* at its most threatening – for the powerful, and for Nietzsche. The locus of Nietzsche's concern with slaves who have conceived themselves as victims of slavery is not that they will become resubordinatively attached to this identity, but that they will use this identity as a vehicle through which to become something other than slaves. The theorizations of feminist *ressentiment* examined in the previous chapter all interpret creative *ressentiment* as the death of politics and its replacement with moralism. But my reading suggests that creative *ressentiment* produces moral concepts that enable politicization to occur at all, concepts that enable the slaves to politicize their situation and to potentially, as Nietzsche describes, 'confound and overthrow' what dominates them (GOM: I, 11).

As Mark Katz (1999) has observed, the reach of creative *ressentiment* is 'maximum-goal revolution' (p. 64). Nietzsche is very clear about the political threat that creative *ressentiment* can pose to the social order in which it appears. In the third essay of the *Genealogy*, by which time the honest democrat is persuaded, Nietzsche observes that creative *ressentiment* is 'the most dangerous of all explosives' (GOM: III, 15). Creative *ressentiment* has an explosive quality and poses the threat of 'anarchy' (GOM: III, 13): dissolution of the socio-political order that brought it into being, rescinding of 'the privilege of the full-toned bell over the false and cracked' (GOM: III, 12). An apt way to conceptualize the threat posed by *ressentiment* is provided in Rosemary Hennessey's (2000) discussion of the radical character of outlawed need. Hennessey observes that capitalism's production of surplus value is necessarily also 'the production of outlawed need' (p. 216). Beyond the generic deprivations attending the commodification of labour power, Hennessey discusses deprivations introduced through minimum wage setting, longer working hours, high rates of unemployment and cuts to health and welfare provision, which affect 'human capacities for sensation and affect' no less than needs for 'food, clothing, housing, health care, education, and time for intellectual and creative development' (p. 216). Capitalist arrangements forge distinctions between 'allowed and illegitimate needs', accumulating a ground of 'unmet needs' which form capitalism's 'monstrous', 'unassimilable' yet 'necessary' outside (p. 228). Outlawed needs assume a radical character since 'they cannot be brought back into capitalism without abolishing the very terms of the extraction of surplus value' (p. 228). Explosive *ressentiment* has precisely the character of a monstrous, unassimilable, necessary outside.

Earlier I observed that the theorizations of feminist *ressentiment* are based on a relatively narrow reading of the theory of *ressentiment* – one that is shaped by the task of diagnosis rather than by critical exegesis of the theory. Their readings of the theory of *ressentiment* elide the dimension of *ressentiment* described above, but also elide the dimension of *ressentiment* I discuss in the following section, the phase of *ressentiment* I am calling explosive/contained. This is the phase in which *ressentiment* is 'brought to terms' and proves to be acutely vulnerable to recuperation and redirection. In terms of using Nietzsche's theory of *ressentiment* to read contemporary feminism and victim politics, I contend that this third phase of *ressentiment* is the most relevant. I suggest a strong notion of feminism as creative *ressentiment* belongs to earlier moments in history. As implied by the title of Ruth Rosen's (2000) history of the second wave of feminism, *The World Split Open*, feminist versions of Nietzsche's slave revolt have well and truly already occurred. Women's movements have already well begun the complex work of 'becoming political' and opening gendered social being to contingency – work that is continuously renewed and that remains incomplete, but that has already established a rich field of carefully wrought concepts, evolving gestures of disidentification, and strongly fought campaigns and debates. Existing theories of feminist *ressentiment* posit the question: how will feminism overcome its descent into *ressentiment*? According to the reading of Nietzsche's theory I provide here, however, the more pertinent question at this point may be: how have feminism's creative-explosive *ressentiments* been recuperated, redirected, brought to terms?

Governing *ressentiment*: law and the priest

That creative *ressentiment* has an explosive quality and poses a threat to the socio-political order within which it appears is clear from Nietzsche's account of this threat (anarchy) but also from the time he spends detailing the two primary strategies the powerful employ to diffuse the threat posed by slaves who contest their social constitution as slaves. The first strategy is legalism, the 'institution of law' (GOM: II, 11), which works to contain the *ressentiment* of the slaves by furnishing it with 'a target and a limit' (Ridley, 1998, p. 132). Legalism makes the slaves' indigestible hopes over into digestible complaint by governing the arbitration of injustice, imposing parameters of right and recognition upon phenomena of victimization, and articulating a set of ostensibly repairable wrongs towards which a *ressentimental* populace can direct complaint. Law, on this reading, works for the powerful as does the muleta for the matador, enticing and diverting the treacherous ire of the bull. I will unpack this strategy before discussing the one that, according to Nietzsche, is far more thoroughly successful: priestly asceticism.

In his discussion of the strategy of legalism Nietzsche is sparring with the philosopher from whose work he drew the term '*ressentiment*', Eugen Dühring. In his book *Der Werth des Lebens: Eine philosophische Betrachtung [The Value of*

Life: A Course in Philosophy], Dühring (1865) argued that 'all concepts of justice' are to be attributed to 'the feeling of *Ressentiment*' (pp. viii, 220).[6] For Dühring, justice – the means by which we express distinctions between right and wrong – 'exists for and springs from the ancient sense of vengeance' (p. 220). Dühring argues that *ressentiment* – 'a reaction, a sensation that belongs alongside revenge and fits with it in the same category of emotion' (p. 220) – is a configuration of affect to which no human is immune: insofar as one is human, one feels *ressentiment*. On this basis, Dühring reads criminal justice systems as organic extensions of an essentially natural doctrine of revenge, a naturally occurring human capacity to distinguish the just from the unjust and to contrive a system through which the unjust may be avenged and deterred. Nietzsche appropriates Dühring's use of the term *ressentiment* but rebuffs his thesis on *ressentiment* with a 'blunt antithesis' (GOM: II, 11).

Observing that Dühring presents justice as 'at bottom merely a further development of the feeling of being aggrieved', Nietzsche counters Dühring's naturalization of justice systems: 'legal conditions can never be anything other than *exceptional conditions*' (GOM: II, 11):

> 'Just' and 'unjust' exist, accordingly, only after the institution of the law (and *not*, as Dühring would have it, after the perpetration of the injury). To speak of just or unjust *in itself* is quite senseless; in itself, of course, no injury, assault, exploitation, destruction can be 'unjust', since life operates *essentially*, that is in its basic functions, through injury, assault, exploitation, destruction and simply cannot be thought of at all without this character.
>
> (GOM: II, 11)

In a sense, Nietzsche counters Dühring's order of naturalization with a different order of naturalization. The 'injustices' to which justice systems are addressed come as part of the essential operation of life, and as such can only be construed as 'injustices' via a kind of anti-nature, a 'partial restriction of the will to life, which is bent on power' (GOM: II, 11). This basic disagreement between Nietzsche and Dühring about the relation of nature to law is the ground on which Nietzsche posits his alternative account of the institution of law. As opposed to Dühring's 'communistic cliché' in which law is understood as 'a means of *preventing* all struggle in general' – a means of deterring the unjust – Nietzsche proposes that law be understood as 'a means in the struggle between power complexes' (GOM: II, 11). Where Dühring sees the institution of law as an extension of humanity's reactive feelings, Nietzsche argues the institution of law is the means by which the powerful 'struggle *against* the reactive feelings' (GOM: II, 11) emanating from lower social strata. The powerful, on Nietzsche's view, contrive 'exceptional conditions' through which the explosive *ressentiment* of the lower orders can be diverted and thereby contained. Hence the powerful's 'need for law':

in which sphere has the entire administration of law hitherto been at home—also the need for law? In the sphere of reactive men, perhaps? By no means: rather in that of the active, strong, spontaneous, aggressive. From a historical point of view, law represents on earth . . . the struggle against the reactive feelings, the war conducted against them on the part of the active and aggressive powers who employed some of their strength to impose measure and bounds upon the excesses of the reactive pathos and to compel it to come to terms. Wherever justice is practiced, one sees a stronger power seeking a means of putting an end to the senseless raging of *ressentiment* among the weaker powers that stand under it (whether they be groups or individuals)—partly by taking the object of *ressentiment* out of the hands of revenge, partly by substituting for revenge the struggle against the enemies of peace and order, partly by devising and in some cases imposing settlements, partly by elevating certain equivalences for injuries into norms to which from then on *ressentiment* is once and for all directed.

(GOM: II, 11)

For Nietzsche, then, legal systems do not spring from *ressentiment*, instead they work to redirect and in this way quell *ressentiment*, enabling the powerful to preserve their power by compelling a *ressentimental* populace to 'come to terms'. Hence, law is not an expression of slave morality; it is a recuperation of slave morality and a site for continual recuperation of slave moralities. The concepts of free will, the wronged victim, accountability, guilt and blame are reified as legal categories, their definition, arbitration and manner of arbitration taken out of popular hands through a new division of law and extra-law. Law recognizes a spectrum of defined forms of victimization, while also taking the place of the wronged victim. In European systems of law, victims are plaintiffs and witnesses: it is law itself (rather than the victim) that is wronged in the commission of a crime.

As we saw in Chapter 3, the place of law in feminist politics is a key theme in the theorizations of feminist *ressentiment*, and in view of Nietzsche's discussion of *ressentiment* and law I want to bring those theorizations back into focus, in particular, Brown's view that the 'effort which strives to establish racism, sexism, homophobia as morally heinous in the law, and to prosecute its individual perpetrators there, has many of the attributes of what Nietzsche named the politics of *ressentiment*' (Brown, 1995, p. 27). I disagree with the idea that turning to the law is germane to the politics of *ressentiment* as Nietzsche describes it. As the above discussion indicates, in Nietzsche's theory, *ressentiment* is not characteristically disposed to legalism. Rather, law is a venue contrived for containing the threat posed by *ressentiment*, which at its maximum reach wants to mount a deeper and more thorough-going challenge to the social order than that afforded by case-by-case justice. Yet Nietzsche's discussion of the role of law affirms the concerns Brown and other theorists raise about the dominant place of legalism as a political strategy in feminism and identity politics. Law reform is no substitute for substantive socio-political change, and has the effect of extending the power of law to divert, contain and recuperate radical political projects and energies. As I argued in Chapter 2, however, in the era of neoliberalism, we also need to be wary of anti- or extra-legalism, or the argument that law reform has no place in the politics of emancipation. In the current context, anti-legalism powerfully reflects neo- liberalism's privatization of social risk, its situating of the citizen as individually responsible for ensuring that their vulnerabilities do not give way to victimization, and that their victimization does not give way to victim mentality. Anti-legalism disregards the important work of bearing witness to the differend, or the effort to signify unacknowledged suffering within and beyond law, which always involves politicizing the terrain of law, its categories, systems of arbitration and address to the wrong, rather than simply submitting to recuperation by law.

The second strategy Nietzsche identifies for diffusing the threat posed by creative *ressentiment* is priestly asceticism. A genuine departure Nietzsche makes from Hegel's master–slave dialectic is that in the *Genealogy* the master–slave relation is eventually tripartite: the priest is a key figure in this relation. The figure of the ascetic priest occupies a liminal position between master and slave. The ascetic priest hosts 'a *ressentiment* without equal', which positions him as slavish, yet his 'will to power is intact', he exhibits 'mastery', and he 'despises more readily than he hates',[7] which suggests the ascetic priest is a kind of noble (GOM: III, 15). Nietzsche insists that master and slave are bound to misunderstand one another because their respective realities are fundamentally incommensurable. But the liminal figure of the ascetic priest is able to prevail equally within and to mediate between slavish and noble spheres: he is at once 'profoundly related to the sick' and able to 'walk among the other beasts of prey with bearlike seriousness and feigned superiority' (GOM: III, 15).

The significance of this liminal figure consists in the labour they perform when they achieve '*dominion over the suffering*' (GOM: III, 15). The ascetic priest 'defends his herd . . . against the healthy [the nobility]' while also discouraging the herd from 'envy of the healthy' (GOM: III, 15). Discouraging envy while being also sensitive to suffering is key to the priest's ability to stabilize and maintain 'segregation' between 'sick' and 'healthy' (GOM: III, 15). The 'essential art' and 'supreme utility' of the priest, Nietzsche writes, are that in his dominion over the suffering he effectively '*alters the direction of ressentiment*' (GOM: III, 15). The priest induces the slaves to self-blame, in this way providing a consummate solution for the powerful to the threat of *ressentiment* from below:

> 'I suffer: someone must be to blame for it'—thus thinks every sickly sheep. But his shepherd, the ascetic priest, tells him: 'Quite so, my sheep! Someone must be to blame for it: but you yourself are this someone, you alone are to blame for it—*you alone are to blame for yourself!*'—This is brazen and false enough: but one thing at least is achieved by it, the direction of *ressentiment* is *altered* . . . You will guess what, according to my idea, the curative instinct of life has at least *attempted* through the

ascetic priest, and why it required for a time the tyranny of such paradoxical concepts as 'guilt', 'sin', 'sinfulness', 'depravity', 'damnation':
to render the sick to a certain degree *harmless*, to work the self-destruction
of the incurable, to direct the *ressentiment* of the less severely afflicted
sternly back upon themselves ('one thing is needful')—and in this way to
exploit the bad instincts of all sufferers for the purposes of self-discipline,
self-surveillance, and self-overcoming.

(GOM: III, 15, 16)

According to Nietzsche, the priest's inducement of the slave to self-blame is a
substantially more effective solution than that provided by law. The redirection and
internalization of *ressentiment* introduce a spiritualized species of self-loathing by
which the slaves are perfectly disarmed. We see here one of the reasons why
Nietzsche's *Genealogy* was generative for Foucault. Nietzsche's ascetic priest
embarks upon the conduct of conduct: his ministrations diffuse the threat of
ressentiment by reconstituting the slaves as self-disciplining, self-surveilling, self-
blaming subjects – subjects who, in the active practice of self-government, return
themselves to docility.

The priest contains the explosive threat of *ressentiment* by directing the sufferer
to seek the cause of their suffering 'in *himself*, in some *guilt*, in a piece of the past'
so they will interpret their suffering 'as *punishment*' (GOM: III, 20). The slave is
thereby 'transformed into "the sinner"' (GOM: III, 20). Nietzsche enumerates a
range of labours the priest performs through this interweaving of suffering, guilt and
sin, all of which are designed to dispel the slave's 'discontent with his lot' (GOM:
III, 18) by encouraging them towards obedience rewarded with redemption in the
afterlife. When the priest is not administering guilt, they engage in discursive play
and resignification, showing 'ingenuity in name-changing and rebaptizing' to make
the slaves 'see benefits and a relative happiness in things they formerly hated'
(GOM: III, 18). Hence, for Nietzsche, the priest represents 'life *against* life': the
priest works on behalf of 'life' in maintaining a social order which segregates the
'sick' from the 'healthy', but does so by intensifying the sickness of the sick (GOM:
III, 13). Self-blaming *ressentiment* is, it seems, the worst kind of *ressentiment*.
Through priestly asceticism the slaves are, in effect, returned to *victima*, but their
suffering has been spiritualized and accrues a completely new meaning. Their
suffering is not a necessary sacrifice; it is instead an experience they have brought
upon themselves. A wrong has occurred, but a wrong committed by the slave: the
slave's suffering is punishment for sin. Hence the passage through brute-creative-
explosive/contained *ressentiment* can be interpreted as a movement from *victima*,
to the wronged victim, to the wrongdoer or 'sinner'. In the transition from the
wronged victim to the wrongdoer, the morality created by the slaves in protest
against the conditions of their existence is recuperated, reversed and turned back
on them. The ascetic priest engages principally and trenchantly in the activity of
victim-blaming, re-positioning the slaves as the subjects of the other-blaming
morality they created, which, when 'internalized', becomes a morality of self-blame

and victim-blame. At least, this is ideally what takes place in the third phase of *ressentiment*, from the perspective of Nietzsche's ascetic priest – an outcome that is not guaranteed. Observing their similar mobilization of discursive play and the activity of victim-blaming in response to political threats and instability, in what remains of this section I develop an analogy between asceticism as Nietzsche describes it and neoliberal victim theory.

Nietzsche observes that the ascetic priest 'appears in almost every age' (GOM: III, 11). In our age, where would we say the priest appears? Where is social suffering attributed to individual fault? Where do ascetic practices of self-discipline, self-surveillance and self-blame take on the role of stopping complaint about social suffering? I propose that an analogy can be drawn between priestly asceticism and the anti-sociological heuristics of neoliberal victim theory. The victim-blaming discourses of neoliberalism and their logic of victim-bad/agent-good are doing the work of the priest today. As I observed in Chapter 1, the era of neoliberalism is characterized by a condition of 'rising inequality everywhere' (Harvey, 2005, p. 119), yet discourses of victim-blame operate to disguise this condition, veiling the social foundations of suffering and attributing suffering instead to the subjectivity of the sufferer. Like the priest, the neoliberal rubric of individual responsibility for individual socio-economic fate obscures social relations and forces, enabling structural inequality, disadvantage and discrimination to be 'rebaptized' as personal failure. Nietzsche's ascetic priest spiritualizes social suffering, while neoliberal victim theory psychologizes it. Victimization is seen to be brought on by victim mentality, and to introduce the risk of victim mentality. In both cases, remedy is sought in improved individual orientation to practices of personal responsibility rather than collective efforts towards socio-political change. The 'sinner' in priestly asceticism has offended a god and finds redemption in penance, while the 'victim' in neoliberal victim theory has offended the market and finds redemption in the agency of market-readiness. In a new twist on *victima*, vulnerability becomes an ineluctable condition: the only thing one can do is assume responsibility for developing self-protective practices of risk management and survival. Vulnerability is rebaptized as personal responsibility, and vulnerability that gives way to victimization becomes the fault of the victim.

For asceticism to work, its governmentality has to succeed: it requires the active participation of subjects in their own resignification as responsible, resilient agents and the recognition of its norms at the level of conduct and in speech. Asceticism thus needs to be abundantly present in everyday practices, speech and writing, its values reverberating in established gestures for professing disapproval of the egoistic, complaining sufferer and for signifying one's own or others' status as self-coerced 'good sufferers' – uncomplaining, self-blaming and actively directing victim-blame towards 'bad sufferers'. That neoliberal victim theory enjoys this degree of prominence is proven rather than disproven by the fact that the gesture of renouncing victimhood is now thoroughly clichéd. The prominence of neoliberal victim theory geopolitically is shown in existing accounts of the rise of anti-victimism in North America (Cole, 2007) and Europe (Dean, 2010; Naqvi, 2007) and, as I have previously discussed, in the generalization of the 'Agents Not Victims' trope within intellectual culture and in the politics of globalization and development (Wilson, 2011; Dahl, 2009).

The analogy I am drawing here is suggested particularly by Nietzsche's emphasis on the ascetic priest's penchant for discursive play, for 'name-changing and rebaptizing' (GOM: III, 18). As we saw in Chapter 1, these are principal activities in the critiques of victim feminism, which very literally engage in the spin-doctoring work of name-changing and rebaptizing as they produce a suite of depoliticizing conceptual makeovers of issues in feminist politics, and launch their re-naming and re-claiming of 'feminism'. Name-changing and rebaptizing are also principal activities in the broader resignification of 'feminism' Nancy Fraser (2009) describes as the neoliberal production of feminism's 'uncanny doubles'. In the bodies of work that frame victim identity as a forfeiting of responsibility and victim politics as harmful sanctimony we find the work of the priest. The neoliberal negation and co-option of second-wave feminism's 'best ideas' are discursive asceticism in Nietzsche's sense. As Richard White (1994) remarks, 'the priest can always assume new masks, though the ultimate effect of his machinations will always be the same' (p. 71). As in all asceticism, neoliberalism's victim-blaming resig-nifications are characteristically 'brazen and false' (GOM: III, 18), but where their governmentality succeeds, this advances rather than impedes what is essential to asceticism: the promotion of the unegoistic, non-complaining sufferer as ideal.

Nietzsche encourages us to recognize ascetic constructions as brazen and false – not in order to instruct us in resisting its constructions, but instead to show their power to protect and stabilize a body politic that relies on what will inevitably be strongly contested relations of domination, and presumably to admire the ability of the ascetic priest to conserve a space for the potential unfolding of human greatness among an elite social class. If, however, in reading Nietzsche's text we are in a position of wanting to refuse neoliberal asceticism and to avoid Nietzschean elitism, it is significant that his theory of *ressentiment* leaves open the prospect of a further phase of *ressentiment* characterized by dissonance and the refusal of ascetic constructions – by critical foreclosure, avoidance, remaking or undoing of asceticism's ability to 'alter the direction of *ressentiment*' and blunt the political challenges of subordinated political subjects. This suggests that, just as I earlier asked, where today we find Nietzsche's ascetic priest, we need to also ask where today do the efforts of the priest collapse? Where do we find signs of refusal to accept the anti-sociological heuristics of neoliberal victim theory and efforts to counter these resignifications through new and reclaimed political strategies and idioms – in Isin's (2002, p. 275) terms, moments of 'becoming political' and constituting ourselves differently from the dominant images of neoliberal victim theory? In terms of using Nietzsche's theory of *ressentiment* to interpret contemporary feminism, this notion of a fourth phase in the politics of *ressentiment* characterized by the refusal of asceticism noticeably aligns with the way Fraser (2009) shapes a key task for feminists in the current political moment: the task of disrupting 'the easy passage from [feminist] critique to its neoliberal double' in order to 'distinguish ourselves from' and 'avoid resignification by' neoliberalism (p. 115). In terms of the analogy I have drawn, Fraser is here describing what potentially takes place in the fourth phase of *ressentiment*: a refusal of asceticism that assumes the form of 'reclaiming' slave morality and undertakes the work of disarticulating its 'best ideas' from their ascetic double.

That the priest appears and reappears historically is perhaps not for Nietzsche evidence of the abiding strength or heroism of asceticism, but instead a sign of its instability, its failures, an indication that its resignifications are vulnerable to refusal and growing disaffiliation. After concluding my analysis in this chapter of Nietzsche's theory of *ressentiment*, I will return in the conclusion to this book to the question of where today we find anti-ascetic responses to neoliberal victim theory, and consider the prospects for anti-asceticism in the making of what Fraser (2009) invokes as 'post-neoliberal' feminism.

Conclusion

This chapter's analysis of Nietzsche's theory of *ressentiment* demonstrates the emancipatory dimension of the category 'victim' – its creative capacity to resist *victima* through the denaturalization of social suffering – and provides a way to interpret not only feminist efforts to politicize victimization, but also the kinds of responses these politicizations can expect, namely, ascetic responses that characteristically turn the victim's *ressentiment* 'sternly back upon themselves' (GOM: III, 16) through gestures of responsibilization and victim-blame. In this way, despite its elitism and presence as a resource for neoliberal victim theory, Nietzsche's theory of *ressentiment* is valuable because it offers alternative perspectives on victim identity and the dynamics of victim politics. Rather than support the prejudices and confines of neoliberal victim theory and its associated body of anti-victim critiques, Nietzsche's theory of *ressentiment* shows us what the category victim can do, while also providing a powerful way to interpret, through the concept of asceticism, the derogation of victim identity and victim politics in neoliberal times. But the insights of Nietzsche's theory can only be gained through critical exegesis of the overall theory, and not through the narrow diagnostic usage, for, as I have argued, the diagnostic operation reduces the concept of *ressentiment* to a referent for a disease, producing a flattened portrait of *ressentiment* as well as that which is diagnosed. While the interpretation of feminism and *ressentiment* I have provided here departs from those articulated in existing theorizations of feminism and *ressentiment*, I do ultimately agree that the goal is to move 'beyond *ressentiment*'. However, I see this in the sociological sense of moving beyond socio-political and economic arrangements that institute conditions of gaping inequality. Such a movement necessarily involves critiquing and countering the forms of discursive asceticism that attempt to rebaptize these conditions as the final shape of human freedom.

Notes

1 See Introduction, n. 8.
2 While I think theorizations of political *ressentiment* tend to link the two by fore-grounding memory as a problem of *ressentiment* and forgetting as an antidote to it, there is value in Connolly's (1988) distinction between 'civic' *ressentiment*, pertaining to the way *ressentiment* plays out in socio-political relations, and existential *ressentiment*, concerning the relationship between mortality and time, transience and eternity, responding to Nietzsche's characterization, in *Thus Spake Zarathustra*, of *ressentiment* as 'ill-will against time' (TSZ: II, On Redemption. See also PTG: 1–4 and TI: The Problem of Socrates). Richard Ira Sugarman (1987) provides an unsurpassed reading of the existential element of Nietzsche's concept of *ressentiment*, in which time is figured as the 'original injury', in his book *Rancor Against Time*.
3 As Robin Small (1997, 2001) has shown, the term '*ressentiment*' first appears in one of Nietzsche's unpublished notebooks from 1875 (Nietzsche, [1875] 1973), 12 years before it appeared in his published work (GOM: I, 10). In the 1875 notebook Nietzsche appraises the discussion of '*ressentiment*' in Eugen Dühring's *Der Werth des Lebens: Eine philosophische Betrachtung [The Value of Life: A Course in Philosophy]* (1865). Nietzsche's use of the French '*ressentiment*' (resentment) is borrowed from Dühring. This is the same Dühring Frederick Engels critiqued in his book *Anti-Dühring: Herr Eugen Dühring's Revolution in Science* ([1894] 1969).
4 Regarding the noble's immunity to *ressentiment*, Nietzsche writes: '*Ressentiment* itself, if it should appear in the noble man, consummates and exhausts itself in an immediate reaction, and therefore does not *poison* . . . Such a man shakes off with a *single* shrug many vermin which eat deep into others' (GOM: I, 10).
5 The key term Nietzsche uses to describe the slave's weakness is impotence, which captures at once a social position that is 'denied the true reaction, that of deeds' (GOM: I, 10) and a physiologically imperfect state when compared with the master's appar-ently consummate masculinity. As this suggests, Nietzsche's theory of *ressentiment* is animated by gendered metaphorics. Nietzsche identified the slave type with women ('How much slave is still residual in woman, for example!' [BGE: 261]) and conceives of the slave's *ressentiment* as emasculating, describing it as a 'shameful emasculation of feeling' (GOM: III, 14). Deleuze similarly ascribes to *ressentiment* a 'dreadful feminine power' (Deleuze, 1983, p. 119). Bound up in Nietzsche's condemnation of *ressentiment* is the fear that, when men are consumed by *ressentiment*, they cease to be manly, engaging instead in a subjective process of becoming-woman.
6 There is to date no English translation of Dühring's book. I am very grateful to Dougal McNeill for translating these passages from Dühring's *Der Werth des Lebens* for me. McNeill's translations are included with permission.
7 Nietzsche distinguishes between despising and hating. Despising 'looks down' on others and as such is noble; hating 'looks up', so is plebeian.

CONCLUSION

Feminism after neoliberal victim theory

My analysis in this book has shown that the hallmarks of neoliberal victim theory – the victim-bad/agent-good formulation, the pattern of reverse victimology and the motif of resentment – are strongly present in feminist critiques of 'victimhood', obviously so in the case of the popular press critiques of victim feminism, and more ambiguously, but no less troublingly, in scholarly feminist critiques of anti-rape feminism and feminist *ressentiment*. My analysis has thus explored 'coincidences' of feminism and neoliberalism – a direct coincidence characterized by complicity and the articulation of neoliberal feminism (Chapter 1), and more ambiguous coincidences that I have framed as examples of Harvey's (2005) notion of 'vulnerability to incorporation into the neoliberal fold' – examples of progressive discourses in which stated derogations of 'victimhood' and 'resentment' provide unavowed discursive support for the widely resonant constructions of neoliberal victim theory, aligning with rather than obstructing neoliberal resignifications of 'feminism', 'victimhood', 'agency' and 'resentment' (Chapters 2 and 3).

In parallel, my analysis has also sought to identify conceptions of victimhood that, set against the context of neoliberal victim theory, are unique, atypical or, in Deleuze and Guattari's sense, 'minor' – that is, able to show the fragility and impermanence of the current community in a way that is only possible from its margins and minor literature; and able 'to express another possible community and to forge the means for another consciousness and another sensibility' (Deleuze and Guattari, 1986, p. 17). In this case, I have sought ways of theorizing victimhood that permit analysis of the constructions, erasures and paradoxes of neoliberal victim theory and provide resources for challenging its dominance in contemporary victim talk, finding these in the work of Lyotard and Nietzsche as well as in the work of a range of feminist theorists and activists, some unearthed from under the label 'victim feminism'. In conclusion, I want to indicate how these resources can be mobilized in feminist theory and politics going forward, and address the question of what feminists and other progressives might now gain from the gesture of 'reclaiming' victimhood amidst the dominance of neoliberal victim theory.

I want to first invoke research about feminism, neoliberalism and victimhood that, pursuing a different methodology to the approach of theory and textual analysis that I have adopted in this book, shows vividly the presence of neoliberal victim theory beyond the texts of anti-victimism, and the effectiveness of its governmentality. Joanne Baker's (2008, 2010) interview research with 55 Australian women aged 18–25 shows the discursive impact of neoliberal victim theory in terms of shaping the way the majority of her respondents conceptualize and talk about their life experiences and life chances. Baker's research found neoliberal discourses of choice and personal responsibility are strongly present and are articulated through rejection of 'victimhood' and avoidance of 'any appearance of vulnerability' (Baker, 2010, p. 192). As Baker describes,

> Young women will actually go to great lengths to avoid being regarded as a victim . . . Neoliberal and post-feminist discourses have closed down the space available for articulating any sense of unfairness or oppression . . . instead, participants preferred to emphasize their sense of agency and self-determination.
>
> (p. 190)

Aligning with 'the overarching message of neo-liberalism [that] success and failure are determined by personal skills and shortcomings' (Baker, 2008, p. 59), Baker's participants actively signify their experiences of disadvantage and violence as opportunities for personal growth and self-improvement (pp. 59–60). Illustrating the way in which neoliberal victim theory rebaptizes compassion for the victim as, practically, a lack of compassion – a 'tough love' position that situates the victim's character and not the social world as the target of intervention and transformation – many of Baker's participants demonstrate lack of empathy in the appraisal of others' experiences of disadvantage and adversity (p. 60). Baker also discerns her participants' ironically very circumscribed relationship to feminist identity – their adherence to feminist principles of equality, but inability to 'freely choose' to identify as feminist. As Baker describes, 'young women who identified as feminist reported that they would be "careful" where they espoused feminist beliefs, not wanting to be regarded as "a manhater, you know, an aggressive woman"' (p. 62).

Significantly, Baker (2010) highlights a participant who held 'atypical' views and showed a 'lack of investment in neoliberal discourses' (p. 198). This participant refused to 'obscure or revise the extent of her disadvantage and its profound impact on her life' (p. 198), and demonstrated empathy for others' experiences of disadvantage and adversity: 'She voiced none of the commonly expressed expectations that individual strength could overcome great disadvantage, but rather identified the ongoing difficulties that can result from the experience of being sexually abused' (p. 198). Baker observes that in the context of her study the presence of this atypical view underlines the ubiquity of neoliberal discourses among the majority of participants: 'Her lack of investment in neoliberal discourses underscored the consistent and robust investment of the other respondents' (p. 198). The atypical view present in Baker's study also, I suggest, marks a crucial site of feminist investigation: victim talk that contests the values and constructions of neoliberal victim theory; the appearance of 'minor' views amidst the 'major' language of victimhood; zones and instances of anti-asceticism where, as I posited in Chapter 4, the efforts of asceticism collapse. In a powerful example of this kind of victim talk, feminist blogger Emi Koyama has recently framed contra- or post-neoliberal feminism as beginning with an anti-ascetic gesture of reclaiming the notion of 'victim'.

Instead of moving to avoid victim identity and erase disadvantage and adversity, Koyama's piece 'Reclaiming "Victim" and "Victimhood"' (2011) provides a robust critique of the neoliberal expectation that she should participate in such avoidance and erasure. Koyama critiques what she sees as neoliberal capitalism's 'trauma recovery industry' (p. 1), which – in a familiar resignification of feminist conceptions of survivorship – is dominantly characterized not by compassion for victims, but by the withdrawal of compassion for victims who do not make the prescribed progression from 'victimhood' to 'survivorship', framed as a celebration of human resilience. In its resignifications of 'victimhood' and 'survivorship', neoliberalism has situated victimhood as 'something to be overcome' (p. 1). In the neoliberal capitalist climate of 'forced optimism' and 'mandatory healing', those suffering the effects of social subordination are urged to 'quickly transition out of victimhood into survivorship, so that we can return to our previous positions in the heteronormative and capitalist social and economic arrangements' (p. 1). Rather than invalidate the knowledge and perspectives that arise from experiences of victimization, and in order to mark resistance to the imposition of 'compulsory hopefulness and optimism in the service of neoliberal capitalist production', Koyama argues that feminists need to reclaim the language of victimhood, which she frames as a gesture of embracing vulnerability as a source of strength, instead of 'blaming and invalidating victims' (p. 1). She writes:

> I argue that feminist anti-violence movements and communities must embrace unproductive whining and complaining as legitimate means of survival in a world that cannot be made just by simply changing our individual mentalities. We must acknowledge that weakness, vulnerability, and passivity are every bit as creative and resilient as strength and activeness.
>
> (p. 1)

More than being a legitimate means of survival, I interpret complaint such as Koyama's as marking a significant disaffiliation from neoliberal victim theory. Koyama refuses to refuse 'victimhood', and this activity of 'reclaiming' victimhood is not a mere reversal. It is 'minor', or combining elements of contamination and political rebellion: Koyama speaks the 'major' language of victimhood (for example, opposing weakness and strength) but reiterates it rebelliously, critiquing the erasure of structural oppression in the reduction of 'victimhood' to individual mentality, and affirming the legitimacy of complaint. Koyama argues that a robust feminist critique of neoliberal capitalism 'begins' (p. 1) with the gesture of reclaiming victimhood, suggesting that this gesture is an opening rather than a resolution – an opening onto new avenues of politicization rather than an end in itself. In other words, the gesture of reclaiming victimhood is necessary but not sufficient.

In a familiar irony, neoliberalism leaves little choice but to engage in a reclaiming of 'victimhood'. Quietly avoiding the 'language', 'politics' of 'paradigm' of victimhood or actively abandoning these as too fraught (among other modes of refusing victimhood) corroborates the construction of 'victimhood' as inherently troubled, and marks one more place in which there is no active refusal to renounce victimhood, one more moment in which a cogent critique of the neoliberal reorganization of 'victimhood' and a challenge to the dominance of market logic in the language of social suffering, fails to genuinely materialize. Neoliberal victim theory thus bequeaths progressive scholars and activists the ostensibly unenviable task of reclaiming the much-maligned concept of 'victim'. If we do not move to visibly use and revalue this term, we corroborate its neoliberal reorganization as a ghettoizing term unless it is naming a protected party – the Real Victim; and we fail to obstruct the dominant place of market logic in the available language of social suffering and complaint. My analysis in this book suggests, however, that the task of reclaiming 'victim' perhaps only appears unenviable specifically through the categories of neoliberal victim theory itself, where in feminism's case it seems as though reclaiming victimhood means resuscitating a famously failed, sweeping alignment of 'woman' with 'passive victim'. My analysis has shown that reclaiming the notion of 'victim' in fact means consulting the rich and noticeably anti-ascetic heritage hidden behind the construction 'victim feminism': robust feminist critique and politicization of victim-blame, critiques of the intersections of gender, race-ethnicity, colonialism, imperialism and class in the politics and social construction of victimhood, conceptions of 'victimhood' and 'agency' that refuse the victim/agent dichotomy, genuinely politicizing conceptions of 'survivorship', and an ethical orientation to subjugated knowledge, in this case, the dissonant forms of victim talk, characterized by the (real or imagined) egoistic assumption of authority on the victim's part, that trigger reactive victim-scapegoating and secondary victimization. These are all good resources for challenging neoliberal victim theory and forging new political terrain. Politically, reclaiming the notion of 'victim' is necessary, but it is not on that count a 'necessary evil', and nor is it, theoretically, a poor prospect, as shown in my discussion in this book of a range of different theoretical concepts and approaches to 'victimhood'.

Reminding us that, 'if we forfeit our vocabulary, we risk losing our ability to talk about structural inequality, systemic domination, and collective life', Cole (2007) observes that in response to the 'anti-victimist challenge . . . we should neither celebrate victimhood, nor jettison it altogether' (p. 177). I suggest that a repertoire of gestures of 'reclaiming' lies between the poles of celebration and jettison, making 'reclaiming' a satisfactory way to frame the response that is needed. As Fraser (2009) has argued, precisely the activity of 'reclaiming' will be essential to the political work of 'post-neoliberal' feminism, if it is to disrupt 'the easy passage from [feminist] critique to its neoliberal double' (p. 115). Fraser suggests the necessary work of reclaiming feminism's 'best ideas' – the critiques of economism, androcentrism, étatism and Westphalianism – will not be sufficient without also moving to 'reconnect feminist critique with the critique of capitalism – and thereby re-position feminism squarely on the Left' (p. 116). Feminism's best ideas need to be reclaimed and, beyond this, focused on the 'post-traditional' and 'market-mediated' forms of gendered structural subordination that have proven to be 'the very lifeblood of neoliberal capitalism' (p. 115). Neoliberal victim theory has sought to representationally erase and thereby materially conserve these enduring and renewed forms of gendered structural subordination. This indicates the need to include 'victimhood' among the ideas that are reclaimed. Such reclaiming, I suggest, is necessary but only likely to become sufficient if it acts as an opening onto new terrain in the theorization and politicization of victimhood, found in the kind of ethical practices and heuristics Van Dijk figures as 'critical victimology' and in the alternative conceptions and modes of analysis of victimhood and victim politics I have marshalled here. These resources lead me to welcome the prospect of an intersectional feminist approach to the theorization and politicization of victimization that is alert to the social construction of victimhood and its cognate categories and terms, sees the role of asceticism in the dynamics of victim politics, and undertakes the work of bearing witness to the differends that inhere in the dominant constructions of neoliberal victim theory, 'brazen and false' as those constructions are.

In concluding, I am mindful of Redfern and Aune's (2013) observation of the tendency to dismiss young women as 'insufficiently political' (p. 11) and ignore their engagement in feminist activism. I suggest that an important part of challenging neoliberal resignifications will be to recognize and amplify the critiques of neoliberalism that young feminists are already articulating – the disputes that are already taking place with feminism's uncanny doubles. In Chapter 2, I framed the SlutWalk movement as a powerful feminist critique of neoliberalism's victim-blaming rubric of personal responsibility as it is brought to bear on legal and social perceptions of rape. I suggest the example of SlutWalk impresses the need to recognize the sites at which post-neoliberal feminism is already underway and to support the critiques that are unfolding there, discerning and building on their modes of critical refusal and complaint and, most crucially, co-insisting that feminist political and theoretical interventions be shaped intersectionally – for, as my analysis has shown, the interventions of feminism's uncanny doubles certainly are not shaped in this way, instead serving to revive the universalizing and essentializing discourses of Western feminism. In the strongest examples of neoliberal feminism that I have discussed – the popular press critiques of victim feminism – we see the 'uncanny double' resignify and depoliticize second-wave feminism's 'best ideas', while also powerfully reviving the aspects of feminism that have been most consistently and persuasively challenged in the long moment of the second wave. In the move to downsize and depoliticize feminist political terrain, these critiques redraw cultural essentialism and the emancipated/emaciated binary, and on the way to emptying 'gender' of its sociological meaning and significance they perversely reassert the primacy of gender, militating against the more politically threatening conception of gender as existing among an intersecting array of engines of social hierarchy and difference, thus a wider field of political contestation. In what may be its most significant political weakness – and in what should, ethically, be its political undoing – neoliberal feminism has resignified second-wave feminism's best ideas while also faithfully reviving its least edifying constructions, a fate our work of reclaiming need not share.

BIBLIOGRAPHY

Abbey, R. (1996). Beyond misogyny and metaphor: Women in Nietzsche's middle period. *Journal of the History of Philosophy XXXIV*(2) (April): 233–256.

Abramovitz, M. (2002). Still under attack: Women and welfare reform. In Holstrom, N. (Ed.) *The socialist feminist project: A contemporary reader in theory and politics*. New York: Monthly Review Press.

Abrams, K. (1995). Sex wars redux: Agency and coercion in feminist legal theory. *Columbia Law Review 95*(2): 304–376.

Ainley, A. (1988). 'Ideal selfishness': Nietzsche's metaphor of maternity. In Krell, F. D. and Wood, D. (Eds) *Exceedingly Nietzsche: Aspects of contemporary Nietzsche interpretation*. New York: Routledge.

Alcoff, L. and Gray, L. (1993). Survivor discourse: Transgression or recuperation? *Signs: Journal of Women in Culture and Society 18*(2) (Winter): 260–290.

Allen, A. (1998). Rethinking power. *Hypatia 13*(1): 21–40.

Allison, J. A. and Wrightsman, L. S. (1993). *Rape: The misunderstood crime*. Thousand Oaks, CA: Sage.

Améry, J. (1980). *At the mind's limits: Contemplations by a survivor on Auschwitz and its realities* (S. Rosenfeld and S. P. Rosenfeld, Trans.). Bloomington and Indianapolis: Indiana University Press.

Amir, M. (1971). *Patterns in forcible rape*. Chicago: University of Chicago Press.

Anderson, I. and Doherty, K. (2008). *Accounting for rape: Psychology, feminism and discourse analysis in the study of sexual violence*. London: Routledge.

Angelides, S. (2005). The emergence of the paedophile in the late twentieth century. *Australian Historical Studies 126*: 272–295.

Appel, F. (1997). The Übermensch's consort: Nietzsche and the 'eternal feminine'. *History of Political Thought 18*(3): 512–530.

Apple, M. W. (2001). *Educating the 'right' way: Markets, standards, God, and inequality*. New York: RoutledgeFalmer.

Armstrong, N. (1998). Captivity and cultural capital in the English novel. *Novel: A Forum on Fiction 31* (Summer): 373–398.

Armstrong, N. and Tennenhouse, L. (1992). *The imaginary puritan: Literature, intellectual labour, and the origins of personal life*. Berkeley, CA: University of California Press.

Aschheim, S. E. (1992). *The Nietzsche legacy in Germany, 1890–1990*. Berkeley, CA: University of California Press.

Atmore, C. (1999). Victims, backlash, and radical feminist theory. In Lamb, S. (Ed.) *New versions of victims: Feminists struggle with the concept.* New York: New York University Press.

Bail, K. (1996). *Do-it-yourself feminism.* Sydney: Allen & Unwin.

Baird, B. (2008). Child politics, feminist analyses. *Australian Feminist Studies 23*(57): 291–305.

Baker, J. (2008). The ideology of choice. Overstating progress and hiding injustice in the lives of young women: findings from a study in North Queensland, Australia. *Women's Studies International Forum 31*: 53–64.

Baker, J. (2010). Claiming volition and evading victimhood: Post-feminist obligations for young women. *Feminism & Psychology 20*(2): 186–204.

Balibar, E. (1991). Is there a 'neo-racism'? (C. Turner, Trans.). In Balibar, E. and Wallerstein, I. (Eds) *Race, nation, class: Ambiguous identities.* London: Verso.

Bannon, I. and Correia, M. C. (Eds) (2006). *The other half of gender: Men's issues in development.* Washington, DC: The World Bank.

Bar On, B.-A. (Ed.) (1994). *Modern engendering: Critical feminist readings in modern western philosophy.* Albany, NY: State University of New York Press.

Bartky, S. (1990). *Femininity and domination: Studies in the phenomenology of oppression.* New York: Routledge.

Baudrillard, J. (1997). *Le paroxysme: entretiens avec Philippe Petit.* Paris: Bernard Grasset.

Behler, D. (1993). Nietzsche and postfeminism. *Nietzsche-Studien 22*: 355–370.

Bell, D. and Nelson, T. N. (1989). Speaking about rape is everyone's business. *Women's Studies International Forum 12*: 403–416.

Bell, V. (1999). *Feminist imagination: Genealogies in feminist theory.* London: Sage.

Bergoffen, D. (1989). On the advantage and disadvantage of Nietzsche for women. In Dallery, A. B. and Scott, C. E. (Eds) *The question of the other: Essays in contemporary continental philosophy.* Albany, NY: State University of New York Press.

Bergoffen, D. (1994). Nietzsche was no feminist . . . . *International Studies in Philosophy XXVI*(3): 23–31.

Berns, N. (2004). *Framing the victim: Domestic violence, media and social problems.* Hawthorne, NY: Aldine de Gruyter.

Bernstein, E. (2010). Militarized humanitarianism meets carceral feminism: The politics of sex, rights, and freedom in contemporary anti-trafficking campaigns. *Signs: Journal of Women in Culture and Society 36*: 45–71.

Bertram, M. (1984). 'God's second blunder': Serpent woman and the *Gestalt* in Nietzsche's thought. *Southern Journal of Philosophy 19*(3): 259–277.

Blair, T. (1996). *New Britain: My vision of a young country.* London: Fourth Estate.

Bloom, A. (1987). *The closing of the American mind.* New York: Simon & Schuster.

Boltanski, L. and Chiapello, E. ([1999] 2005). *The New Spirit of Capitalism.* London: Verso.

Breitenbecher, K. H. (2006). The relationships among self-blame, psychological distress and sexual victimization. *Journal of Interpersonal Violence 21*(5): 597–611.

Brennan, L. (2013). *Lani's story: Not a victim. A survivor.* Sydney: HarperCollins.

Bridenthal, R., Grossman, A. and Kaplan, M. (Eds) (1984). *When biology became destiny: Women in Weimar and Nazi Germany.* New York: Monthly Review Press.

Brodie, J. (2005). Globalisation, governance and gender: Rethinking the agenda for the twenty-first century. In Amoore, L. (Ed.) *The global resistance reader.* London: Routledge.

Brown, W. (1995). *States of injury: Power and freedom in late modernity*. Princeton, NJ: Princeton University Press.

Brown W. (2000). Nietzsche for politics. In Schrift, A. (Ed.) *Why Nietzsche still? Reflections on drama, culture and politics*. Berkeley, CA: University of California Press.

Brown, W. (2001). *Politics out of history*. Princeton, NJ: Princeton University Press.

Brown, W. and Halley, J. (Eds) (2002). *Left legalism/left critique*. Durham, NC: Duke University Press.

Bumiller, K. (1987). Rape as a legal symbol: An essay on sexual violence and racism. *University of Miami Law Review 42*(75): 75–91.

Bumiller, K. (1990). Fallen angels: The representation of violence against women in legal culture. *International Journal of the Sociology of Law 18*: 125–142.

Bumiller, K. (2008). *In an abusive state: How neoliberalism appropriated the feminist movement against sexual violence*. Durham, NC: Duke University Press.

Burckhardt, J. ([1860] 1995). *The civilisation of the Renaissance in Italy*. London: Phaidon Press.

Burgard, P. J. (Ed.) (1994). *Nietzsche and the feminine*. Charlottesville, VA: University of Virginia Press.

Burney-Davis, T. and King, R. S. (1989). The Vita Femina and truth. *History of European Ideas 11*: 841–847.

Butler, J. (1990). *Gender trouble: Feminism and the subversion of identity*. New York: Routledge.

Callinicos, A. (2001). *Against the third way: An anti-capitalist critique*. Cambridge: Polity Press.

Castaglia, C. (1996). *Bound and determined: Captivity, culture-crossing, and white womanhood from Mary Rowlandson to Patty Hearst*. Chicago: University of Chicago Press.

Chow, R. (2002). *The Protestant ethnic and the spirit of capitalism*. New York: Columbia University Press.

Clark, L. M. G. and Lange, L. (Eds) (1979). *The sexism of social and political theory: Women and reproduction from Plato to Nietzsche*. Toronto: University of Toronto Press.

Clark, M. (1994). Nietzsche's misogyny. *International Studies in Philosophy 26*(3): 3–12.

Cocks, J. (1989). *The oppositional imagination: Feminist, critique and political theory*. London and New York: Routledge.

Cocks, J. (1991). Augustine, Nietzsche and contemporary body politics. *Differences 3* (Spring): 144–158.

Cocks, J. (1997). Review: Wendy Brown, *States of Injury*. *American Journal of Sociology 103*(3): 810–811.

Cole, A. M. (2007). *The cult of true victimhood: From the war on welfare to the war on terror*. Stanford, CA: Stanford University Press.

Connolly, W. (1988). *Political theory and modernity*. Oxford: Blackwell.

Connolly, W. (1997). Reworking the Democratic imagination. *The Journal of Political Philosophy 5* (June): 183–193.

Conway, D. (1993). *Das Weib an Sich*: The slave revolt in epistemology. In Patton, P. (Ed.) *Nietzsche, feminism and political theory*. Sydney: Allen & Unwin.

Cooper, D. (2010). The pain and power of sexual interests: Responding to *Split Decisions*. *International Journal of Law in Context 6*(1): 94–99.

Coulter, A. (2009). *Guilty: Liberal 'victims' and their assault on America*. New York: Crown Forum.

Coulthard, G. (2007). Subjects of empire: Indigenous peoples and the 'politics of recognition' in Canada. *Contemporary Political Theory 6*(4): 437–460.

Coulthard, G. (2012). Seeing red: Recognition, reconciliation and resentment in indigenous politics. Public lecture, Dalhousie University, Halifax, Canada. Available at: http://halifax.mediacoop.ca/events/9499 (accessed 10 September 2013).

D'Souza, D. (1991). *Illiberal education: The politics of race and sex on campus*. New York: Free Press.

Dahl, G. (2009). Sociology and beyond: Agency, victimization and the ethics of writing. *The Asian Journal of Social Science 37*: 391–407.

Davis, M. (1997). Crying in public places: Neoconservatism and victim panic. In Mead, J. (Ed.) *Bodyjamming: Feminism, sexual harassment and public life*. Sydney: Vintage.

Dean, C. (2010). *Aversion and erasure: The fate of the victim after the Holocaust*. Ithaca, NY: Cornell University Press.

Del Caro, A. (1990). The pseudoman in Nietzsche, or the threat of the neuter. *New German Critique 50* (Spring/Summer): 133–156.

Deleuze, G. (1983). *Nietzsche and philosophy* (H. Tomlinson, Trans.). New York: Columbia University Press.

Deleuze, G. and Guattari, F. (1986). *Kafka: Toward a minor literature* (D. Polan, Trans.). Minneapolis, MN: University of Minnesota Press.

Denfeld, R. (1995). *The new Victorians: A young woman's challenge to the old feminist order*. Sydney: Allen & Unwin.

Derrida, J. (1979). *Spurs/eperons: Nietzsche's styles* (B. Harlow, Trans.). Chicago: University of Chicago Press.

Derrida, J. and McDonald, C. (1982). Interview: Choreographies. In McDonald, C. (Ed.) *The ear of the other: Otobiography, transference, translation*. Lincoln, NB: University of Nebraska Press.

Deutscher, P. (1993). 'Is it not remarkable that Nietzsche . . . should have hated Rousseau?' Woman, femininity: Distancing Nietzsche from Rousseau. In Patton, P. (Ed.) *Nietzsche, feminism and political theory*. Sydney: Allen & Unwin.

Dever, M. (2008). *Gender differences in post-PhD employment in Australian universities: The influence of PhD experience on women's academic careers—final report*. Brisbane: The University of Queensland Social Research Centre.

Devine, M. (2004, 29 February). Crying Wolf belittles plight of real victims. *The Sydney Morning Herald*, p. 15.

Diethe, C. (1989). Nietzsche and the woman question. *History of European Ideas 11*: 865–875.

Diethe, C. (1996). Nietzsche and the Early German feminists. *Journal of Nietzsche Studies 12* (Autumn): 69–82.

Diprose, R. (1989). Nietzsche, ethics and sexual difference. *Radical Philosophy 52* (Summer): 27–33.

Diprose, R. (1994). *The bodies of women: Ethics, embodiment and sexual difference*. New York: Routledge.

Dow, B. J. (1996). *Prime-time feminism: Television, media culture, and the women's movement since 1970*. Philadelphia, PA: University of Pennsylvania Press.

Due, C. and Riggs, D. W. (2012). The terms on which child abuse is made to matter: Media representations of the Aurukun Case. *Australian Feminist Studies 27*(71): 3–18.

Duggan, L. (2003). *The twilight of equality? Neoliberalism, cultural politics and the attack on democracy.* Boston: Beacon Press.

Dühring, E. (1865). *Der Werth des Lebens: Eine philosophische Betrachtung.* Breslau.

Duménil, G. and Lévy, D. (2004). *Capital resurgent: Roots of the neoliberal revolution* (D. Jeffers, Trans.). Cambridge, MA: Harvard University Press.

Dworkin, A. (1976). *Our blood: Prophecies and discourses on sexual politics.* New York: Perigee Books.

Dzodan, F. (2011). MY FEMINISM WILL BE INTERSECTIONAL OR IT WILL BE BULLSHIT! Available at: http://tigerbeatdown.com (accessed 7 June 2012).

Ehrenreich, B. (2009). *Smile or die: How positive thinking fooled America and the world.* London: Granta.

Ehrenreich, B. and Hochschild, A. (Eds) (2004). *Global woman: Nannies, maids and sex workers in the new economy.* New York: Owl Books.

Eisenstein, Z. (1997). Feminism of the north and west for export: Transnational capital and the racialising of gender. In Dean, J. (Ed.) *Feminism and the new democracy: Resiting the political.* London: Sage.

Elder, L. (2000). *Ten things you can't say in America.* New York: St Martin's Press.

Engels, F. ([1894] 1969). *Anti-Dühring: Herr Eugen Dühring's revolution in science.* Moscow: Progress Publishers.

Estrich, S. (1987). *Real rape: How the legal system victimises women who say no.* Cambridge, MA: Harvard University Press.

Evans, R. J. (1976). *The feminist movement in Germany 1894–1933.* London: Sage.

Faludi, S. (1992). *Backlash: The undeclared war against women.* London: Chatto & Windus.

Faust, B. (1993). *Backlash? Balderdash! Where feminism is going right.* Sydney: University of New South Wales Press.

Felson, R. B. (2002). *Violence and gender reexamined.* Washington, DC: American Psychological Association.

Foucault, M. ([1979] 1984). Nietzsche, genealogy, history. In Rabinow, P. (Ed.) *The Foucault reader.* New York: Pantheon.

Frank, T. (2006). *What's the matter with America? The resistible rise of the American Right.* London: Vintage Books.

Fraser, N. (2009). Feminism, capitalism and the cunning of history. *New Left Review 56*: 97–117.

French, M. ([1978] 1992). *The women's room.* London: Warner.

Friedan, B. (1963). *The feminine mystique.* London: Penguin.

Fukuyama, F. (1992). *The end of history and the last man.* New York: The Free Press.

Galinsky, E. and Friedman, D. (1995). *Women: The new providers* (Whirlpool Foundation Study, Part 1). New York: Families and Work Institute.

Garner, H. (1995). *The first stone: Some questions about sex and power.* Sydney: Picador.

Gatens, M. (1996). *Imaginary bodies: Ethics, power and corporeality.* New York: Routledge.

Gavey, N. (1999). 'I wasn't raped, but . . .': Revisiting definitional problems in sexual victimisation. In Lamb, S. (Ed.) *New versions of victims: Feminists struggle with the concept.* New York: New York University Press.

Gavey, N. (2005). *Just sex? The cultural scaffolding of rape.* London: Routledge.

Gelles, R. J. and Straus, M. A. (1990). *Physical violence in American families: Risk factors and adaptations to violence in 8,145 families.* Piscataway, NJ: Transaction Publishers.

Giddens, A. (2001). *The Third Way and its critics*. Cambridge: Polity Press.

Gill, R. (2007a). Critical respect: The difficulties and dilemmas of agency and 'choice' for feminism: A reply to Duits and Van Zoonen. *European Journal of Women's Studies* *14*(1): 69–80.

Gill, R. (2007b). Postfeminist media culture, elements of a sensibility. *European Journal of Cultural Studies 10*(2): 147–166.

Gill, R. (2008). Culture and subjectivity in neoliberal and feminist times. *Subjectivity 25*: 432–445.

Gill, R. and Scharff, C. (Eds) (2011). *New femininities: Postfeminism, neoliberalism and subjectivity*. London: Palgrave Macmillan.

Gotell, L. (2008). Rethinking affirmative consent in Canadian sexual assault law: Neoliberal sexual subjects and risky women. *Akron Law Review 41*(4): 878–879.

Gotell, L. (2010). Canadian sexual assault law: Neoliberalism and the erosion of feminist-inspired law reform. In McGlynn, C. and Munro, V. (Eds) *Rethinking rape law*. London: Routledge.

Gotell, L. (2012). Third wave antirape activism on neoliberal terrain: The mobilization of the Garneau sisterhood. In Sheehy, E. (Ed.) *Sexual assault in Canada: Law, legal practice and women's activism*. Ottawa: University of Ottawa Press.

Graybeal, J. (1998). *Ecce Homo*: Abjection and 'the feminine'. In Oliver, K. and Pearsall, M. (Eds) *Feminist interpretations of Friedrich Nietzsche*. Philadelphia, PA: Pennsylvania State University Press.

Green, D. G. (2006). *We're (nearly) all victims now: How political correctness is undermining our liberal culture*. London: Civitas.

Greenfeld, L. A. (1997). *Sex offenses and offenders: An analysis of data on rape and sexual assault*. Washington, DC: Bureau of Justice Statistics, Office of Justice Programs, U.S. Department of Justice. Minnesota Center Against Violence and Abuse. Available at: http://www.mincava.umn.edu (accessed 4 April 2013).

Greer, G. (1971). *The female eunuch*. London: Paladin.

Gruber, A. (2009). The feminist war on crime. *Iowa Law Review 92*: 741–833.

Haag, P. (1996). 'Putting your body on the line': The question of violence, victims, and the legacies of second-wave feminism. *Differences 8*(2): 24–67.

Hall, R. (2004). 'It can happen to you': Rape prevention in the age of risk management. *Hypatia 19*(3): 1–19.

Halley, J. (2002). Sexuality harassment. In Brown, W. and Halley, J. (Eds) *Left legalism/Left critique*. Durham, NC: Duke University Press.

Halley, J. (2006). *Split decisions: How and why to take a break from feminism*. Princeton, NJ: Princeton University Press.

Halley, J., Kotiswaran, P., Shamir, H. and Thomas, C. (2006). From the international to the local in feminist legal responses to rape, prostitution/sex work, and sex trafficking: Four studies in contemporary governance feminism. *Harvard Journal of Law & Gender 29*(2): 335–423.

Handler, J. and Hasenfeld, Y. (2007). *Blame welfare, ignore poverty and inequality*. Cambridge: Cambridge University Press.

Haraway, D. (1991). *Simians, cyborgs and women: The reinvention of nature*. New York: Routledge.

Harding, S. (1986). *The science question in feminism*. Ithaca, NY: Cornell University Press.

Hartsock, N. (1983). The feminist standpoint: Developing the ground for a specifically feminist historical materialism. In Harding, S. and Hintakka, M. B. (Eds) *Discovering reality: Feminist perspectives on epistemology, metaphysics, methodology and philosophy of science*. Dordrecht: Reidel.

Harvey, D. (2005). *A brief history of neoliberalism*. Oxford: Oxford University Press.

Hatab, L. J. (1981). Nietzsche on woman. *Southern Journal of Philosophy 19*(3): 333–345.

Hays, S. (2003). *Flat broke with children: Women in the age of welfare reform*. Oxford: Oxford University Press.

Heberle, R. (1996). Deconstructive strategies and the movement against sexual violence. *Hypatia 11* (Fall): 63–76.

Helliwell, C. and Hindess, B. (2005). The temporalizing of difference. *Ethnicities 5*(3): 414–418.

Helliwell, C. and Hindess, B. (2013). Time and the others. In Seth, S. (Ed.) *Postcolonial theory and international relations: A critical introduction*. London: Routledge.

Hennessey, R. (2000). *Profit and pleasure: Sexual identities in late capitalism*. London and New York: Routledge.

Hindess, B. (2002). Neo-liberal citizenship. *Citizenship Studies 6*(2): 127–143.

Hoeveler, D. L. (1998). *Gothic feminism: The professionalization of gender from Charlotte Smith to the Brontës*. Philadelphia, PA: Pennsylvania State University Press.

Hoffman, J. and Graham, P. (2006). *Introduction to political theory*. Harlow: Pearson.

hooks, b. (1984). Sisterhood: political solidarity between women. In *Feminist theory: From margin to center*. Boston: South End Press.

hooks, b. (1999). *Outlaw culture: Resisting representations*. New York: Routledge.

Hosking, J. (2002, 31 March). The rape survivor who faced fear to fight back. *Sunday Star Times*, C5, C10.

Huggins, J. et al. (1991). Letter to the Editor Re. Diane Bell. *Women's Studies International Forum 14*: np.

Hughes, R. (1993). *The culture of complaint: The fraying of America*. Oxford: Oxford University Press.

Humphries, D. (2006, 23 September). Woman most likely. *The Sydney Morning Herald*. Available at: www.smh.com.au (accessed 25 September 2006).

Irigaray, L. (1991). *Marine lover of Friedrich Nietzsche* (G. C. Gill, Trans.). New York: Columbia University Press.

Isin, E. (2002). *Being political: Genealogies of citizenship*. Minneapolis, MN: University of Minnesota Press.

Jameson, F. (1981). *The political unconscious*. Ithaca, NY: Cornell University Press.

Kapur, R. (2002). The tragedy of victimisation rhetoric: Resurrecting the 'native subject' in international/post-colonial feminist legal politics. *Harvard Human Rights Journal 15* (Spring): 1–38.

Kapur, R. (2012). Pink Chaddis and SlutWalk couture: The postcolonial politics of feminism lite. *Feminist Legal Studies 20*(1): 1–20.

Katz, B. L. and Burt, M. R. (1988). Self-blame in recovery from rape: Help or hindrance? In Burgess, A. W. (Ed.) *Rape and sexual assault II*. New York: Garland.

Katz, M. N. (1999). *Reflections on revolutions*. New York: St Martin's Press.

Kaye, M. and Tolmie, J. (1998). Discoursing dads: the rhetorical devices of fathers' rights groups. *Melbourne University Law Review 22*: 162–194.

Keay, D. (1987, 23 September). Interview with Margaret Thatcher. *Woman's Own*, pp. 8–10.

Kelly, L. (1988). *Surviving sexual violence*. Minneapolis, MN: University of Minnesota Press.

Kelly, L., Burton, S. and Regan, L. (1996). Beyond victim or survivor: Sexual violence, identity and feminist theory and practice. In Adkins, L. and Merchant, V. (Eds) *Sexualising the social: Power and the organisation of sexuality*. London: Macmillan Press.

Kempadoo, K. (1998). Introduction: Globalizing sex worker rights. In Kempadoo, K. and Doezema, J. (Eds) *Global sex workers: Rights, resistance, and redefinition*. New York: Routledge.

Kennedy, E. (1987). Women as *Untermensch*. In Kennedy, E. and Mendus, S. (Eds) *Women in western political philosophy*. Brighton, Sussex: Wheatsheaf Books.

Kidd, R. and Chayet, E. (1984). Why do victims fail to report? The psychology of criminal victimisation. *Journal of Social Issues 40*(1): 39–50.

Knowles. G. (2013). SlutWalk Speech 2013. Available at: http://rapecrisisdunedin.tumblr. com (accessed 15 October 2013).

Kofman, S. (1994). A fantastical genealogy: Nietzsche's family romance. In Burgard, P. J. (Ed.) *Nietzsche and the feminine*. Charlottesville, VA: University of Virginia Press.

Koyama, E. (2011, 22 November). Reclaiming 'victim': Exploring alternatives to the heteronormative 'victim to survivor' discourse. *Eminism*. Available at: http://eminism. org (accessed 11 October 2013).

Laclau, E. and Mouffe, C. (1985). *Hegemony and socialist strategy: Towards a radical democratic politics*. London: Verso.

Lamb, S. (1996). *The trouble with blame: Victims, perpetrators, and responsibility*. Cambridge, MA: Harvard University Press.

Lamb, S. (1999). Constructing the victim: Popular images and lasting labels. In Lamb, S. (Ed.) *New versions of victims: Feminists struggle with the concept*. New York: New York University Press.

Larbalestier, J. (1990). The politics of representation: Australian Aboriginal women and feminism. *Anthropological Forum 6*(2): 143–166.

Laster, K. and Erez, E. (2000). The Oprah dilemma: The use and abuse of victims. In O'Malley, P. (Ed.) *Crime and the criminal justice system in Australia: 2000 and beyond*. Sydney: Allen & Unwin.

Le Dœuff, M. (1987). Ants and women, or philosophy without borders. In Griffiths, A. P. (Ed.) *Contemporary French philosophy*. Cambridge: Cambridge University Press.

Logan, L. (1993). Mary Rowlandson's Captivity and the 'place' of the woman subject. *Early American Literature 28*: 225–277.

Lougheed, P. (2002). 'Then began he to rant and threaten': Indian malice and individual liberty in Mary Rowlandson's captivity narrative. *American Literature 74*(2): 287–313.

Lyotard, J.-F. (1988) *The differend: Phrases in dispute* (G. V. D. Abbeele, Trans.). Minneapolis, MN: Minnesota University Press.

MacDonald, E. and Tinsley, Y. (2011) *From 'real rape' to real justice: Prosecuting rape in New Zealand*. Wellington: Victoria University Press.

Macintyre, S. and Clark, A. (2003) *The history wars*. Melbourne: Melbourne University Press.

Manzo, K. (2008). Imaging humanitarianism: NGO identity and the iconography of childhood. *Antipode 40*(4): 632–657.

Marcus, S. (1992). Fighting bodies, fighting words: A theory and politics of rape prevention. In Butler, J. and Scott, J. (Eds) *Feminists theorise the political*. New York: Routledge.

Mardorossian, C. M. (2002). Towards a new feminist theory of rape. *Signs: Journal of Women in Culture and Society 27*(3): 743–775.

Maushart, S. (2007) *What women want next*. London: Bloomsbury.

McCaffrey, D. (1998). Victim feminism/victim activism. *Sociological Spectrum 18*(3): 263–284.

McDermott, P. (1995). On cultural authority: Women's studies, feminist politics, and the popular press. *Signs: Journal of Women in Culture and Society 20*: 668–684.

McLaughlin, K. (2012) *Surviving identity: Vulnerability and the psychology of recognition*. London: Routledge.

McLeer, A. (1998). Saving the victim: Recuperating the language of the victim and reassessing global feminism. *Hypatia 13* (Winter): 41–55.

McRobbie, A. (2004). Post-feminism and popular culture. *Feminist Media Studies 4*(3): 255–264.

Mead, J. (Ed.) (1997). *Bodyjamming: Sexual harassment, feminism and public life*. Sydney: Random House.

Mendieta, E. (2005). *Abolition democracy: Beyond empire, torture and prisons*. New York: Seven Stories Press.

Meyer, D. (1980). *The positive thinkers: A study of the American quest for health, wealth and personal power, from Mary Baker Eddy to Normal Vincent Peale*. New York: Pantheon Books.

Minow, M. (1993). Surviving victim talk. *UCLA Law Review 40*: 1413–1428.

Mohanty, C. T. (1986). Under Western eyes: Feminist scholarship and colonial discourses. *Boundary 2*(12): 333–358.

Moreton-Robinson, A. (2003). Tiddas talkin' up to the white woman: When Huggins et al. took on Bell. In Grossman, M. (Ed.) *Blacklines: Contemporary critical writing by indigenous Australians*. Melbourne: Melbourne University Press.

Moreton-Robinson, A. (2009). Imagining the good indigenous citizen: Race war and the pathology of patriarchal white sovereignty. *Cultural Studies Review 15*(2): 61–79.

Moreton-Robinson, A. (2011). The white man's burden: Patriarchal white epistemic violence and aboriginal women's knowledges within the academy. *Australian Feminist Studies 26*(70): 413–431.

Morrison, T. (ed.) (1992). *Race-ing justice, en-gendering power: Essays on Anita Hill, Clarence Thomas, and the construction of social reality*. New York: Pantheon Books.

Mouffe, C. (1996). Democracy, power and the 'political'. In Benhabib, S. (Ed.) *Democracy and difference: Contesting the boundaries of the political*. Princeton, NJ: Princeton University Press.

Naqvi, F. (2007). *The literary and cultural rhetoric of victimhood: Western Europe, 1970–2005*. New York: Palgrave Macmillan.

Narayan, U. (1997). *Dislocating cultures: Identities, traditions and Third World feminism*. New York: Routledge.

Nietzsche, F. W. ([1870–2] 1998). *Philosophy in the tragic age of the Greeks* (M. Cowan, Trans.). Washington, DC: Gateway.

Nietzsche, F. W. ([1875] 1973). *Kritische Gesamtausgabe: Werke*, Colli, G. and Montinari, M. (Eds). Berlin, vol. IV/1.

Nietzsche, F. W. ([1878] 1994). *Human, all too human* (M. Faber and S. Lehmann, Trans.). London: Penguin Books.

Nietzsche, F. W. ([1881] 1995). *Daybreak: Thoughts on the prejudices of morality* (R. J. Hollingdale, Trans.). Cambridge: Cambridge University Press.

Nietzsche, F. W. ([1882–6] 1974). *The gay science: With a prelude in rhymes and an appendix of songs* (W. Kaufmann, Trans.). New York: Vintage Books.

171

Nietzsche, F. W. ([1883–5] 1961). *Thus spoke Zarathustra: A book for all and none* (R. J. Hollingdale, Trans.). London: Penguin Books.

Nietzsche, F. W. ([1886] 1989). *Beyond good and evil: Prelude to a philosophy of the future* (W. Kaufmann, Trans.). New York: Vintage Books.

Nietzsche, F. W. ([1887] 1989) *On the genealogy of morals: A polemic* (W. Kaufmann, Trans.). New York: Vintage Books.

Nietzsche, F. W. ([1889] 1990) *Twilight of the idols* (R. J. Hollingdale, Trans.). London: Penguin Books.

Nietzsche, F. W. ([1901] 1989). *Ecce Homo: How one becomes what one is* (W. Kaufmann, Trans.). New York: Vintage Books.

Nissim-Sabat, M. (2009). *Neither victim nor survivor: Thinking toward a new humanity.* Lanham, MD: Lexington Books.

Oliver, K. (1995). *Womanizing Nietzsche: Philosophy's relation to the 'feminine'.* New York: Routledge.

Oliver, K. and Pearsall, M. (Eds) (1998). *Feminist interpretations of Friedrich Nietzsche.* Philadelphia, PA: Pennsylvania State University Press.

O'Malley, P. (1992). Risk, power and crime prevention. *Economy and Society 21*(3): 252–275.

Osborne, P. and Segal, L. (1996). Gender as performance: Judith Butler. In Osborne, P. (Ed.) *A critical sense: Interviews with intellectuals.* London and New York: Routledge.

Paglia, C. (1994). *Vamps and tramps: New essays.* London: Viking.

Paltrow, L. (2008). Lessons from the U.S. experience of unborn victims of violence laws. New York: Advocates for Pregnant Women. Available at: http://advocatesfor pregnantwomen.org (accessed 1 May 2008).

Pateman, C. (1988). *The sexual contract.* Cambridge: Polity Press.

Pateman, C. (1989). *The disorder of women: Democracy, feminism and political theory.* Stanford, CA: Stanford University Press.

Peterson, Z. and Muehlenhard, C. (2004). Was it rape? The function of women's rape myth acceptance and definitions of sex in labeling their own experiences. *Sex Roles: A Journal of Research 51*(3–4): 129–144.

Pettit, B. and Western, B. (2004). Mass imprisonment and the life course: Race and class inequality in U.S. incarceration. *American Sociological Review 69*(2): 151–169.

Picart, C. J. S. (1999). *Resentment and the 'feminine' in Nietzsche's politico-aesthetic.* Philadelphia, PA: Pennsylvania State University Press.

Pizzey, E., Shackleton, J. R. and Urwin, P. (2000). *Women or men: Who are the victims?* London: Civitas Institute for the Study of Civil Society.

Pollin, R. (2000). Anatomy of Clintonomics. *New Left Review 3* (May/June): 17–46.

Power, N. (2009). *One dimensional woman.* London: Zero Books.

Radner, H. (2011). *Neo-feminist cinema: Girly films, chick flicks and consumer culture.* New York: Routledge.

Rancière, J. (1992). Politics, identification and subjectivization. *October 61* (Summer): 58–65.

Redfern, C. and Aune, K. (2013). *Reclaiming the F word: Feminism today* (2nd edn). London: Zed Books.

Ridley, A. (1998). *Nietzsche's conscience: Six character studies from the 'genealogy'.* Ithaca, NY: Cornell University Press.

Riley, R. L., Mohanty, C. T. and Pratt, M. B. (Eds) (2008). *Feminism and war: Confronting US imperialism.* New York: Zed Books.

Ringrose, J. and Renold, E. (2012). Slut-shaming, girl power and 'sexualisation': Thinking through the politics of the international Slutwalks with teen girls. *Gender and Education 24*(3): 333–343.

Roberts, D. (1997). *Killing the black body: Race, reproduction and the meaning of liberty*. New York: Vintage.

Robinson, D. (2006). *The status of higher education teaching personnel in Australia, Canada, New Zealand, the United Kingdom and the United States* (Report Prepared for Education International). Ottawa: Canadian Association of University Teachers.

Rock, P. (2004). *Constructing victims rights: The Home Office, New Labour and victims*. Oxford: Oxford University Press.

Roiphe, K. (1993). *The morning after: Sex, fear and feminism*. London: Hamish Hamilton.

Roiphe, K. (2011, 12 November). In favor of dirty jokes and risqué remarks. *The New York Times*. Available at: www.nytimes.com (accessed 13 November 2011).

Roiphe, K. (2013, 8 October). Was philosophy Prof. Colin McGinn's story really a clear-cut case of sexual harassment? *Slate*. Available at: www.slate.com (accessed 11 October 2013).

Ronai, C. R. (1999). In the line of sight at *Public Eye*: In search of a victim. In Lamb, S. (Ed.) *New versions of victims: Feminists struggle with the concept*. New York: New York University Press.

Ronell, A. (1991). Avital Ronell (interview A. Juno). *Re/Search: Angry women*. San Francisco: Re/Search Publications.

Rose, S. and Hartmann, H. (2004). *Still a man's labor market: The long-term earnings gap*. Washington, DC: The Institute for Women's Policy Research.

Rosen, R. (2000). *The world split open: How the modern women's movement changed America*. London: Penguin Books.

Rowlands, S. and Henderson, M. (1996). Damned bores and slick sisters: The selling of blockbuster feminism in Australia. *Australian Feminist Studies 11*(23): 9–16.

Sales, E., Baum, M. and Shore, B. (1984). Victim readjustment following assault. *Journal of Social Issues 40*(1): 117–136.

Sartre, J.-P. (1969). *Being and nothingness* (H. E. Barnes, Trans.). London: Methuen.

Schaffer, K. and Randall, D. (2001). Transglobal translations: The Eliza Fraser and Rachel Plummer captivity narratives. In Harper, G. (Ed.) *Colonial and postcolonial incarceration*. London: Continuum.

Scharff, C. (2011). Disarticulating feminism: Individualization, neoliberalism and the othering of Muslim women. *European Journal of Women's Studies 18*(2): 119–134.

Scheler, M. ([1915] 1961). *Ressentiment* (W. H. Holdheim, Trans.). New York: Free Press.

Schmidt, R. (1993). 'Dissonance is the voice of the future': Lily Braun's *Memoiren einer Sozialistin*. In Keith-Smith, B. (Ed.) *German women writers, 1900–1933: Twelve essays*. New York: The Edwin Mellen Press.

Schram, S. (2000). *After welfare: The culture of postindustrial social policy*. New York: New York University Press.

Schrift, A. D. (1994). On the gift-giving virtue: Nietzsche's feminine economy. *International Studies in Philosophy XXVI*(3): 33–44.

Schutte, O. (1984). *Beyond nihilism: Nietzsche without masks*. Chicago: University of Chicago Press.

Schutte, O. (1994). Nietzsche's psychology of gender difference. In Bar On, B.-A. (Ed.) *Modern engendering: Critical feminist readings in modern western philosophy*. Albany, NY: State University of New York Press.

Scott, J., Crompton, R. and Lyonette, C. (eds) (2010). *Gender inequalities in the 21st century: New barriers and continuing constraints.* Cheltenham: Edward Elgar.

Sharpe, J. (1993). *Allegories of empire: The figure of woman in the colonial text.* Minneapolis, MN: University of Minnesota Press.

Sherman, Y. D. (2011). Neoliberal femininity in *Miss Congeniality.* In Radner, H. and Stringer, R. (Eds) *Feminism at the movies: Understanding gender in contemporary popular cinema.* New York: Routledge.

Shklar, J. (1984). *Ordinary vices.* Cambridge, MA: Harvard University Press.

Singer, L. ([1983] 1998). Nietzschean mythologies: The inversion of value and the war against women. In Oliver, K. and Pearsall, M. (Eds) *Feminist interpretations of Friedrich Nietzsche.* Philadelphia, PA: Pennsylvania State University Press.

Small, R. (1997). *Ressentiment,* revenge, and punishment: Origins of the Nietzschean critique. *Utilitas 9* (March): 39–58.

Small, R. (2001). *Nietzsche in context.* Burlington, VA: Ashgate.

Smith, A. M. (1997). Feminist activism and presidential politics: Theorising the costs of the 'Insider strategy'. *Radical Philosophy 83* (May/June): 25–35.

Smith, C. (2002). *Proud of me.* London: Penguin Books.

Solomon, R. C. (1994). One hundred years of *ressentiment*: Nietzsche's *Genealogy of Morals.* In Schacht, R. (Ed.) *Nietzsche, genealogy, morality: Essays on Nietzsche's Genealogy of Morals.* Berkeley, CA: University of California Press.

Sommers, C. H. (1994). *Who stole feminism? How women have betrayed women.* New York: Simon & Schuster.

Sommers, C. H. (2000). *The war on boys: How misguided feminism is harming our young men.* New York: Simon & Schuster.

Sommers, C. H. (2002). The case against ratifying the United Nations Convention on the Elimination of All Forms of Discrimination Against Women (CEDAW). Testimony to the Senate Foreign Relations Committee (Washington, June 2002). Available at: www.aei.org/publications (accessed 18 April 2008).

Sommers, C. H. (2007). The subjection of Islamic women. Washington, DC: American Enterprise Institute for Public Policy Research. Available at: www.aei.org/publications (accessed 18 April 2008).

Sommers, C. H. (2013). *Freedom feminism: Its surprising history and why it matters today.* Washington, DC: American Enterprise Institute Press.

Sontag, S. (1978). *Illness as metaphor.* New York: Farrar, Straus and Giroux.

Spivak, G. C. (1985). Three women's texts and a critique of imperialism. *Critical Inquiry 12*: 234–261.

Spivak, G. C. (1988). Can the subaltern speak? In Nelson, C. and Grossberg, L. (Eds) *Marxism and the interpretation of culture.* Urbana, IL: University of Illinois Press.

Staten, H. (1990). *Nietzsche's voice.* Ithaca, NY: Cornell University Press.

Stringer, R. (2000). 'A Nietzschean breed': Feminism, victimology, *ressentiment.* In Schrift, A. (Ed.) *Why Nietzsche still? Reflections on drama, culture and politics.* Berkeley, CA: University of California Press.

Stringer, R. (2001). Blaming me, blaming you: Victim identity in recent feminism. *Outskirts: Feminisms Along the Edge 8.* Available at: www.chloe.uwa.edu.au/outskirts/ (accessed 2 February 2002).

Stringer, R. (2006). Fact, fiction and the foetus: Violence against pregnant women and the politics of abortion. *Australian Feminist Law Journal 25*: 99–117.

Stringer, R. (2011). From victim to vigilante: Gender, violence and revenge in *The Brave One* and *Hard Candy*. In Radner, H. and Stringer, R. (Eds) *Feminism at the movies: Understanding gender in contemporary popular cinema*. New York: Routledge.

Stringer, R. (2012). Impractical reconciliation: Reading the Northern Territory intervention through the Huggins–Bell debate. *Australian Feminist Studies 27*(71): 19–36.

Sugarman, R. I. (1987). *Rancor against time: The phenomenology of ressentiment*. Hamburg: Felix Meiner Verlag.

Sykes, C. (1992). *A nation of victims: The decay of the American character*. New York: St. Martin's Press.

Talbot, M. (2005). Choosing to refuse to be a victim: 'Power feminism' and the intertextuality of victimhood and choice. In Lazar, M. M. (Ed.) *Feminist critical discourse analysis: Gender, power and ideology in discourse*. London: Palgrave Macmillan.

Tapper, M. (1993). *Ressentiment* and power: some reflections of feminist practices. In Patton, P. (Ed.) *Nietzsche, feminism and political theory*. Sydney: Allen & Unwin.

Tennenhouse, L. (1996). The case of the resistant captive. *The South Atlantic Quarterly 95*(4): 919–946.

Thomas, H. R. (1983). *Nietzsche in German politics and society 1890–1918*. Manchester: Manchester University Press.

Thonnessen, W. (1973). *The emancipation of women: The rise and decline of the women's movement in Germany Social Democracy 1863–1933*. Frankfurt: Pluto.

Tirrell, L. (1994). Sexual dualism and women's self-creation: On the advantages and disadvantages of reading Nietzsche for feminists. In Burgard, P. J. (Ed.) *Nietzsche and the feminine*. Charlottesville, VA: University of Virginia Press.

Trioli, V. (1996). *Generation F: Sex, power and the young feminist*. Melbourne: Minerva.

Ullman, S. E. (2006). Social reactions, coping strategies, and self-blame attributions in adjustment to sexual assault. *Psychology of Women Quarterly 20*(4): 505–526.

US Census Bureau (2009). *The American Community Survey: 2008*. Washington, DC: US Census Bureau.

US Census Bureau (2011). *Income, poverty and health insurance coverage in the United States: 2010*. Washington, DC: US Census Bureau.

Van Dijk, J. (1999). Introducing victimology. In Van Dijk, J., Van Kaam, R. R. H. and Wemrners, J. (Eds) *Caring for crime victims*. New York: Criminal Justice Press.

Van Dijk, J. (2009). Free the victim: A critique of the western conception of victimhood. *International Review of Victimology 16*(1): 1–33.

Vetten, L. (2011). Politics and the fine art of preventing rape. *Feminism and Psychology 21*(2): 268–272.

Walter, N. (1998). *The new feminism*. London: Little, Brown and Company.

Walters, M. (1998). American gothic: Feminism, melodrama and the backlash. In Oakley, A. and Mitchell, J. (Eds) *Who's afraid of feminism? Seeing through the backlash*. London: Hamish Hamilton.

White, R. (1994). The return of the master: An interpretation of Nietzsche's *Genealogy of Morals*. In Schacht, R. (Ed.) *Nietzsche, genealogy, morality: Essays on Nietzsche's Genealogy of Morals*. Berkeley, CA: University of California Press.

Wilson, K. (2011). 'Race', gender and neoliberalism: Changing visual representations in development. *Third World Quarterly 32*(2): 315–331.

Wininger, K. J. (1998). Nietzsche's women and women's Nietzsche. In Oliver, K. and Pearsall, M. (Eds) *Feminist interpretations of Friedrich Nietzsche*. Philadelphia, PA: Pennsylvania State University Press.

Wolf, N. (1990). *The beauty myth: How images of beauty are used against women.* London: Vintage.

Wolf, N. (1993). *Fire with fire: The new female power and how it will change the twenty-first century.* London: Chatto & Windus.

Wolf, N. (2004, 1 March). The silent treatment. *New York Magazine*, pp. 10–15.

Wolfe, P. (2006). Settler colonialism and the elimination of the native. *Journal of Genocide Research 8*(4): 387–409.

Wolfgang, M. (1958). *Patterns of criminal homicide.* Philadelphia, PA: University of Pennsylvania Press.

XX [Anonymous] (1997). Sticks and stones. In Mead, J. (Ed.) *Bodyjamming: Feminism, sexual harassment and public life.* Sydney: Vintage.

Yeatman, A. (1993). Voice and representation in the politics of difference. In Gunew, S. and Yeatman, A. (Eds) *Feminism and the politics of difference.* Sydney: Allen & Unwin.

Yeatman, A. (1995). Interlocking oppressions. In Caine, B. and Pringle, R. (Eds) *Transitions: New Australian feminisms.* Sydney: Allen & Unwin.

Yeatman, A. (1997). Feminism and power. In Shanley, M. L. and Narayan, U. (Eds) *Reconstructing political theory: Feminist perspectives.* Cambridge: Polity Press.

Young, I. M. (1990) *Justice and the politics of difference.* Princeton, NJ: Princeton University Press.

Zaslow, E. (2009). *Feminism Inc.: Coming of age in girl power media culture.* New York: Palgrave Macmillan.

INDEX

177

Printed in Great Britain
by Amazon